The Rise of

Mystery Babylon

Vol. I: The Way of Cain
(Part 1)

Hi Kim,

Enjoy the book!

Brett

Brett Lee Thomas

Parallel World Books

The Rise of Mystery Babylon
Vol. I: The Way of Cain (Part 1)

ISBN-13: 978-0-9995257-3-9
Parallel World Books

Cover photos courtesy of Adi Nes

Email:
  brettleethomas@protonmail.com

www.mysterybabylon.com

*Those who cannot remember the past
are condemned to repeat it.*

- George Santayana

Table of Contents

Preface

The Ancient Parallel to Today's World:
"The Days of Noah"

*You have to know the **past** to understand **the present**.*
- Carl Sagan[1]

There is much in this volume that was once common knowledge in ancient times. Life was very different back then. The whole world was very different. The people of our past probably thought and did things that, today, many might find a little surprising. Yet, there were *some* ideologies and ways of life practiced back then which are surprisingly similar to those practiced today. Why? What's going on? Why the return of some elements in our past? Could there actually be a *parallel* of what might have happened back then to now?

Two Parallel Worlds

*But as the **days of Noe (i.e. Noah)** were, so shall also the coming of the Son of man be.*   *- Mat. 24:37 (KJV)*

Just what do these prophetic words mean, spoken by Jesus himself?[2] Two thousand year ago, Jesus' disciples asked him to describe the "end times," and what would be the approaching signs of the apocalypse. As the above explanation seems to provide, there actually would be a parallel between two eras of existence: how life was lived in *the days of Noah (or Noe)* and how life would be lived in the future.

This above verse tells us so much. If the lifestyles of the two eras would have to match then it gives us a fairly good clue towards understanding whether or not we might be near the end of our age, or the so-called "end times." This also gives us a rationale for understanding why God had to destroy the working order of the ancient world (at the time of Noah). Obviously, they were sinning immensely. There were severe cracks in their ideologies and ways of living. And, if we want to discover what good and evil most probably *is*, and when will be these "end of times," all we need to do is discover what depravities may have been going on in these ancients days and use it as the probable model for our future. Obviously, if these lifestyles of old were bad enough for God to pass His horrible judgment on the entire world then they must be of some merit.

The purpose of this volume is, first off, to show the reader a lot of what could have gone on back then, in those times of early Genesis, and how there could actually be a *parallel* of two real eras of existence. In our current times, we are bombarded by so many angles, bombarded with people telling us what *they* feel is right and wrong. Beauty is truly in the eye of the beholder today. There are so many diverse opinions around that most of us probably do not have a solid moral grasp at a foundation anymore. From the ancient side of this parallel however we can absolutely learn what was considered right and wrong back then, and run with it. The utilization of this knowledge will really help us understand how to solidify our own moral foundations, and our own daily walk.

What is Bringing it All Back

There is something truly evil out there, something beyond our world, lurking in the shadows of everyday life; something which has continually manipulated cultures, politics, and religions throughout history. This is the system that the Bible coins *Mystery Babylon.*

> *And upon her forehead was a name written,* **MYSTERY, BABYLON**...
> - *Rev.* 17:5 (KJV)

The word *Babylon* has almost always been thought of as headquarters of the greatest religious apostasy ever known, both literally and symbolically. It was and is the true enemy of the Bible. The city itself was lost over the years, but this "capital of corruption" continued on, in many different forms, and as a symbol of all that is against God. And, on top of this, there are a number of *mysteries* associated with this once-great city. There were cultural, political and religious *systems* established in these early times that have continued on, throughout empires, throughout world-changes. All of what began around the era of Babylon would eventually manifest itself into so many different forms and faces it would never really lose its punch since then, even over time. That's why the Bible calls it **Mystery** *Babylon*: it resides "under the surface" of so much even today. These systems are ever-working to manipulate us, the way we think, the attitudes we take, the things we believe in, all with the hopes of bringing our world right back to the same existence as these earliest times, as the times of Babylon itself.

Is the future just like the past? Does history truly repeat itself? And, what is working to bring so much of these same ancient ideologies and world views back to us, again?

> *The result of the* **serpent** *nature in mankind is the conglomerate world* **system** *- economic, political, and religious - prophetically called Mystery Babylon... (and) he is "that ancient serpent called* **the devil and Satan**, *which deceiveth the whole world"...* ("The World System", n. d., p. 2)[3]

Just who or what would be this *Serpent*, in regards to the whole scheme of things? What *system* is bringing our world right back to the same estate as it was in Noah's day? Could this Serpent be the same serpent who deceived Eve back in the earliest part of Genesis, back in the time of the Garden of Eden?

This first volume (*The Way of Cain*) will concentrate on earth's history before, and leading up to, the building of Babylon, as well as what socio/cultural influences this Serpent may have had on this ancient world. The second volume (*The Tower of Babel*) will take us deeper into the Babylonian *systems* themselves, political and religious systems of influence instigated by the Serpent himself. The Serpent's role in our past (and present) begins through the discovery of what really may have happened in early Genesis, especially up to the time of the Biblical Flood. This would be the ancient parallel time the Bible refers to as "the days of Noah."

Obscured History, and Meant to Stay That Way

> *When words lose their meaning, people will lose their liberty.*
> - *Confucius*

Words were manipulated back then. Words are manipulated today. Why don't we already know about the *Serpent* and *Mystery Babylon*? Why have so many of us been kept "in the dark" about a lot of what is in this book? Could the information contained herein have been, for the most part, *purposely* obscured?

To begin our quest, we'll delve into many of the little-known or obscured interpretations of early Genesis. Much of this information comes from a variety of alternate or ancient texts, texts which could help us understand the whole truth of Genesis, and of our world. Since the Bible does not give us exact meanings and stories in exact detail, it is necessary to search out these other texts. They will help "fill in the gaps" on what may be the whole story here. It shouldn't be a problem to search where we can to find what we need to fill these gaps, as long as we utilize God's gift of *discernment* He may have given to each and every one of us. Once we know the entire story here, the mysteries of ancient Babylon should become more and more clear.

There are those who say *Genesis* and *Revelation* are the books of the Bible that Satan hates the most, the reason being that Genesis exposed his plans of the past and Revelation exposes his plans of the future. It is for these very reasons that full comprehension of what they say is so vital. They represent the framework for understanding the evil Serpent, *Mystery Babylon* and how our world is currently being manipulated for the worse (and not better). Since much of our history has been changed, or even obscured, the probability of "connecting the dots" in this cause were next to none… until now. Only a detailed revival of information can provide one a foundation for rediscovering what so many of us may have been missing, all of these years.

To "complete" these stories, we'll incorporate the most accurate, most relevant and most respected ancient works on Genesis first, down to the most questionable. We can come up with one (conglomerate) "story" of what might have really happened, if we're work hard enough. This will also help us identify the definitive *parallel* of these ancient "days of Noah," then to now.

Putting these volumes together was not easy. The information had to have been put together in a way much the same way one would assemble a jigsaw puzzle. It took a while, but this end-result is very, very telling. It's also necessary we study the *earliest* and most original texts for one important reason:

*The farther you are away from the originals the farther you are away from the **truth**.*
- Unknown

These volumes do help bring an essence of probable *truth* to our history. They allow for one compelling view of the Genesis story, which helps us strengthen our foundations and religious beliefs. It also helps "blow the lid" off of false information which has been fed to us, for far too long.

The theme of these volumes are twofold: one, to understand how these Serpent *systems* of Babylon work; secondly, to strengthen our own moral and religious foundations, making it easier for us to go out into this world and extol confidence in whatever we're saying or thinking. Many of us have been taught to just do what we are told, as spoken of by politicians and religious authorities. Many of us, as well, may concentrate on good, positive elements of the Judeo/Christian belief, but few really comprehend how our **enemies** are working against us, and how to deal with it. We must also learn and understand *this* side of coin here. We need to know *all* of what we could be up against in this world, in order to survive. As they say: "know thy enemy."

"Out of Touch" Ideals?

This all may begin to sound a little simple to accomplish, at least at first, but there is a lot in the way of our comprehension of *Mystery Babylon*. There is a lot of "smoke and mirrors" out there, and that's probably by design. There's no scientific proof to most everything in this book, as well. But, one's comprehension of anything religious relies on *belief* itself, a belief in these ancient stories of Genesis as factual, as well a belief in the original Greek and Hebrew words of the Bible as the undisputed word of God.

So, with that said and done, a lot of these volumes deal with elements in our world one might find really fantastic, even downright folklore (especially regarding the supernatural world, fallen angels, the existence of demons, etc). It seems there's a lot around us working against our understanding already:

The late eighteenth and early nineteenth centuries saw a massive decline in the popularity of the Christian Church in many parts of Protestant Europe… churches everywhere were being neglected and left to fall into ruin under the impact of Newtonian science and the arrival of the Industrial Revolution. In an age of reason and learning, there were little place for the alleged transgressions of **angels**, **fallen** *or otherwise. Most of the general public were simply not interested…*
(Collins, 1996, p. 20)[4]

In ancient days, however, the masses believed most of these fantastic elements. They attributed the supernatural as more than just folklore. So, with that, we must ask ourselves: just because a lot of people today may try to ridicule this information or put it down, does that mean it never existed, or isn't still relevant? The world truly is a complex place, full of intricate and interrelated processes. Who's to say the supernatural elements of our ancient past really disappeared or faded into obscurity! As the Bible clearly state: "there is nothing new under the sun." The past never really goes away.

True, a number of people may read the following information and claim, "Well, this is just one man's opinion." Yes, there really is no proof, but can one really prove anything supernatural or religious? In the book's defense, these volumes are not filled with a lot of wild speculation or "pet-theories." We, for the most part, just let all of the ancient authors and texts speak for themselves.

When it all boils down to is: even the "big bang theory," the theory of evolution and many other things we are fed today are, at best, just *theories*. No one is alive today who could *definitively* tell us what happened back then because no one today was alive back then! These are only a consensus of accredited *opinions*, and there are other people out there who give these accredited people their own accreditations! Where does it end? Who has the true keys to knowledge? In this age of science and reason it's easy to assume that there will probably be a consensus of thought *against* the contents of this book. But, that doesn't mean there isn't more beyond this world that we can see and touch. There are agendas to everything, even opinions.

We will also see that there are so many out there who have some kind of stake in telling us what they are telling us, what they think *should* be our history and what should be our morality. There's politics in everything, even if we don't see it initially.

If this is true, then how do we find the real truth? How do we find the real story? It takes an open mind, a mind to seek out "other" sources of information which could help us decipher why things are the way they are, and how things became the way they did. Sometimes, we need to wade through the vast amount of muck presented to us, to find true answers in this world. We need to go beyond most of the predetermined **denials** we will be facing, to discover all of what we really may have been missing.

So, to begin our reinterpretation of many widely-held thoughts about our past, and expose this ancient system of *Babylon* in the process, let's take a step back, and look at what might have really happened *"in the beginning."*

Chapter 1

In the Beginning…
With a Gap in Between

*Earth **made** waste and empty by judgment.*
                 - *Gen.* 1:1-2 (The Scofield Bible, notes)

If we want to delve into some of the more obscure viewpoints of religious theology we really need to take a good, hard look at a few alternate views of Genesis. As we begin to dive into these early accounts, we may also begin to decipher this ancient side of the Noachic *parallel*. So, to start at the beginning, we really need to go to the very first verse of Genesis, where we have the words "in the beginning."

Creationists tell us that the earth is up to 12,000 years old. Evolutionists say billions. Which is right? Or, could there be still another scenario, a scenario which might represent something a little different? Could there be something somewhere *in between*, a scenario that may even give us an entirely new way to look at our world?

Many of us who are religious were taught that God created this world in six days, and rested on the seventh. For centuries we have accepted this story, as well as other early stories in Genesis, as absolute truth. We trusted the men who first translated the Bible into English, and that they made no mistakes in their translation. What if, however, these people were not entirely correct in their interpretations? What if the original language of the Bible, perhaps, said something fairly *different* than what the early translators tried to portray? What if there could be a lot more to these early stories than we were always taught?

To start off, if we add in a few of these alternate, ancient texts, we already get a different interpretation on world creation:

*In the beginning God created **numerous worlds**, destroying **one after the other** as they failed to satisfy Him. All were inhabited by man, a thousand generations of whom He cut off, leaving no record of them.*   (Graves and Patai, 1964, p. 45)[1]

Strangely enough, this may sound a little more like our modern view of *evolution* than it may the Bible. Evolutionists often may hold that the ecosystem of our earth was destroyed and "brought back to life" again and again, even six or seven times. There were numerous worlds before ours that didn't make it. Case in point: the rise and fall of the dinosaurs. To clarify our stance in this volume, however, we want to make something totally clear: this book is *not* trying to promote the theory of evolution, nor compromise Biblical scripture in any way. On the other extreme, we are not trying to make the Bible "fit in" with modern, secular views of the world. What we want to do is show there could be *other* ways to look at Biblical creation, and early stories of Genesis. If they show some similarities to the evolutionary concept, then so be it. With all of this said and done, let's see how there could be something very interesting and different on the horizon, a different *but Biblically sound* view of our earliest of days!

As many may know, the Old Testament was originally written in Hebrew, the New Testament in Greek. As one saying goes, "if you really want to understand the Bible, you need to read it in its original Hebrew." So, to gather the entire story of these earliest *days of Noah* we attempted to do just that, whenever possible. Most of us know English was not the original language of the Bible. No matter how well the Bible was translated, no matter how many variable translations we have out there, the English word cannot totally grasp the original meaning of the Hebrew. As with the English language, there could be more than one meaning to most Hebrew words in the Bible. Because of this fact, could there be different meanings, even completely different elements, to some of these early accounts? Could our whole Biblical narrative, perhaps, be different? What this may point to is a simple concept: perfect words of the Bible, *imperfect translators.*

The learned scholars who translated King James Bible, for example, probably translated the words with the best of intentions. They probably believed most of they've always been *taught*, using their preconceived notions to build upon their interpretation. It's simple. The Creation of Genesis 1 becomes a perfect example of this. Their attempt to keep up with tradition may have swayed them to insert *one* meaning of the original Hebrew over another, to make it all sound "politically correct." Once we look at the original Hebrew in more detail, however, and discover that there may be *other* ways to interpret these words, a whole new realm of possibilities open up! If there truly could be variations to these early stories how significant would that be to our understanding of everything? How much could these changes also manipulate the way we look at religious or political views in our present-day world? Quite a bit (as we'll see). This will be a permeating theme throughout the book.

Also, some elements of these early stories could have been left out (or beautifully concealed) on accident, or for a very good reason:. they might have been able to help us discover the Serpent's *true* nature and origins, the true origin of *Mystery Babylon*, etc. Learning more about these obscured elements could also help us to determine just *who* or *what* is behind the attempts to bring back most of these same thoughts and ideals (those of "the days of Noah") into our mainstream.

Genesis and Revelation

To begin grasping these alternate concepts, we need to take a good, hard look at Genesis and Revelation, arguably two of the most important books in the Bible. This first volume will concentrate more on Genesis, the second on both Genesis and Revelation. The reason we need to understand so much about Genesis is because Genesis obviously gives us the ancient parallel of the *days of Noah*, the "background" to it all. Revelation gives us the modern equivalent to it all. If we dare challenge what most of the modern Christian academics have accepted as the only story, if we dare desire to find out what *really* may be influencing our world "behind the scenes," let's continue further.

The Gap Between the Worlds

One interesting but obscured theory must first arise, regarding Biblical creationism. This theory is fairly old, and most of us probably have never heard of it. This is one example of a school of thought where our modern population has been kept "in the dark." This first theory, commonly known as the *Gap Theory*, is an incredible way of looking at creation. It could really turn one's assumptions of the first chapter of Genesis "on its ear."

This theory, along with the rest of the alternative views in these volumes, requires the reader to maintain a sense of openness and plausibility. Along with this, we'll discuss a number of other topics. The relevance of *angels* in our past and present world, for example, will be discussed in great detail. If we believe the Bible is the word of God then, hopefully, we'll believe in angels as well. The ancients who scribed the Bible surely believed in them! so, ultimately, there is really nothing in this book that intentionally contradicts the words of the Bible. We only offer other possible interpretations to it all.

The Gap Theory is quite simple: the first verse of the Bible signifies the *beginning* of God's entire creation. But, between the first and second verses, there was a **gap** of time. The exact temporal expanse between these two verses is unknown. Whatever may have existed during this time was also unknown. The original creation took place "in the beginning" (Gen. 1:1), with at least one "re-creation" occurring since then, probably many of them. First creation, another "re-creation" and then another… all the way up to the time of the "Six-Day Creation" of Genesis.

As the Bible states:

In the beginning God created the heaven and the earth.
                    - Gen. 1:1 (KJV)

This is the first creation of everything. And, next, the verse states:

And the earth was without form, and void…
                    - Gen. 1:2 (KJV)

This represents time skipping ahead, just before the time of the Six-Day Creation. We will see why it is perfectly plausible to have a gap in time here. According to C.I. Scofield, Thomas Chalmers and other scholars, it was just before the time of this second verse that something horrible happened. Marginal notes in the Scofield Bible, for example, gives us an explanation for what might have went on:

Earth made waste and empty by judgment.

There are also clues in the Bible which might help to support this theory. As we'll see, the earth itself may be old, it might even be *extremely* old, and there could have been more than one "destruction and re-creation" cycle before our present Six-Day Creation. If that's the case, could there have been a major catastrophe right before Genesis' Six-Day Creation?

As we review these first two verses of Genesis, we may need to begin looking at the original Hebrew. If we accept the modern interpretation of how it all went down, the "beginning" of our world we know of occurred somewhere in the area of six thousand years ago. This was, more or less, the time Adam and Eve were said to have been placed in the Garden of Eden. With the Gap Theory, however, we cannot assume that this time was also the time of the creation of *everything*. That could have been long before.[2]

Let's look at the first verse:

In the beginning God created the heaven and the earth.
- Gen. 1:1 (KJV)

The word *beginning* comes from the Hebrew word *reshiyth*. *Reshiyth* means "first in place, time, order or rank."[3] So, could this have signified the *first* creation, the first harmonized world in a cycle? Could there have been a second, third, or even more?

The Differences Between the Words "Earth" and "World"

*Before the mountains were brought forth, or ever thou hadst formed the **earth** <u>and</u> the **world**, even from everlasting to everlasting, thou art God.*
- Psa. 90:2 (KJV)

In the Bible, we also seem have an anomaly. As we see in the above, the words *earth* and *world* appear to represent two different things, two distinct terms. They are not the same. Simply, we might be able to theorize that the *world* (such as in the verse above) represents the **present, organized order of things**, the *earth* represents the **physical land** itself. The *world*, then, would be the organized *cosmos*, or how the earth was made up to be, not physical ground, substance, rock, etc. So, as we begin to look at it this way, we could now postulate that there may have been *more than one* cosmos, or organized *world*, on the earth during different periods, yet one physical earth was here the whole time.

> *Now Moses saith in the beginning of the Pentateuch, "In the beginning God made the heavens, and the **earth existed of old"***...   - *Bakhayla Mikael*[4]

Perhaps there were several of these "organized" worlds, with the Six-Day Creation of Genesis being the latest!

Make sense?

It's interesting how the Greek word *kosmos* was (in the New Testament) often used as the English *world*. This word *kosmos*, in Classical Greek, represents "a harmonious order, system or arrangement."[5] Again, it seem to connect with the above. God created the physical earth a long time ago, and also fashioned the first organized, harmonious order to the earth at the same time! This harmonized *world* is the only thing that God manipulates directly over the years. Today, we see the most current, refashioned *world* He put together (at the exact time He began the Six-Day Creation). The first harmonized *order* changed a number of times, destroyed and refashioned once again.

Whatever went on during these times "of old," before our previous cosmos or *world*, we just don't know. Maybe we weren't supposed to know. Also, we don't know why God wasn't satisfied with the organized *worlds* before us, and why they were all destroyed. One thing we can surmise, however: our present, organized world was formed out of the ashes of a former world's undistinguishable ruin, "reworked" by God once again.[6]

More Than One World?

There seems to be more Scriptural evidence that describes how at least one *world* was created by God:

*Through faith we understand that the **worlds** were framed by the word of God, so that things which are seen were not made of things which do appear.*
- *Heb.* 11:3 (KJV)

*Hath in these last days spoken unto us by his Son, whom he hath appointed heir of all things, by whom also he made the **worlds**...* - *Heb.* 1:2 (KJV)

Interestingly enough, the Greek word for *worlds*, in the above, is *aion*. Interestingly, this word was not used in the context of space here, but of *time*. It does not only mean a "perpetuity of time," but "a period of time" or an "age"... just like the Hebrew word for *beginning* in Genesis 1:1.[7] In other words, the original Greek may be referring to these *worlds* as in being in a *succession of order* – one of these simultaneous world refashioned after another (rather than *separate*, distinct worlds themselves)![8]

Digging deeper: the root word of the Greek *aion* is *aei*, which can mean "at any and every time: when according to the circumstances something is or ought to **be done again**."[9] So, it seems to further supports our thought here: each time one world was destroyed the cosmos of the earth was made anew, or refashioned again, into something different. The physical earth was always there. Picture this as an area of land which was "baptized" by a violent storm, or huge rain spell. Things have changed on the surface, but the earth is still there, ready to sustain life again.

Interestingly:

*Remember this, and shew yourselves men: bring it again to mind, O ye transgressors. Remember the **former things** of old: for I am God, and there is none else... Declaring the **end from the beginning**, and from **ancient times** the things that **are not yet done**...*
- *Isa.* 46:9-10 (KJV)

The more we ponder the possibilities of our earth having more than one *world* in the past the more sense verses like the above seem to make.

A World Formed Without Form, and Void?

> *And the earth was **without form**, and **void**…*
> *- Gen.* 1:2 (KJV)

As we'll now see, the Hebrew word *tohuw* was translated into English as "without form." The word *tohuw*, however, can also mean "that which is wasted" or to have "laid waste," as well a "place of chaos," "vanity" or "confusion."[10] The Hebrew *bohuw* was translated into the English as *void*, but this could also mean a state of "waste" or "emptiness."[11] Put them all together and we could have another possible scenario to our beginnings, the above verse "retranslated":

> *And the earth was **laid to waste**, and **emptied**…*
> *- Gen.* 1:2 (in retranslation)

This seems to be a lot different than what many of us may have assumed about the Six-Day Creation. Common perception was that, at the beginning of our Six-Day Creation, the earth was **created** in a vain, or created as an empty, wasted state, without any form or void. Now, a question that might logically follow: was the earth created this way, or did it *become* this way?

The following verse of the Bible seems to give us an answer:

> *For thus saith the LORD that created the heavens; God himself that formed the earth and made it; he hath established it, he created it **not in vain**, he formed it to be inhabited: I am the LORD; and there is none else.*
> *- Isa.* 45:18 (KJV)

Clearly, God established a working order to the earth (i.e. a *world*) at the time of creation, and formed it *not in vain*. It must have reached that state later on. God did not set out to create the earth *without form* and *void*, but rather to be inhabited in an established, organized way! It only makes sense. The Bible also seems to make it clear the world didn't start out like a typical evolutionist would want us to believe. It was fashioned as a structured, clean and organized cosmos. It began this way, and, for whatever reason, did not last.

The World "Was"

> *And the earth **was** without form, and void...*
> *- Gen. 1:2 (KJV)*

The English use of the word **was**, in this verse, also becomes somewhat of a convincer for the Gap Theory. The English *was* originates in the Hebrew word *hayah*.[12] Looking at *Strong's Concordance and Lexicon* we clearly see the word means "to be," "to come to pass" or to "come about." *Hayah*, also, can mean "to happen" or "fall out." Again, with all of this in mind, we can see the verse might be able to take on a whole new meaning if we apply the above:

> *In the beginning God created the heaven and the earth. And the earth **had fallen out; to be laid to waste, and emptied**...*   *- Gen. 1:1-2 (in retranslation)*

As we see, this point could represent a *point of change*, a *destruction* and *recreation* event. Simple.

> *If the Hebrew verb were **eue**, "was" would be an accurate translation; but it is **eie**, the causative form of be which means **become**. This causative form (eie) appears more than twenty times in chapter one of Genesis alone, and everywhere denotes **a change**, and not mere existence.*   (Johnson, 2004, p. 205)[13]

The translators of the 1611 King James Version probably thought the world was created in six days, as they were taught, as do so many in the faith today! They probably inserted the English words they thought were right, to make everything fit in with the assumption of the majority. But, since we are looking into these *other* possible meanings using the original Hebrew, however, we're beginning to discover just how the words of the Bible could take on more than one meaning.

The "Foundation of This World"

As we've already postulated, the established *world* which was present before our own may have been destroyed, for whatever reason, leaving God to do something different the next time. At this moment, He set up the foundations for another, *new* world. So, the word *foundation* could also be of some significance here, in regards to the Gap Theory.

To begin, the English word *foundation*, in the New Testament, comes from the Greek *katabole*. Interestingly enough, the word *katabole* actually originates from the word *kataballo*: a compound word made up of *ballo* ("to cause, to throw") and *kata* ("down").[14] As we can now see, the root of the original Greek for *foundation* could also signify that which was "caused" to be "thrown" down. Could this *foundation*, then, represent the point when one established cosmos was upset, and "thrown down," only to be set up again in another way?[15] This *foundation* now may represent the turning point for a whole new era:

*For we which have believed do enter into rest, as he said, As I have sworn in my wrath, if they shall enter into my rest: although the works **were finished** from the **foundation** of the world.* - *Heb.* 4:3 (KJV)

The above seems to state the works of God were *already in place*, or already *finished*, by the time of our present world's foundation. What does this mean? Could it be that each *foundation* was indeed that time when a former world was thrown down, or *finished*, and a whole new organized cosmos (or world) was set up to replace it?

Throughout these examples, we may begin to understand how the Gap Theory could easily gather momentum. Yet, there is one powerful verse in the Bible which, according to many, seems to stop this momentum cold:

*Wherefore, as by **one man** sin entered into the **world**, and death by sin; and so death passed upon all men, for that all have sinned.* - *Rom.* 5:12 (KJV)

This verse, according to many scholars, is thought to be "proof-positive" that there was no previous world before Adam. There was one man who brought sin into our world according to this verse, so how could there be anything *before* Adam if this was true? It's totally understandable to make this conclusion, but we have to remember the context of how *world* was used here. We know how it could have meant something *different* than the physical earth itself. And, the original Greek word for *world - kosmos -* seems to put things right back into perspective here! Adam brought sin into our *present* organized order of things, and not the overall earth itself. Simple. There may have been sin before our current world, in the previous ones. And this verse also does not deny there could have been more than one organized cosmos or world before. It only affirms that Adam was the person who brought sin into *this* current world![16]

Could there have been human beings on the earth before this current world, bringing it to a point where God felt He had to pass on His judgment? Did this former world go through its own version of the "end times?"

The concept of pre-Adam civilizations was well accepted by early sages. Also in support of the notion of lost civilizations, we read in Psalms (105:8) the words: "He hath remembered his covenant for ever, the world which he commanded to a thousand generations"... The Talmud reveals that this verse indicates that God's Law, the Torah, was given to Moses and all the Hebrews at Mount Sinai after the elapse of 1,000 human generations. Since Moses was of the 26th generation following the first progenitor the human race, this indicates some 974 generations before Adam. (Killian, p. 29-30)[17]

We also recall, from the beginning of this chapter, that one author summarized it as:

In the beginning God created numerous worlds, destroying one after the other as they failed to satisfy Him. All were inhabited by man, a thousand generations of whom He cut off, leaving no record of them. (Graves and Patai, 1964, p. 45)[18]

There are a number of ancient Jewish traditions which give us similar interpretations: the "first week" of God's creation lasted a *long* period of time; none of the ancient worlds fashioned before ours were "ripe" enough to meet God's satisfaction; and, as each world was destroyed, they were reduced to the same existence of "formlessness and void." All of these thoughts also reek of the Gap Theory, as well.

"Being Overflowed With Water"

The following verse also seems to state something in support of our Gap Theory:

*Whereby the world that **then was**, being overflowed with water, perished...*
- II Pet. 3:6 (KJV)

Interestingly, as we know, the original Greek word for *world* was *kosmos*.[19] What "world that then was" are we talking about here? Could these verses be referring to a flood, the flood of Noah, or even a flood which may have occurred *before* our present cosmos? Noah's Flood did devastate the previous cosmos that Noah lived in, but didn't destroy it completely! The entire world did not "perish" as they knew it. It was just flooded for a time. Could this particular flood of water represent what happened *before* the world that was now our own? Interestingly, we also see, according to the Bible, our current world has been called "*this **present** evil world*" (Gal. 1:14). Maybe, before this present evil world, there was another world - with its own story - that perished.

Obviously, we see, in the beginning of our Six-Day Creation:

*...darkness was upon the face of the **deep**. And the Spirit of God moved upon the* ***face of the waters***. *- Gen. 1:2 (KJV)*

If one uses common sense, it seems there may have been a water catastrophe here, due to the physical earth now being covered with water. We're simply not sure.

But, if there could have been a number of these destroyed-and-recreated worlds to our physical earth, could our earth indeed be a lot *older* than the young-world Creationists believe? Science theorizes our earth is a few billions of years old, not a few thousands. Could the Gap Theory lead to the possibility that science and the Bible could have at least *some* common ground here, as far as the physical age of the earth?

Pre-Adamic Flood Vs. Noachic Flood

What about all of that *water* on the earth, mentioned in early Genesis? Could that have helped destroy man's existence before the world of our own?

Psa. 90:
2 *Before the mountains were brought forth, or **ever though hadst
   formed the earth and the world**, even from everlasting to everlasting,
   thou art God.*
3 *Thou turnest man to destruction; and sayest, Return, ye children of
   men...*
4 *Thou carriest them away as with a **flood**...*

Could some Biblical references of a Flood **not** just be representative of the Flood of Noah, but another flood, a flood that could have had a part in destroying the world before the time of Adam? We simply don't know what actually happened in the world before our own, but the Bible does seem to drop us a few hints. As we recall, from the previously-mentioned II Peter 3:6:

*Whereby the world that then was, being overflowed with **water**, perished...*
                                                  - II Pet. 3:6 (KJV)

Obviously, a lot of people have speculated (and still do) that this was nothing but a reference to Noah's Flood. Yet, as we now could speculate, the Bible might be mentioning what could be another flood, a flood with a lot of the same destructive attributes.

How so? Let's look at a few possible verses:

2 Sam. 22:
2 *And he said, The LORD is my rock, and my fortress, and my deliverer;*
3 *...thou savest me from violence.*
5 *When the waves of death compassed me, the floods of ungodly men made me
   afraid;*
8 *Then the earth **shook and trembled**; the foundations of heaven **moved and shook**,
   because he was wroth.*

10 He bowed the heavens also, and came down; and darkness was under his feet.

*12 And he made **darkness** pavilions round about him, **dark waters**, and thick clouds of the skies.*

15 And he sent out arrows, and scattered them; and discomfited them.

*16 And the channels of the sea appeared, **the foundations of the world were discovered**, at the rebuking of the LORD.*

In the flood mentioned above, the earth "shook and trembled," arrows came and scattered the inhabitants, water and darkness were the result. The Bible does not mention any like this during the time of Noah's Flood. In almost a mirror-image of the above, we have:

<u>*Psa. 18:*</u>

1 I will love thee, O LORD, my strength.

4 The sorrows of death compassed me, and the floods of ungodly men made me afraid.

*7 Then the earth **shook and trembled**; the foundations also of the **hills moved** and were **shaken**, because he was wroth.*

9 He bowed the heavens also, and came down: and darkness was under his feet.

*11 He made **darkness** his secret place; his pavilion round about him were dark waters and thick clouds of the skies.*

*12 At the brightness that was before him his thick clouds passed, **hail stones** and **coals of fire**.*

13 The LORD also thundered in the heavens, and the Highest gave his voice; hail stones and coals of fire.

*14 Yea, he sent out his **arrows**, and scattered them; and he shot out **lightnings**, and discomfited them.*

*15 Then the channels of **waters** were seen, and **the foundations of the world were discovered** at thy rebuke, O LORD.*

Again, we have *hailstones*, *lightning* and *coals of fire* being launched upon the earth. We have great *earthquakes* and mountains *shaking*. Although all of this could have possibly occurred during the Flood of Noah, nothing was mentioned in the Biblical account.

It's interesting to note there's even a famous *pagan* legend which claims a lot of the same here. The Icelandic legend of *Ragnarok* reports that, at one time, the whole world had been turned upside down. Rocks and gravel rained down from the sky. Flames were in the air. A great heavenly fire was followed by our world being totally submerged in water. The gods at the time and others living were totally wiped out, with only two people left there to repopulate the earth. The end of this here sounds a lot like what we find at the beginning of Genesis, with *two* people - Adam and Eve - spreading their seed out upon the land.

It's also interesting that we find the word "**foundations**" again, used in both blocks of verses. Could this then, as we recall, actually be significant of the turning point, from one world to another. Could there have possibly been a flood that occurred before the foundation of our present world, as well? In both of these verses above, they end with the mention of a **new** foundation. Could this signify a new *world* on its way? There was no new world after Noah's flood, no need for a new foundation.

In the next set of verses, we see "foundations" was used again:

Psa. 104:
4 *Who maketh his angels, spirits; his ministers a flaming fire:*
5 *Who laid the **foundations** of the earth, that is should not be removed forever.*
6 *Thou coveredst it with the **deep** as with a garment: that **waters** stood above the mountains.*
7 *At thy rebuke they (the angels) fled; at the voice of thy **thunder** they hasted away.*
8 *They go up by the mountains; they go down by the valleys unto the place which thou hast founded for them.*
9 *Thou hast set a bound **that they may not pass over**; that they **turn not again** to cover the earth.*

It seems whoever lived during this time did not survive the disaster at hand, not so for Noah's Flood. And, there's more. The following verses, similar to the above, seem to take things a little further:

*I beheld the earth, and, lo, it **was without form**, and **void**; and the heavens, and they had **no light**.* - *Jer. 4:23 (KJV)*

Wow, this is surprising. Even though this verse sounds like it should be coming out of Genesis 1, it is in the Book of Jeremiah. Could Jeremiah be describing this same time, the time just before Adam? As we read further, we see:

Jer. 4:
*24 I beheld the **mountains**, and, lo, they trembled, and all the hills moved lightly.*
*25 I beheld, and, lo, there was **no man**, and all the birds of the heavens were fled.*
26 I beheld, and, lo, the fruitful place was a wilderness, and all the cities thereof were
broken down at the presence of the LORD, and by his fierce anger.
27 For thus hath the LORD said, The whole land shall be desolate; yet will I not make
a full end.
*28 For this shall the earth mourn, and the **heavens above be black**; because I have*
spoken it, I have purposed it, and will not repent, neither will I turn back from it.

Jer. 4:25 again makes it known that there was *no man* in the world around or after this time. This could not be Noah's flood. We know there were survivors! Again, we see that mountains moved and trembled about, not mentioned in Noah's flood. The word "trembled," interestingly enough, comes from the Hebrew *raash*, which means *to undulate*. Assumedly, there were great shocks, or earthquakes, which *undulated* this entire world before Adam. The shocks caused mountains to rise and fall and move from side to side, in smooth, wave-like motions.[20] The Hebrew word for "moved lightly," in the above, was *qalal*, meaning "to be light in the sense of weight." So, we now know that the mountains must have moved around like waves on the ocean, the hills tossing about like featherweights. There seems to be *major* cataclysmic change with this flood, a change which shook the earth to its core! In Noah's Flood, however, we recall there wasn't earthquakes or the shaking of mountains like this, nothing.

There are another block of verses which say almost the same:

Job 9:
4 He… is mighty in strength…
*5 Which **removeth the mountains**, and they know not: which **overturneth** them in*
his anger.
*6 Which **shaketh** the earth **out of her place**, and the pillars thereof tremble.*
*7 Which commandeth the **sun**, and **it riseth not**; and sealeth up the stars.*

Interesting, though, we also see the Lord shook the earth "out of her place." Again, major change had occurred.

Another ancient source give us this: after the flood of Noah, God assures Noah that, "I will not again destroy together all living as I have done."[21] Interesting. Why would God say "again" and "as I have done?" Maybe He did bring a flood upon the earth more than one time. The ancient historian, *Philo*, also interprets this promise to Noah in the same way, but with a little bit more:

> *...therefore I (God) will not now proceed to smite all living flesh **as I have done at other times**...*
>
>   - *Works of Philo Judaeus* Questions and Answers on Genesis 2(54)[22]

Could these *other times* be the other times our world was reconfigured before the Six-Day Creation?

If this happened again and again, then why don't we know a great deal more information about the other times before us?

No Memory of Former Things?

From the former verses, we might be able to assume that, in the flood before Adam (or, the so-called "pre-Adamic" Flood), this former world was entirely cut off, and all of human life ended.[23] This was an abrupt halt to everything. There was no direct genetic link of any ancient human being before this to our present day.[24] And, we do seem to have an interesting piece of information which might support this: one 12,000 year-old strand of human hair was reportedly discovered in Woodburn, Oregon in 2001. The "DNA analysis of hair follicles found at the site have so far failed to find a match with any known human racial type living on earth today," says William Orr, a professor who analyzed it. "The geneticists found the hair didn't match any Asian hair DNA. It didn't match African, European. It didn't match anything."[25] Interesting: this hair's DNA had *no* match with any modern human. Why? Could the reason be that those who existed before this Adamic flood were entirely wiped out? As we recall, in Jeremiah:

> *I beheld, and, lo, there was **no man**...*
>
>   - *Jer.* 4:25 (KJV)

As we'll discover next, there could be good reason why there wasn't very many written accounts about this time before our own. This could also be the reason why we, as human beings, really don't have any manner of "collective memory" of any life before the Adamic Flood. We don't much except, possibly, the divinely-inspired hints we get from God in the Bible.[26]

Along these lines, the Bible also tells us that:

There is no remembrance of former things…
- Eccl. 1:11 (KJV)

Maybe this pre-Adamic information is something God feels we really don't need to know too much about. Yet, although we might not know a lot about this era, that doesn't mean it never happened.

Willingly Ignorant?

As we begin our journey through the earliest parts of Genesis, we seem to have some scriptural evidence of a world before our Six-Day Creation. If this was the case, then why do so many people - Christian and no - scoff so easily at the possibility of things such as the Gap Theory? Why do so many learned people of the past, and in this day and age, automatically seem to debunk alternate thoughts such as this and others we'll begin discover in the rest of this book? The answer is simply:

*…the time will come when they will **not** endure sound doctrine; but after their own lusts shall they heap to themselves teachers, having itching ears; And they shall **turn away their ears** from the truth, and shall be turned unto **fables**.*
- II Tim. 4:3-4 (KJV)

*…This people honoreth me with their lips, but their heart is far from me. Howbeit in vain do they worship me, teaching for doctrines the commandments of men. For laying aside the commandment of God, ye hold **the tradition of men**… ye reject the commandment of God, that ye may keep your own **tradition**.*
- Mark 7:6-9 (KJV)

The following verses also seem to affirm that, in the **last days** (our modern times, maybe?), there will be a great "falling out." People will begin to *scoff* at the very idea of most any other thoughts other than tradition, and what a few overseers have taught the masses. Please note the last verse in this block, especially:

<u>II Pet. 3</u>:
3 *Knowing this first, that there shall come in the last days scoffers, walking after **their own lusts**,*
4 *And saying, Where is the promise of his coming? for since the fathers fell asleep, all things continue as they were from the beginning of the creation.*
5 *For this they **willingly** are **ignorant of**, that by the word of God the heavens were **of old**, and the earth standing out of the **water** and in the **water**…*

II Peter even says here that people will become willingly ignorant of how old the heavens and probably the earth are, and the concept that our earth was placed in and out of the water at certain times. Does this make affirmation of our Gap Theory concept? Could this be what it all means? The next verse or two of this chapter seems to clear it up, without confusion:

<u>II Pet. 3</u>:
6 *Whereby **the world** that **then was**, being overflowed with water, **perished**:*
7 *But the heavens and the earth, **which are now**, by the same word are kept in store, reserved unto fire against the day of judgment and perdition of ungodly men.*

Wow! This tells us so much. It seems to state that there was once a world once in and out of the water. This same world which overflowed with water had perished. Finally, there obviously had to have been a heaven and earth (i.e. a *world*) reformulated, to make them into what we have here *now*. It's so right in front of us, but we also have so much dissention about this possibility.

As we look further, we see the Greek word for *willingly*, in the above, means "to choose." So, it seems that people will *choose* to believe what they were always taught (i.e. tradition) or make a conscious *choice* to be ignorant of something alternative, something which, very well, could be the truth. How true this has become.

So many out there do not want to accept change, nor open their ears to any other theories around. Sounds like a good reason why so many of us have never heard of the Gap Theory? How often are scientists, for example, willing to accept anything *other* than pet theories of the scientific community (such as evolution)? Anything else is shouted down, or torn down. Today, the Bible seems to have been demoted to a collection of false myths, or stories, but believers know there is more.

Why Don't More People Question Tradition?

There are a number of fossils which seem to show us that there could indeed be a lot more to our history than only 6,000 years. Science claims the world is much older than this. Maybe it is. But, that doesn't necessarily mean Bible is false, however! Not at all. A lot of these upcoming "reinterpretations" of Genesis might sound as unbelievable as the Gap Theory, at first. That's why these volumes were written however, to give us a chance to see *other* things that we were intentionally being steered away from - the *other* side of culture, politics and religion. This is all important, and deserves an audience. Maybe the Bible isn't as full of unscientific myths as so many portray it to be. Maybe there is something to all of the verses above, maybe something to the Gap Theory itself. We will eventually see this represents knowledge, knowledge the present "powers that be" feel we shouldn't know, don't need to know, or has nothing to do with supporting their agenda.

It's time to make sense of the "politically incorrect" and see these verses for what they might actually be saying!

*Thou sendest forth thy spirit, they are **created**: and thou **renewest** the face **of the earth**.* - *Psa.* 104:30 (KJV)

Maybe there is a lot more truths in the Bible than we were previously taught, or had even ever thought!

More Biblical Re-interpretations

We should also realize that our main focus in life today doesn't really have to depend on knowing all the information *before* the time of Adam and Eve. We no longer live in that world. For whatever reason God did not grace us with much information. What we really need to do is to concentrate on the world *that is now*, with the possibility of the Gap Theory in the back of our minds. Since the Bible is the *book of the generations of Adam* (Gen. 5:1), it's a book that's more concerned with the world that existed *since* his formation. Any hints of a world before our own were probably secretly and divinely inserted by God, to help us begin to question secular tradition and manipulation.

As we begin to take the next steps in understanding, we'll continue to take a deeper look at the stories of Genesis. They say that understanding the past is a key to understanding our future. The reason we try to decipher what happened so long ago is because it just may be the first step to help us find real *truths* in our present age.

Yet, the **Serpent's** system does not want our progression beyond what we already have. It does not want exposure, because it will feel much like a cockroach who scatters after being found hiding under an overturned rock. But, regardless, let's continue onward. Let's discover more alternate views of the Six-Day Creation, up to the era of the Garden of Eden and beyond.

Chapter 2

Angels From
"The Well of Lost Souls"

*When he (God) comes, Fire shall be **darkness** in the midnight black.*
- Sibylline Oracles 1st Fr. (notes)[1]

*...thy (God's) judgments are a great **deep**...*
- Psa. 36:6 (KJV)

In the last chapter, we discovered how the world may actually be a lot older than what many creationists think. We've postulated how the earth's organized *cosmos* may have been destroyed, and refashioned, a number of times, climaxing at the Six-Day Creation of Genesis! In this chapter, we're going to discover there may also have been something to what people call the underworld, a place of punishment below the earth, etc. We'll also discover there may have been human beings (and more) alive during worlds past, even our previous world. And that almost every man, angel, or whomever occupied the earth at this time, *died* (or somehow fell from their present state of being). We'll soon see how it all of it might have gone down, and what happened to these individuals.

Although the former *world* may have been destroyed, could there have been anyone who survived… into this one? Did anything of any special significance pass from one world to another? To answer this, we may need to sound a little esoteric, or spiritual. We need to go into the supernatural realm of understanding a bit, and ask: what if the *spiritual* remnants of the former world were brought back, into our current world, by God? What if even the spiritual part of human individuals - their *soul* – were temporarily cast down into some dark, temporary state of abyss, at the time of the previous world's destruction? What if these same souls were then brought **back up again**, into this world, at the time of our Six-Day Creation? Sounds like reincarnation, but is it *really*?

This becomes an intriguing, and somewhat difficult, topic to delve into, but the Bible does seem to get into this topic a little bit (believe it or not). As we'll soon discover, the words ***darkness*** and ***deep***, as in the above quotes, often show up in Biblical narrative.

What do they stand for? Why does this have relevance to our expose on the Serpent and *Mystery Babylon*?

First, we'll discover these words could actually stand for a supernatural place, or abode - a spiritual place. It could actually represent a temporary place were human souls could have been placed. Call it the "Well of Lost Souls," if you will. In the case we will examine, this *Darkness* and the *Deep* could then be considered the spiritual place where remnants of our former world (as the souls of everyone alive during that time) were stored, and held. It would be where souls would just sit, ready and waiting for whatever God had in store for them next. Think the descriptions of *hell*, here. Think *purgatory*, *hades* or *Sheol*. All of these touch somewhat on this concept. They all have similarities to the Darkness and the Deep, but are not exactly the same.

Regarding the Darkness: the "remnants" previously mentioned would be comprised of, for the most part, human souls, possibly some *angelic* souls as well, whatever may have been taken out at the time of God's judgment, here. It may sound a little difficult to comprehend here. It may even sound a little like reincarnation, until we read further.

First, the Bible makes an interesting statement: we were *already* accounted for *before the foundations* of this world:

*According as he hath chosen us in him **before the foundation** of the world.*
                                                    - Eph. 1:4 (KJV)

*Then shall the King say unto them… Come, ye blessed of my Father, inherit the kingdom prepared for you **from the foundation** of the world…*
                                                    - Mat. 25:34 (KJV)

How could this happen? Why would God even consider us before the foundations of this world? Could the possibility be that each of us had a part of God's plan *before* this time? And, if so, we need to ask ourselves: why would *we* be so relevant if we were not even close to being born yet? Could there have been *one* piece of us already there, at the time before our Six-Day Creation, that mattered? To a number of us, these ideas might sound like they're going down a totally pagan pathway of reincarnation, but they aren't. It takes a bit of explanation, but it leads to a fascinating way to really look at things here.

So, to comprehend what the *Darkness* and the *Deep* may have really stood for, let's dive into even *more* esoteric topics. Let's first decipher what would be considered the spiritual "antithesis" of such a dismal place known as the *Darkness* or the *Deep*. Let's look into what the Bible calls "*the Light*."

Divisions of "Light" and "Dark"

As we proceed, one thought that may come into our minds is: if no human was *physically* able to be pass on from the former world, then what's the possibility of something *spiritual* passing? Could human *souls* have made it through? And, what about the *angelic* beings who may have existed during this time? What if they also became a part of God's destruction, as well?

According to our theory, all individuals were silenced at the time of God's judgment. There was probably no "second coming" to take the pious away. What if some individuals (human and angel) really didn't *deserve* to have such a harsh judgment dictated against them? What if some fell as a victim of circumstance, living at the wrong place at the wrong time? In this carpeted approach to judgment, someone's moral stance would not be put into play. Wouldn't it be up to God to devise a plan for the just? It's quite possible the previous world didn't have the same pathways to reach heaven as we have today. And God is a fair God. Maybe God decided there was to be a way for the previous world's just.

Let's look deeper.

The "Light of Face"

We continue our look at early Genesis, with the second half of Genesis 1, verse 2:

Gen. 1:
2 ...and **darkness** was upon the face of the **deep**. And the spirit of God moved upon the face of the **waters**.
3 And God said, Let there be **light**: and there was light.

As many people might accept, there could be two "hemispheres" of existence: the natural and the supernatural; the corporeal and the spiritual; the terrestrial and the extraterrestrial. Most of us understand common, everyday meanings to words we bring up here. Could the words *darkness*, *deep* and *water* all have deeper, supernatural meanings here, as well? How about the word *light* (in contrast to the supernatural *darkness*)? Could the two, each, be thought of as an opposite, spiritual extreme?

We already know the *world* could have a few of different meanings, beyond the obvious. There could be more meanings to light and darkness, as well:

Gen. 1:
4 *And God saw the **light**, that it was good: and God divided the light from **the darkness**.*
5 *And God called the light Day, and the darkness he called Night. And the evening and the morning were the first day.*

The above concept of *light*, for example, could be referring to one's esoteric, or supernatural, "light" if you will, their "angelic light." The English word for *light*, in the above, comes from the Hebrew *owr*, which could symbolize *the light of someone's face*. Often, the features of one's face represented the defining nature of a person in ancient days. A person's race, color, national identity, and other factors often were summed up by looking at their face. So, *light*, in the Bible, could also be used in conjecture with the *brightness* (or countenance) of one's face (as in Job 29:24, Psa. 4:7, 44:4 and 104:15, for example). Even Prov. 16:15 states, "when the king's *face* shineth..." Could *light*, in the above verses, also refer to the countenance, or shine, of one's face? What beings could emanate such a bright, shining countenance such as this?

*O Lord, is there in the world another god besides You, who created **angels** and filled **them with light**...*
> *- First Book of Adam and Eve (The Conflict of Adam and Eve with Satan) 27:10[2]*

Supernatural beings - angels - were traditionally thought to have the ability to be "of the light," or "show" light. The ancient Christian theologian *Augustine* once made this statement:

> *Where Scripture speaks of the world's creation, it is not plainly said whether or when the **angels** were created... when all things, which are recorded to have been completed in six days, were created and arranged, how should the angels be omitted, as if they were not among the works of God, from which on the seventh day He rested?... There is no question, then, that if the angels are included in the works of God during these six days, they are that **light** which was called Day... For when God said, Let there be light, and there was light, if we are justified in understanding in this light the **creation of the angels**, then certainly they were created partakers of the eternal light which is the unchangeable Wisdom of God, by which all things were made... so that they, being illumined by the Light that created them, might themselves become light and be called Day... The true Light, which lights every man that comes into the world, John 1:9 - this Light lights also every pure angel, that he may be light not in himself, but in God...* - *Augustine* City of God 11:9[3]

So, we can define this supernatural *light* as:

- Spiritual awareness; illumination.
*- A prominent or distinguished person; a **luminary**.*[4]

In the Bible, there are many examples of this *light* as symbolic of God's Holiness, as well as some manner of *angelic* illumination.

> *...LORD, lift thou up the **light** of thy **countenance** upon us.*
> - *Psa.* 4:6 (KJV)

> *...God is **light**, and in him is no darkness at all.*
> - *I John* 1:5 (KJV)

The Elohim

Another controversial element in all this lies in the word *Elohim*. The Bible seems to state that God *alone* formed and reformed the heavens and the earth. Curiously enough, by the end of our Six-Day Creation however God was said to have a group of angels alongside Him (Gen. 2:1). Some schools of thought believe, collectively, that God and his angels were, together, known as the *Elohim* or *bene Elohim*.[5] If this is the case, just *when* did He pick up these angels up? Could they have always been there, or did He fashion them at some time? Could the time He stated "let there be *light*" (i.e. the first day of creation) actually be the time He decided to form them, or call the *up* from somewhere?[6]

Angelic Beings "Created" on Day One?

> *...These are the holy angels of God, who were **first** created...*
> - *Shepherd of Hermas* Visions 3:4[7]

> *...on the **First** Day... God created... the hosts which are invisible (that is to say, the **Angels**...), and all the ranks and companies of Spiritual beings...*
> - *Cave of Treasures* The Creation. First Day[8]

> *For on the **first** day He (God) created... all the spirits which serve before him - the **angels**...* - *Book of Jubilees* 2:2 (also 2:8)[9]

On this **first** day (of the "six"), did God lay out the groundwork for the *supernatural* cosmos, as well? It states, in the classic *Legends of the Jews*, that God taught the Biblical Enoch (a great teacher of ancient days) about His creation of all things, including the earth, man, and the *light*.[10] We see that:

> *I commanded **in** the very **lowest parts**, that **visible** things should come down from invisible...* - *2 Enoch* 25:1[11]

> *...God revealed unto him (Enoch) great secrets, which even the angels do not know. He told him how, out of the **lowest darkness**, the visible and invisible were created...*
> (Ginzberg, 1909, p. 135)[12]

As we see here, out of the lowest *darkness* God brought up the visible and invisible. The visible and invisible *what*? Could the *invisible* actually be the souls of the former world's angelic beings? And, if they were, who could be the *visible* beings to be brought up also? Could these be the humans of the previous world's destruction?

Their souls may all have been held somewhere, waiting to come back in existence:

> ...*He (God) willed, and heaven, earth, water, air, fire,* **and the angels** *and* **darkness**, *came into being...*   - *Book of the Bee* Ch. II[13]

Well, what about this *Darkness*? Could it *really* be considered as a spiritual abode for lost souls of the previous *world*?

The Dark Extreme

Now, if we look at Genesis Chapter 1, again:

> <u>Gen. 1:</u>
> 2 ...*and* **darkness** *was upon the face of the deep.*
> 3 *And God said, Let there be* **light**: *and there was light.*

The above verses of Genesis state the *darkness* was upon the face of the deep, and *light* brought up soon after. What if this *light* came up from that "holding area" - the *Darkness*?[14]

> ...*God... commanded the* **light** *to shine* **out of darkness**...
>   - *II Cor.* 4:6 (KJV)

Could this also help to further solidify our assumptions about the two being at "extreme," polarizing supernatural sides?

> ...*from whom if an angel turned away, he becomes impure, as are all those who are called unclean spirits, and* **are no longer light in the Lord**, *but* **darkness** *in themselves, being deprived of the participation of* **Light** *eternal...*
>   - *Augustine* City of God 11:9[15]

*...(He created) the **abysses** and the **darkness**, eventide (and night)...*
- Book of Jubilees 2:2[16]

*This earth is above the **water**, and, below the **Ocean**, is the **awful abyss of water**, and below the abyss is a rock, and below the rock is SIOL (Sheol - i.e. Hell, Hades, etc.), and below SIOL is the wind, and under the wind is the boundary of **darkness**.*
- Bakhayla Mikael, p. 12[17]

So, to progress here, we need to look into this other supernatural term, the *opposite* of what a bright, lively state of being is. Being *dark*, or living in *darkness*, can also stand for:

- absence of light; lacking enlightenment
- characterized by gloom; dismal
- having depth
- concealed or secret; mysterious; obscure
- exhibiting or stemming from evil characteristics or forces[18]

One Biblical resource defines *darkness* (figuratively) as misery, destruction, death, ignorance or wickedness.[19] So, along these same lines, *night* could also stand for:

- a time or condition of gloom, obscurity, ignorance, or despair
- a time or condition marked by absence of moral or ethical values[20]

Now that we know *darkness* and *night* could be close in a number of spiritual ways, we know they could also be in sharp contrast to all that is *light* or *day*. Col. 1:13 even stated that some **angels** possessed the powers of *darkness*! So, it only makes sense to assume that some angels could be associated with *light*, the *brightness of day*, etc., while others might take on the spiritual significances of all that is opposing?

*Ye are all the children of **light**, and the children of the day: we are not of the **night**, nor of **darkness**.*
- I Cor. 5:5 (KJV)

II Cor. 6:

14 _Be ye not unequally yoked together with unbelievers: for what fellowship hath righteousness with unrighteousness? and what communion hath_ **light** _with_ **darkness**_?_

15 _And what concord hath_ **Christ** _with_ **Belial**_? or what part hath_ **he that believeth** _with an_ **infidel**_?_

Maybe there were angels out there who, either _came up_ from the darkness, or were still _of the darkness_. We've already postulated that this darkness was a "well" of sorts, a "holding place" of souls from the previous world. Maybe at the time of the first day of creation God brought up the ones He considered moral and worthy, leaving the others there, still in that unenlightened state.

There is a good deal of ancient written evidence to support this. Ancient Jewish lore, for example, mentions the place where souls of the unborn are kept, _the Guff_. Could this be the same thing? Could this _Darkness_, then, represent some gloomy place of _unenlightened absence_, where the souls of our previous world had to be temporarily placed, of course, until God decided it was time to do something with them?[21]

> _...in mythology the underworld was imagined as a_ **chthonic** _place of_ **darkness**, _contrasting with the celestial realm..._
> ("Black and White Dualism", n. d., p. 1)[22]

The word _chthonian_, in the above, literally stands for, "belonging to the earth" or "in, under, or beneath the earth."[23]

The Darkness... Of the Deep

So, if this _Darkness_ could be an actual, _spiritual_ plane of existence, and it's beneath our world, then the _Deep_ could also have some deeper, supernatural significances here. Could it represent some other sort of spiritual "area" which, perhaps, may surround this _Darkness_, a place where the Darkness was inserted?[24] Let's see.

*Thy righteous is like the great mountains; thy **judgments** are **a great deep**...*
                                                      - Psa. 36:6 (KJV)

If we acknowledge there could be *supernatural* elements to words such as the above, then we may be able to assume that God could have designated a huge number of souls from the previously-destroyed world to enter the *Darkness*. It was part of His judgment, and only for a limited time. This dark, holding cell was set in a spiritual abyss, far beneath our earth, known as the *Deep*.

Interestingly, there are Biblical meanings of the *Deep* which seem to support this:

- the deepest part of the sea (e.g. Psa. 69:15)
- a state of **chaos** (e.g. Gen. 1:2)[25]
- the grave or abyss (e.g. Rom. 10:7, Luke 8:31)
- the bottomless pit, or hell (e.g. Rev. 9:1-2, 11:7, and 20:13)

So, if we accept that how *deep* could have also been used in these ways, it could mean a whole lot more than a body of water:

> *It is not unreasonable, then, to see "the deep" in Genesis signifying something greater than simply deep water... it has other shades of meaning as well, including the abyss and the grave... The Deep does refer to the ocean. But it also symbolic of a **judgment** against wrongdoing and bolsters the overall feel that all things **are not right** in creation as the opening passage of Genesis unfolds.*   (Quayle, 2005, p. 16-17)[26]

What it all boils down to is: since we've already postulated our previous world, and every one in it, was destroyed by judgment of God, in a massive, chaotic flood. This was just before the Six-Day Creation of Genesis 1. And, this *Darkness of the Deep* was the gloomy, 'holding area' which held the previous world's (human and angelic) souls.

There poured the *souls* of every human and angelic being alive at the time: the righteous with the unrighteous; the good with the evil; the dedicated with the indifferent. Since the souls of **everyone** were bunched together in such a way, it literally became the enactment of the phrase, "destroy them all. God knows His own."

It wasn't hell. It wasn't eternal damnation. It wasn't even Purgatory. It was just a temporary place to hold future inhabitants of the new world.

Next, at the time of Gen. 1:2, the time was ripe for God to "hover over the face of the waters" and take action. It was ripe to "sort them out." Thus began our Six-Day Creation.

But, Isn't This Reincarnation?

On the surface, this concept might begin to sound a lot like pagan reincarnation. There may be some similarities on the surface but there also are some *major* differences:[27]

> *The first earth age was inhabited by us, by our souls in a different form... in this earth age we have flesh bodies because we were created and formed from the dust of the earth... Your spirit (your intellect) and your soul will either live forever or will be consumed in the lake of fire (hell)... Every **soul goes through each earth age only one time**, but it is the **same one soul**... So this second earth age... became necessary so as to allow every soul to come through it and make a **choice** between following God or following satan... God placed a veil between this earth age and the first so that we cannot know what side we were on in that revolt, nor do we possess any memory of it... this is not saying there is any reincarnations... Each soul can only pass through each earth age **one** time; just like we live in this earth age but we can also live in the next earth age, **referred to as Heaven**... what would be the use of this earth age, which itself is nothing more than a **proving** ground, a place and a time for us to decide whom we will love and follow?*
> ("When Was the Beginning?", n. d., p. 8-12)[28]

We are not "progressing" upward *on our own*, progressing towards some "god-like" state, as the typical believer of reincarnation would want to believe. None of it happened without the hand of God, refashioning the world into what He wanted next! This was not This was another chance for those who may have been prematurely destroyed in the past, and hadn't yet been able to make up their mind in the right way.

> *He shook the earth and then covered it with water, to give it a good cleansing. This was NOT Noah's flood, because everything on the earth perished! Everything. After God "washed" away those evil rudiments, He began to prepare this old earth for a new age... By allowing His children to be born **as innocent babes**, through their mother's womb, they would have no remembrance of that great rebellion in the*

*world **that then was**.*   ("3 World Ages", n. d., p. 1)[29]

The victims of this blanket destruction would not have any remembrance of the world *that then was*. As a result, those human souls not brought back up as the light (i.e. former angelic souls) were allowed one more chance in the world... the world which is **now** (II Pet. 3:6-7). Any souls placed in the Darkness of the Deep - human or angelic - would now be brought up, by God, and placed somewhere (and, at some time) in His brave new world.

Now, in regards to the undecided individuals of the past world, *this* was their second chance. In this brave new world, *they* will have another opportunity - to make a decision on now show where their loyalty lies. Our present world now become a **proving ground** for a number of ancient, undecided souls… those of the past.

Whether or not it happened this exact way before our current world's formation, the Darkness was as least used to harbor souls who had passed on during this era. The following situations seem to point towards this, as well:

*Or, Who shall descend into the **deep**? (that is, to bring up Christ again from the **dead**).*
- Rom. 10:7 (KJV)

<u>Luke 8</u>:
30 *And Jesus asked him, saying, What is thy name? And he (the demon-possessed man) said, Legion: because many devils were entered into him.*
31 *And they besought him that he would not command them to go out into the **deep**.*

There are more supernatural elements relevant to our story than just this "holding cell."

The "Sea"

Along these same lines, we need to quickly look into another often-misunderstood term of the Bible: the *Sea* or *Seas*.

Gen. 1:
9 *And God said, Let the waters under the heaven be gathered together unto one place, and let the dry land appear: and it was so.*
10 *And God called the dry land Earth; and the gathering together of the waters called he* **Seas***: and God saw that it was good.*

The *Deep* can be defined as more than a body of water in the Bible. How about the *Sea.*[30] Could it have a supernatural aspect to it, as well? How do we go about showing this angle? First, we'll see that one of the greatest theological arguments *against* the *Gap Theory* (in the previous chapter) lies with the following verse:

For **in six days** the LORD **made** heaven and earth, the **sea**, and all that in them is, and rested the seventh day...   - *Ex.* 20:11 (KJV)

At first glance, it looks a bit damaging. It states that God only took *six days* to create the heavens and earth. Nothing apparently existed before that. Sounds pretty "open and shut." But, in order to find *true* meanings to a verse we often need to go look at the original Hebrew. It might actually be saying something a little different, here. As well, another important thing for one who really wants answers: to get the real meanings behind a verse we need to look at how a verse is used *in context* with its surrounding verses.

Let's look at the original Hebrew word for *made* in the above. It is the word *asah*, meaning "to do," "fashion" or "accomplish." Interestingly enough, it is not the same Hebrew as the word used for the English "created," in Gen. 1:1! You think they would be almost the same, if not exact, if they represented the same creation. But, right off the bat, this now begins to support the thought that maybe they were two separate acts, representative of two different times. One verse described the primary creation of our heavens and earth, the other described this *reorganization* of some former world. So, what if the above verse, then, only stood for the reorganization of our previous world? And, when we view the *context* of which this verse resides, we may further begin to understand what it all really means. Let's look at a few verses directly before it:

Ex. 20:
9 *Six days shalt thou labour, and do all thy* **work***:*
10 *But the seventh day is the sabbath of the LORD thy God: in it thou shalt not do any work, thou, nor thy son, nor thy daughter, thy manservant, nor thy maidservant, nor thy cattle, nor thy stranger that is within thy gates:*
11 *For in six days the LORD* **made** *heaven and earth,* **the sea***, and all that in them is, and rested the seventh day: wherefore the LORD blessed the sabbath day, and hallowed it.*

These verses seem to deal with the *seven-day* time-frame, set forth as an example of how God wanted Moses to promote to the ancient Israelites (to work six days and keep Sabbath on the seventh). If we look at the *context* of these verses we clearly see they refer to *work*. Simply, one should work for *six* days, and rest on the seventh… which is just how God did with our Six-Day Creation. It doesn't necessarily mean He fashioned the entire heavens and earth in six days.

We also notice, during this same six-day timeframe, God made *the sea*. Now, what would be this "sea," exactly? Did God create just one sea of water at this time, and what was so significant about it? Why would the Bible mention one lonely *sea* here, when there were vast amounts of water (i.e. oceans) to be created, mountains, and other things which were much larger? Even the original Hebrew word for *sea*, here, doesn't mean anything like "water in general." It is something specific. Could this *sea* stand for something *deeper*, a blanket-name for something *supernatural*, as well?

Looking at a verse in the book of Revelation, we discover:

And I saw a new heaven and a new earth: for the first heaven and the first earth were passed away; and there was **no more sea***.*　　　　　　- *Rev.* 21:1 (KJV)

Wow, this verse in Revelation, in ways, parallels the above verse of Exodus. Now, does Revelation, here, state that, after the time Jesus returns, there will be *no more water* on the earth or something? What would be so important about God removing one particular sea of water from the earth at this time? Makes no sense, unless we open it up for the opportunity of it being something else.

Job 38:
1 *Then the LORD answered Job out of the whirlwind, and said...*
4 *Where wast thou when I laid the* **foundations** *of the earth? declare, if thou hast understanding...*
8 *Or* **who shut up the sea** *with doors, when it brake forth, as if it had issued out of the womb?*
9 *When I made the cloud the garment thereof, and thick darkness a swaddlingband for it...*

The above verses seem to say that, when God laid the foundations of the earth, He *then* shut up the sea! So, at the foundations of our current cosmos, God both created and shut up the sea. Could this *sea* actually stand for the **supernatural** world, the way it was first laid out in our existence?[31] Could God have created (or refashioned) it, "shut it up" to make it inaccessible to humanity (as it currently is), then, after Christ's return, remove the veil so we no longer will be restricted from seeing into it? It only really makes sense if we interpret it as something like this.

If we've reached the end of our present existence - at this point of Revelation - then it might be a ripe time for God to bring on the "end times": the *last* of these undecided *souls* of the previous world would have already been born! Then, upon Jesus' return (at the end of our current era), there really wouldn't be any more souls left in the supernatural *Darkness* to bring up, and wouldn't be much of a need to retain the *Sea* the way it currently is. So, according to Revelation, there would be no *more Sea*.

Another question that might arise: are we just going to be talking about "holding places" and the supernatural world? And, in what way do these alternate theories of Genesis relate to *Mystery Babylon*? It'll probably all start to come together, as we read on. Knowledge such as this could also begin to give us new perspectives on how things may have really been, and, ultimately, help us see how much the wool has been pulled over our eyes, all of these years.

In the meantime, as we continue on with the chronology of Gen. 1, our next logical question might be: What about the *other* human souls left in the deep, dark depths of the supernatural *Sea*, up to this time? Quite possibly, if we move forward to day *five* of our Six-Day Creation, we'll now see it was time for God to bring another group of individuals up to the earth - as *human beings.*

Chapter 3

The Pre-Adamites

*And Adam gave names to every **animal**, **and** to the **birds of the heaven**, and to every **beast of the open field**. But for Adam, **no partner** was found like himself.*
- *Genizah Manuscripts* Gen. 2:20[1]

The above is a pseudo-biblical account of creation, around the same time the first man of Genesis, *Adam*, was designated to name each animal. If we notice, in the above, he **also** gave names to the *birds of the heaven* and every *beast of the open field*. Now, let's wait a minute: why notate these as two separate, definitive groups? Wouldn't it be easier just to say, "Adam named the animals?" And, of course, the obvious question: why was Adam looking for a partner among animals? Was he looking to make an animal his wife?

So, if the possibility exists that these two groups were not necessarily animals, per se, then just what *were* they? There are a number of ancient sources, including the Bible, who may list these "birds" and "beasts" in similar ways. Why?

Also, the Bible and others state that, at this time, Adam was looking for a partner - a helpmate or wife. What reason would Adam do this? Obviously, this was a time *before* Eve was created. So, the next obvious question must arise: was Adam *really* alone at this time? Could Adam have been, subtly, looking for a *human* mate, within the construct of individuals he was facing here? May there have been a bit *more* to the Garden of Eden story than most of us have once assumed?

In this chapter, we'll show ancient written evidence, even in the Bible, that paves the way towards there being *other* groups of people on the earth at this time, people alive before, and during, this early time of Adam. And these people collectively would be thought of as *pre-Adamites*. Let's take a look at the *fifth* day of creation, and discover how, quite probably, there were other groups of people formed at this time.

Day Five - Out of the Darkness

*The LORD by wisdom hath **founded the earth**; by understanding hath he established the heavens. By his knowledge the depths **are broken up**...*
                                                    - Prov. 3:19-20 (KJV)

*Dead things **are formed** from **under the waters**, and the inhabitants thereof.*
                                                    - Job 26:5 (KJV)

As we already recall (from the previous chapter), God would eventually have to bring a good number of human *souls* from the previous world, from the *Darkness* of the *Deep*. As human beings, the undecided would have to make the greatest decision of their lives. God assuredly knew about each individual and their moral leanings before the foundation of the world (Eph. 1:4, Mat. 25:34), now it was proving time:

*But ye are a **chosen** generation, a royal priesthood, an holy nation, a peculiar people; that ye should shew forth the praises of him who hath called you **out of darkness** into his marvellous light...*   *- I Pet.* 2:9 (KJV)

Interesting choice of words here. God knew "who was who," even when their souls were still in the *Darkness*! We know the *Darkness of the Deep* and the *Sea* both could have supernatural significances, so it shouldn't be too surprising to hear descriptive terms relating to *water*, here. The next time we hear of life "emerging out of some *watery* chaos" we just might be able to assume there's a link to something in the supernatural!

This, for example, leads us to a verse in Genesis 1:

*And God said, Let the **waters** bring forth abundantly the moving creature **that hath life**...*   *- Gen.* 1:20 (KJV)

As we see, Gen. 1:20 could have stated that God commanded life to come out of the supernatural waters of the *Darkness*. It was at this time He wanted to bring forth, abundantly, the moving creatures that *hath life*. Now, just *who* might be these "moving creatures?" And, are these creatures only animals; or something more? And, on top of it, what would be the significance of the phrase "that hath life?"

Our next postulation begins with these three words. When we look at the original Hebrew, they are represented by the word **nephesh**. The word *nephesh* not only means to be "living," to have "breath" or "life," but to also have "a higher intelligence" or "soul."[2] Now, what kinds of beings around us possess this sort of *higher intelligence*?

The Hebrew for the English phrase "bring forth abundantly" (in the above) is *sharats*, which means "to multiply," "bring forth," "swarm," even to "creep." And, the Hebrew for "moving creature" is *sherets*, which can signify "creeping" or "swarming things." Put them together (with these alternate Hebrew meanings) and we get a very different layout than the King James Version:

> *Let the waters bring forth the swarming (human?) creatures who* ***have a soul****...*
> *- Gen.* 1:20 (in retranslation)

Again, what beings on earth have such a *nephesh* or "higher intelligence," other than human beings (or angels)? What animals would have a *soul*?

Groups of Human Souls

> *And Elohim said, Let the waters swarm abundantly with moving creatures that have life... Everything swarmed at the same time, both good waters of holiness and evil waters of the other side... they were intermingled...*
> *- Zohar* Safra Det'zniuta 38[3]

We've already surmised that all of the vanquished souls of the previous world were made to swarm together in the *Darkness* - the good, the bad and the undecided. And, we've also postulated that *angels* might have already been brought up into our current world, via the *Light* (of the First Day). Still more may have brought up, along the way. What about the rest of the souls down there, the *human* souls? Could it be time for them?

Let's look at some of the possible groups of *human* individuals coming up now (in ways the Bible may have notated them):

- The *Beast of the Field*
- The *Cattle*
- The *Creeping Thing That Creepeth*
- The *Fowl of the Air*
- The *Adam* (or "*Adamites*")

Aren't most of these supposed to be animals? Much like the beginning verse of this chapter, why would authors be referring to names such as "birds of the heaven" and "beast of the field" and not just group the animal kingdom collectively? It's interesting, these **same** groups would, not only be mentioned at the beginning of the Six-Day Creation, but a thousand years later, as going aboard and coming off of Noah's ark! They were even mentioned (in the same manner) 1500 years after this time! But, why? What's in a name? It would seem so simple to just blanket the animal kingdom with one mention of "animals?" Why complicate things, with trying to break them up into individual groups, unless they possibly were not *meant* to represent animals in the original Hebrew?

Bird, Beast and Creature… Not Politically Expedient?

If we look at these names, they obviously don't sound like groups of people. So, why would the Bible do this in the first place? Isn't it insulting to even suggest such a thing? And, if they were indeed groups of people, what if the Bible didn't originally mean for it to be offensive? We have to remember that the Bible wasn't written in today's language, or with today's cultural rules of "political correctness." Things were a lot different, back then. Labels such as this weren't really that much out of the ordinary, or even meant to be totally "offensive," as often considered today. That's just the way it was.

The ancient Israelites, for example, often stated a number of nations around them acted "animal-like," because they were involved in idolatry, human sacrifice, etc.[4] Because of their moral leanings, people in general would be called "beasts," "creatures," even "dogs."[5] Again, that's just the way it was.

*His watchmen [are] blind: they are all ignorant, they [are] all dumb **dogs**, they cannot bark; sleeping, lying down, loving to slumber. Yea, [they are] greedy dogs [which] can never have enough, and they [are] shepherds [that] cannot understand: they all look to their own way, every one for his gain, from his quarter.*
$\qquad\qquad\qquad\qquad\qquad\qquad\qquad\qquad\qquad$ *- Isa.* 56:10-11 (KJV)

*For without [are] **dogs**, and sorcerers, and whoremongers, and murderers, and idolaters, and whosoever loveth and maketh a lie.*
$\qquad\qquad\qquad\qquad\qquad\qquad\qquad\qquad\qquad$ *- Rev.* 22:15 (KJV)

As we stated, these references weren't necessarily meant to be totally insulting. Even today, many women will call a man who sleeps with a lot of woman a *beast* or a *dog*, and it's not really considered "the end of the world." In fact, we have enough scriptural evidence to show that these incidents of "name-calling" had no negative ramifications whatsoever:

*For the **creature** was made subject to vanity, not willingly, but by reason of **him** who hath subjected the same in hope...* $\qquad\qquad\qquad$ *- Rom.* 8:20 (KJV)

*And (Jesus) he said unto them, Go ye into all the world, and preach the gospel to every **creature**.* $\qquad\qquad\qquad\qquad\qquad\qquad$ *- Mark* 16:15 (KJV)

*Therefore if any man be in Christ, he is a new **creature**: old things are passed away; behold, all things are become new.* $\qquad\qquad$ *- II Cor.* 5:17 (KJV)

Obviously, these verses weren't referring to animals. They were talking about people. A huge reason that people, back then, used these terms were probably related to a person's own *moral* choices, or their possible moral lean. It wasn't only the ancient Israelites who conversed in these ways. Practically all ancient nations used terms much this, pagan or Hebrew. With that said and done, could our verse in Genesis also be related to the *human* creature?

*And God said, Let the waters bring forth abundantly the moving **creature** that **hath life**...* $\qquad\qquad\qquad\qquad\qquad\qquad$ *- Gen.* 1:20 (KJV)

We must also remember that there wasn't too much around for ancient people to associate things, one to another. It wasn't like today, where we have the internet, the media, and all sorts of things to compare something with. This could have actually been a way for the ancients to "classify" something, such as a person, a particular group of individuals, what have you. Animals were one of the few things people could look at around them, and use to associate their thoughts with, to turn into symbols of something, whatever.

Since thoughts and perceptions have changed over the years, the men who translated the Bible into English may have even begun to turn these human groups into *beasts*, not knowing what they really were. These misconceptions really hurt our interpretations of the Bible, and what it really may be trying to say. So, let's try to undo some of it all, and move forward.

Let's look at one group. We've seen some interesting things in the quote at the beginning of this chapter:

*And Adam gave names to every **animal**, **and** to the **birds of the heaven**, and to every **beast of the open field**. But for Adam, no partner was found like himself.*
                                                                    - Genizah Manuscripts Gen. 2:20

It seems that Adam named animals, *and*, on top of that, named two other groups of animals? Doesn't make sense. Obviously, these groups probably weren't considered animals or they would have been lumped together with the rest of the animals. Could these have been sentient, rational beings?

Here's a quote from another ancient source:

*My lord, Adam, have you not heard the sound of my tears… have not the birds of the heavens and **the beasts of the earth** informed you, for I begged them all that they tell you about it…*
                                                                    - Book of Adam 20:2

Animals wouldn't go around talking to Adam, and informing him of anything. Let's look at this *Beast of the Earth* group.

The Beast of the Earth

It seems that, in the verse below, three groups were fashioned by God at once.

*And God said, Let the earth bring forth the living creature (soul) after his kind, **cattle**, and **creeping thing**, and **beast of the earth** after his kind: and it was so.*
                                        - Gen. 1:24 (KJV)

Starting with the *Beast of the Earth*, we see that the English word *beast* (in the above) originates in the Hebrew word *chay*. The word *chay* could mean "soul," "beast" or even "living creature." With those holding onto traditional beliefs, the translators of the King James Bible, for example, assumed that this *Beasts (or Chay) of the Earth* group was obviously some group of beasts, and not necessarily a specific group of "living creatures." We know the word "creatures" could easily stand for man.

For the sake of reinterpretation, we'll continue with using the *original* Hebrew words to describe groups such as this, using the word *Chay*, and not *beast*. The reason is because it seems a little bit more appropriate to use these Hebrew titles, rather than trying to use English words such as *beasts*, which may begin to sound insulting to some people.

As we proceed, these same ways to label these particular groups apparently goes way beyond the Bible. In other ancient texts, such as the *Book of Jasher*, we, again, see the *Beasts of the Field* and *Fowl of the Air* were mentioned separately from the animal kingdom, as if they were not the same:

*...I (God) will gather to thee all the **animals** of the earth, the **Beasts of the Field** and the **Fowls of the Air**... And thou (Noah) shalt go and seat thyself by the doors of the ark, and all the beasts, the animals, and the fowls, shall assemble... And the Lord brought this about on the next day, and **animals**, **Beasts** and **Fowls** came...*
                                        - Book of Jasher 6:1-3

*And the Lord sent all the **Beasts** and **animals** that stood round the ark.*
                                        - Book of Jasher 6:25

Again, why name these groups individually, and separate them from the rest of the animals, if they are animals, all the same?

How about in the Bible? Does the Bible give us evidence such as this, that some of these *beasts* may indeed be people? Of course, there are a good number of **actual** animals in the Bible who will (and should) definitely be noted as *beasts*, but not all! As we'll now see, there were definitely unsavory, immoral people the Bible described as thinking or acting as a *beast*:

*I said in mine heart, God shall judge the righteous and the wicked... I said in mine heart concerning the estate of the sons of men, that God might manifest them, and that they might see that they themselves are **beasts**.*
- Eccl. 3:18 (KJV)

In other examples, there were people from other pagan lands who, because of their practices, were thought of as *beasts*:

*...The Cretians are always liars, evil **beasts**...*
- Titus 1:12 (KJV)

*If after the manner of men I have fought with **beasts** at Ephesus, what advantageth it me, if the dead rise not? let us eat and drink; for to morrow we die.*
- I Cor. 15:32 (KJV)

These were all talking about people. How about this?

The beast (chay) of the field *shall honour me...*
- Isa. 43:20 (KJV)

What kind of animal knows how to *honor*? Only people do.

In a couple more examples, we know how domesticated animals usually subsist on grass, hay or cereals. These would typically be the "beasts of burden" an unbeliever might assume the Bible is referring to. Yet, some *Beast of the Field* in the Bible were considered flesh-eating (Gen. 9:3-5). Some were even known as *cannibals* (II Sam. 21:10). Not many of these larger animals eat their own. There is more:

> ... *thus said the Lord God;* **Speak** *unto every feathered* **fowl***, and to every* **beast of the field***, Assemble yourselves, and come; gather yourselves on every side to my sacrifice that I do sacrifice for you... that ye may eat* **flesh***, and drink* **blood***... And I will set my glory among the heathen, and all the heathen shall see my judgment that I have executed, and my hand that I have laid upon them.*
>
> *- Ezek.* 39:17 (KJV)

Again, we see that there were fowl and beasts who were *spoken* to, and also flesh-eating. Now, who rationally speaks to animals anyway? Are these verses doing nothing but describing something *metaphorically*, or could there be something more to it? True animals also really don't know, or care about, their own moral character.

With all of these anomalies, one really needs to take a second look at the origin of English words inserted here, such as "fowl" and "beast."

The Behemah

> *And God said, Let the earth bring forth the living creature (soul) after his kind,* **cattle***, and creeping thing, and beast of the earth after his kind: and it was so.*
>
> *- Gen.* 1:24 (KJV)

Going back to Gen. 1:24, we see another Hebrew word - *behemah* - also translated into the English as *beast*, or *cattle*. Could this represent still another group of human individuals?

Interestingly, one major dictionary defines the word *behemah* as "**someone** or something that is abnormally large and powerful" or "**a person** of exceptional importance and reputation."[6] Other dictionaries, such as Merriam-Webster (www.merriam-webster.com), also seem to confirm that a *beast* could also represent a human being. One archaic definition of *beast* has it as "a contemptible **person**" or "something formidable difficult to control or deal with." And, on top of this, the word *cattle* could also be defined as "**human beings** especially in masse (i.e. a group)."

In another interesting example, the following verse of the Bible describes *the Sabbath*, the designated Jewish day of rest:

*But the seventh day is the sabbath of the LORD thy God: in it thou shalt **not do any work**, thou, nor thy son, nor thy daughter, thy manservant, nor thy maidservant, nor thy **cattle (behemah)**, nor thy stranger that is within thy gates...*
                                                            - Ex. 20:10 (KJV)

As we see, the Bible seems to be doing nothing but mentioning people in the verse, with the *Behemah* right in the middle of it all. Why? Why even would *animals* need to "take a break" in these same ways anyhow?

So, now that we have even more evidence of this, could some of these *beasts* in the Bible (and elsewhere) actually be *human beings*, designated for a particular role in the Garden of Eden? Could they been fashioned as individual groups for a reason? What if God had plans for each individual group, with working roles or functions in the Garden of Eden? It, really, makes no sense for God to create individual groups of people for seemingly no reason. And, since one group was called the *Chay of the **Field***, for example, could this group originally have been designated to help *in a field* somewhere, or help out in farming methods? Maybe one group was for farming, one group (such as the *Behemah*) was to care for domesticated animals, etc. We really don't know for sure.

There is more.

The Creeping Thing That Creepeth

*And God said, Let the earth bring forth the living creature (soul) after his kind, cattle, and **creeping thing**, and beast of the earth after his kind: and it was so.*
                                                            - Gen. 1:24 (KJV)

Our last group of the three, the *Creeping Thing that Creepeth*, could in theory be a little different than the Behemah and Beast of the Field. As before, we'll use the Hebrew word **Remes** to replace the translated *Creeping Thing*, to dignify this group as a group of people, as well. There isn't a lot on the *Remes* (*Creeping Thing*) *that Creepeth* in the

Bible, however, but it does seem to be another important group created by God. It's only logical that they were another group of human individuals fashioned at the same time because they continue to be listed, along with the others. And, it's also logical to assume that they too may, somehow, have had a role in the Garden. As time goes on, and our research amplifies, we should be able to provide more speculation on all these above groups, what roles they may have had, and what they all may have been about.

The Fowl of the Air

> And God said, Let the waters bring forth abundantly the moving creature that hath life, and **fowl** that may fly above the earth in the open firmament of heaven.
> - Gen. 1:20 (KJV)

There's a bit more on the Fowl of the Air, however, but it proves to be a lot less believable (at least, with today's standards). But, we urge an open mind through it all, for that is the only way one will begin to see through the "smoke and mirrors" that have been placed over us.

In day *five*, many traditionalists have taken this day as the day God created the birds, or fowl, in the sky. In ancient times, the words *bird* and *fowl* could almost be used interchangeably.[7] The major difference between the two is that *fowl* are considered birds destined to be consumed by mankind (such as ducks, chickens, quails, etc.), and birds are not. All of it sounds "warm and fuzzy," of course, but could there be something more to this group as well, something human-like? If this group represents something beyond birds, then there may actually be real reasons why this group was called *Fowl of the Air*, something beyond what a lot of us might want to think, or believe.

Well, first off, what kind of human beings can fly? That answer would be none, at least in the common sense. To lay it out, plain and simple, the *Fowl of the Air* could actually be another group of humans, rather *human-like* individuals, brought up from the *Darkness*. They were not *totally* human. They also had some *angelic* qualities, as well. Think all of those diminutive, human-like individuals of ancient folklore: fairies, elves, dwarfs, leprechauns, you name it. Of course, at first thought, it may sound a little extraordinary, but many ancient people sure believed in them. In ways, they had what some would consider *higher*, or angelic, qualities. Yet, since they were part human, they also lived out their lives as human beings (at least until they fell back on these angelic qualities to manipulate the world around them).

We even find ancient people who generally held the idea that angels in general, or even beings with angelic qualities, were associated with the *fowl*. One ancient Jewish source claims:

> *When were the **angels** created?... They were created on the fifth day, for it is written, "And let **fowl** fly above the earth" (Gen. 1:20)... (Thus angels too **fall** within the category of **beings that fly**, and were created on the same day as all flying creatures)...*   *- Genesis Rabbah 1:3 (& notes)*[8]

Sound a little fantastic? Well, as we'll see, it all may not be too far from what the Bible stated all along! As we see, in the above, the *fowl* and angels both fall within the category of beings that can "fly." So, in order to cement the theory that these "flying" *birds* and *fowl* may, on occasion, be linked to *angelic beings*, we need to look at a few more verses.

> *And he cried mightily with a strong voice, saying, Babylon the great is fallen, is fallen, and is become the habitation of **devils**, and the hold of every foul **spirit**, and a cage of every unclean and hateful **bird**...*   *- Rev. 18:2 (KJV)*

The mention of a *bird*, in the above, clearly isn't regarding an innocent swallow. We find another Biblical verse that contains the same original Hebrew root word as was used for the *bird*, above:

> *And I saw an **angel** standing in the sun; and he cried with a loud voice, saying to all the **fowls** that fly in the midst of heaven, Come and gather yourselves together unto the supper of the great God...*   *- Rev. 19:17 (KJV)*

This time, it's translated as *fowl*. Not that angels were speaking to all of the "fowls that fly in the midst of heaven." Angels, of course, would have been talking here to other angels here, *not* birds! They would have *no* reason to invite ordinary hawks or eagles to sup with God. Maybe there's another reason angelic beings "fly" in the midst of heaven (as we shall see)!

Looking at another ancient source - *The Book of Adam* - and we discover an verbal exchange involving Adam and Eve. Eve was really upset at Adam, and didn't know where he was. She made an interesting plea to the beings of her immediate area:

> *Is there none among the **birds**, who would go to him and tell him (Adam), "Come help Eve, your spouse." I beg of you, all you **races of heaven**, and when you go to the east, relate my present sufferings to my lord (Adam).*   *- Book of Adam* 19:2[9]

Again, what kind of animal in the ancients could talk (to Eve)? What birds were of a *race*? And, why would Eve even want to call on just *animals*, to have them go talk to Adam, if they weren't cognitive, sentient creatures?[10]

Later on, in this same story, Adam eventually finds Eve, and she says to him:

> *My lord, Adam, have you not heard the sound of my tears… have not the **birds of the heavens** and the beasts of the earth informed you, for I begged them all that they tell you about it…*   *- Book of Adam* 20:2[11]

Again, if we start assuming that these *birds* or *fowl* could be lumped together in many ways, we've already seen examples of ancient works describing how they both can *fly*. Let's now look at some of the other possible meanings of *to fly*, or *flying*. The Bible and other sources seem to hint to this as one's ability to "pass through" something, or as one's "swiftness" in their ability to move in and out, or pass through. But, pass through what? Could this other definition of *flying*, or *flying though the air*, be related to one's own swiftness in *passing* through the supernatural "veil," or ability to *pass* from one world to another? In other words, "to fly," in respect to these particular *birds*, could mean that they have the ability to transcend both planes of existence. Angels have the ability to "fly" in this way, to appear or disappear in the air around us very quickly. Now we see why these particular *birds* or *fowl* could have been thought of as the *Fowl of the Air.*

> *Air* *spirits… were everywhere,* ***moving invisibly on their wings*** *above the world.*
> (Curran, 2010, p. 65)[12]

Interestingly, fairies, elves and other diminutive angelic-like humans of the past were also said to have had this ability. And it's funny, a large segment of the world's population once believed in these beings. There were many sightings of fairies, communications with, or even something more, and all of this began to slowly wane from public consciousness over time, especially beginning in the early 16th century. Why? Did we just becomes "smarter," or did things in the world change, along with our ways of thinking? There does seem to be a correlation with a few things. More on this coming…

But, for now, we could assume these particular *birds* or *fowl* could have existed in the ancients, also having had positions within the Garden of Eden. Maybe they were there to help solve problems, or do things that ordinary humans just couldn't do. Maybe, on occasion, human beings of the day needed to understand more, and didn't have the knowledge or ability to fathom what to do next.

The Adamites

What about the *Adam* group, the group that Adam would, through namesake, was essentially a part of? As we read in:

Gen. 1:
25 *And God made the beast of the earth after his kind, and cattle after their kind, and every thing that creepeth upon the earth after his kind: and God saw that it was good.*
26 *And God said, Let us make* ***man*** *in our image, after our likeness…*

Here, one more group of human beings is mentioned: the group *Adam* (also known as the *Adamites*). This group had the same name as the famous patriarch Adam; and, as one might guess, it could have been because Adam himself was considered patriarch, or something. We're not sure why, exactly. We will soon see that God would want to have Adam head up the Garden, and maybe the group was named in honor of this one famous man, yet to come. We're not sure.

This group, in the Bible, does often seem to be associated with the English word *man*. That's probably because translators - ancient and modern - may have felt the need to inserted it in there. Yet, there are a good number of words in the Bible to describe human beings without using this one, exact word. We're also not saying there were no other living, breathing men in the other groups. Of course there were. But, it seems there were reasons for trying to jumble up one (and only one) group of human individuals with the English word *man*… interesting reasons.

Christian tradition, of course, tells us there was one, and only *one*, man, named Adam. He was the only one formed by God here, and that's all. We have scriptural evidence, however, that may inform us to there actually being a lot *more* people on this earth than the one man:

So God created man in his own image, in the image of God created he him; **male** *and* **female** *created he* **them**.   *- Gen.* 1:27 (KJV)

Them? It seems obvious that God may have created an entire *group* of individuals on this Sixth Day, *male* and *female*, and not just *one* man. The next question that usually follows is: if there were more than one, then why were we almost *always* led to believe that only one man (named Adam) was formed, here?

Not "Father of the Human Race"?

Before we proceed, a lot of skepticism (from all fronts) may begin to rear its head. It's understandable… to a degree. Some people may even contemplate the thought of actual groups of people - the pre-Adamites - as being somehow unjust, racist, or what have you. Still others might not be able to swallow the concept that Adam wasn't the first human being, the father of humanity. Still more may that think we, somehow, evolved, over a long period of time; the first "Adam" and "Eve" ended up as two humanoids evolving out of the jungles of Africa. Maybe there still another option: let's contemplate the validity of there being up to *five* groups of individuals on earth by this time, and Adam being formed on top of it.

There is a dark underbelly of reasons which might motivate people not open to new thoughts such as the above. One reason is control. Another reason may be one's unwillingness to believe anything non-scientific. Let's look at one reason that Christians may quickly discount the possibility of the above. Their argument against pre-Adamites seems to be centered around one particular verse in Acts:

> *And hath made of one **blood** all nations of men for to dwell on all the face of the earth, and hath determined the times before appointed, and the bounds of their habitation…*   - *Acts* 17:26 (KJV)

According to tradition, here, Adam was considered the "blood" who represented the first human being, and the rest of the human race descended from him. This verse, indeed, seems to provide support for the idea. Since all of us are made of *one blood*, then how can we come from the *Darkness*, fashioned to branch out into various groups? If we are of only one blood, then we obviously come from one man. Yet, in this verse, the word *blood* was not even in early versions of the Bible, such as the King James.[13] It was added later, to make the verse "flow" better, or make it seem more "readable." But, we'll soon see that, by looking into the original Greek, it could mean something a lot different.[14]

Regardless if the word "blood" is supposed to be there or not, the verse still implies that we are all of one blood, right? It seems that way, if we take the verse *out* of context. But, we recall how important it is not to take any verses out of context in the Bible. And, understanding that there could be other possible meanings for the original Greek words here, we'll see that words in this verse could also be translated as *bloodshed*. So, when we insert the verse back *into* its original context, and look at some of the other possible meanings for the Greek, we'll see that the verse might take on a whole new meaning:

<u>Acts 17:</u>
24 *God that made the world and all things therein, seeing that he is Lord of heaven and earth, dwelleth not in temples made with hands;*
25 *Neither is worshipped with men's hands, as though he needed any thing, seeing he giveth to all life, and breath, and all things;*
26 **And He (a.k.a. God) made of <u>one's (i.e. Jesus')</u> bloodshed to be for all nations of men to dwell upon, on all the face of the earth, having determined the appointed times and boundaries of the habitation of men.**
        (in retranslation)
27 *That they should seek the Lord, if haply they might feel after him, and find him, though he be not far from every one of us...*

If we look at the verse in context, now, we see the meaning seems to be totally clear: the *one* discussed is really **Jesus**, and it was *his sacrifice of blood* which set the foundation for how man works on earth, from then on. We now see these verses refer to how a person should look to *God* for their satisfaction, and use Jesus' example of how to live. Simple. Yet, the translators tried to use certain words, even *add additional words*, to make things "fit in" with, probably, what they were taught, or their own assumption. Again, perfect original, *imperfect* translation (and translators**)**.

There's a reason why most Christians were taught that we *all* come from one man, even though, for example, modern science has established that the various groups of people in the world do *not* all have the same genetic makeup.[15] Why, then, have we been taught this for so long? Maybe there is something *deeper* here, something a little less than savory.

What is Behind All of this Disbelief Today?

Knowing this first, that there shall come in the last days **scoffers**, *walking after their own lusts...*   *- II Pet.* 3:3 (KJV)

In the last few hundred years or so ago (especially), we as a human race have had another serious struggle to deal with (beyond the iron-clad grip of science over most all interpretation): "political correctness." It's bad enough that we have science practically debunking everything that relates to the Bible, now it's also mean and unfair, or even bigoted, to suggest that any one group of human individuals might possess something that another group doesn't have, or that one group has one quality or characteristic and another group has something else. Politics shape a lot. Especially in today's world, Biblical translators and other movers-and-shakers, then, may try to "revamp" words which could sound even slightly *inoffensive* to other people, even if it compromised the integrity of the original document. That's a problem for seekers.

The same goes for the Bible. Some might feel the need to remove, alter or *change* whatever's in the Bible *they* feel is insensitive, prejudiced or, in any-way, offensive. They may do this, in order to force another, more socially-conscious meaning into the verse (just like inserting *blood* into the verse above). There are a lot of compassionate-minded individuals out there who want books - even books as old as the Bible - to be pleasing to *everyone*, regardless of what the book originally was trying to say. They may want to rectify the words to fit in with current views or standards of a science-based, secular society. But, whatever the seemingly-good, outer reason for these changes, there are also inner thought behind (as we'll eventually see). Those attempts to change what the Bible may have originally said can be very devastating to any individual trying to decipher and understand what the Word of God is all about.

As Peter stated (in the above), there will be people in the last days who will *scoff* at these words of the Bible, trying to interpret it into the ways *they* want - which is *exactly* what is going on today. Now, it's not really what the Bible says that's important, but what people *think* it should say! If "fairness" is one of the goals of this compassionate, politically correct bunch, then how "fair" is that to change the meanings, here? How can we look at what many have said to be the Word of God, and take real meanings out of it, if it has already been "sanitized" by self-serving, politically correct man?

Also, there are those who, in order to believe the Bible, may feel the need to have it "coincide" with modern-day laws of the scientific community. With these people, the *Fowl of the Air* actually being semi-angelic humans, or possibly even fairies, might not sit well too with science. By their laws, they should not exist. And that's the final say, since they are the deciding factor.

And, the concept of pre-Adamites may also not set too well with a number of Christians. In the Christian community, having us all "under one roof" makes it easier for them to claim, "We preach the Bible, and we are all under Adam. And, since the Bible is the book for all of those under Adam, then we, by default, should be designated to have spiritual authority over every individual on earth." Sounds more like a control thing - to make sure no one escapes the fact that *they* have "keys" to the kingdom. No one is immune to their desires to make the final interpretations, or to their need to fill the pews.

Evolutionists also work hard to push a belief known as *Monogenism*: the theory that states we all have a common origin.[16] Their reasons for believing this, however, are a little different. According to these people, the human race was not created by God. We came from two intelligent, "ape-like" ancestors. From a semi-human "Adam" and semi-human "Eve" the leap was finally made. They made the jump from ape-like being to actual human being. Since then, what continued was a gradual evolution of the species (over a couple million years), into what we all are today. This gradual, upward slope was necessary to show how gene-mutations and survivalist adaptations could have been the ones to do their magic, not God.

Yet, the pre-Adamite theory puts holes into those trying to convert us to these other ways of thought. It says practically the opposite: a creator *God* actually fashioned different groups of people from the beginning of our world. They all didn't come from two individuals, and they all didn't come from some kind of mutation or being "the fittest." And, as time marched on, the human race essentially continued with the *same* physical existence it had when it was first created. They replicated "kind after kind."

So, with this, it's really essential that we don't take the Bible out of context, nor maintain a blind eye to what the Holy Scriptures may *really* be saying. It's important we don't change things, for the sake of science, "political correctness," or even greed! Once we change the words of the Bible around, we could easily change the meanings. Once we change the meanings, we could change *history*. Once we change history, we could start to change modern-day reality.

We already have the *Gap Theory*, the *Well of Lost Souls* (the *Darkness of the Deep*) the *Sea*, and now the *pre-Adamites*. Wouldn't these all disrupt the "politically correct" apple cart of our modern world if many more got wind of them? Wouldn't they be against what a lot of people may *want* to be our history?

So, in order to move further into it all, let's now discuss the unique creation of one *man* within the particular Adamite group, and his contribution to the Garden of Eden. This one member would go on to become a major player in the early Bible, and one of the most prestigious men of his time. In today's "politically correct" vernacular: "It doesn't matter where you come from, it's what you make out of it." This one man would shine, at least for a little while, while the rest of the Adamites wouldn't really seem to. Even though the group had his namesake, almost nothing would be mentioned about the other members of this group from this point on, at least in a positive light. It would be this one Adamite, however, who would go on, siring numerous descendants who would each make their choice to follow God, and make something of their lives.

Yes, this man would be the one most of us know, today, as the **viceroy** of what God would brand the up-and-coming *Garden of Eden*, and his name would be *Adam*.

Chapter 4

The Adam is Formed

Disposed he the wild races of the beasts,
And to us mortals made subordinate
*All cattle; the God-formed one (**Adam**) made chief*
Of all things…
                    - Sibylline Oracles 2nd Fr. 13-18[1]

Some apparent mistranslations of the Bible and other works may already have a chance to be explained. As we have already seen, there could have been a *gap* between the actual creation of our world and the Six-Day Creation of Gen. 1; there could be such a thing as the *Well of Lost Souls*; phrases such as *Beast of the Field* and *Fowl of the Air* may not only stand for animals. What's the "next-step" in our reinterpretation of early Genesis? It's the formation of probably the most famous man of the time, known as *Adam*.

Adam was human, no doubt about it. He was from that Adamite group which, as already stated, didn't had much airtime in the Bible, since. And, although those other groups of the Bible did seem to possess a bit more airtime than these Adamites, they still were nowhere near the amount of airtime that Adam received. Why? What's so significant about this one, particular man? And why would the Bible be known as the *book of the generations of **Adam*** (Gen. 5:1)? What did he have over most of the pre-Adamites and Adamites around him? The reason was simple: Adam tried to turn the tables on what would become a generalized, negative direction that many, if not the majority, would begin to follow. Yes, Adam would decide to follow God, or at least want to. And God rewarded him because He thought he would remain loyal, from start to finish. So, let's get a little more into the "why's" of Adam's placement in the Garden of Eden, the rationales behind it all, and what happened to him because of the choices that he made.

This One Particular Man

The year was approximately 4000 B.C. Even though there were probably a number of angels around at this time, even though there were also human groups around at this time, the Adamites - the group that Adam belonged to - were also on the scene, but Adam wasn't yet.

As we recall, in the latter-half of the Sixth Day, we have:

Gen. 1:
26 *And God said, Let us make **man** (Adam) in our image, after our likeness: and let them have dominion over the fish of the sea, and over the fowl of the air, and over the cattle, and over all the earth, and over every creeping thing that creepeth upon the earth.*
27 *So God created man in his own image, in the image of God created he him; male and female created he them.*

In actuality, it seems the formulation of these Adamites were mentioned *two* times in the Book of Genesis, in *two* separate chapters. Why? Why have one creation in two places? This conundrum has baffled Biblical scholars in the past… until *now*. Quite probably, the above verses represented the time when the *entire group* of Adamites were formed. Soon after, in the next chapter of Genesis, the single man - *Adam* - would be formed. Simple. But, of course, not politically expedient to many.

> *…although Adam was the first man he was not the first human being…*
> (Bristowe, 1927, p. 17)[2]

The time for God's Six-Day reformulation of our world has now ended. After this, all there would be left would be the formation of one particular man.[3]

> *In 1655, Isaac de la Peyreira, a converted Jew, published a curious treatise on the Pre-Adamites. Arguing upon Romans v. 12-14, he contended that there were two creations of man; **that recorded in the first chapter of Genesis** and that described in the second chapter **being distinct.*** (Baring-Gould, 1881, p. 28)[4]

We recall, in the last chapter:

*And God said, Let us make **man** (the Adamites) in our image, after our likeness...
male and female created he **them**.*   *- Gen. 1:26-27 (KJV)*

Now, in this chapter, we have:

*And the LORD God formed man (the man, **Adam**) of the dust of the ground, and
breathed into his nostrils the breath of life; and man (the man, Adam) became a living
soul.*   *- Gen. 2:7 (KJV)*

Why mention the same event twice, unless these were two *separate*, distinct
formulations?

To gather even more support for this postulation, there seems to be a difference with
the original Hebrew words used to describe the way God formed the Adamites, as
compared to how He formed Adam. The Adamites (in Genesis, Chapter 1) were **created**
(using the Hebrew word *bara*); the solitary man Adam (in Genesis, Chapter 2) was
formed (using the Hebrew *yatsar*). Again, why were these different, if they were the
same creation? The reason for the different words probably was to show that this one,
particular Adamite was indeed formed *differently*.

The next thing for us to understand is how the word *man* was sometimes used in the
Bible. In Genesis Chapter 2, the original Hebrew words for *man* were configured a little
different differently than in Chapter 1. In Chapter 1, the Hebrew *Adam* was one single
word.[5] In Chapter 2, the word *Adam* is accompanied by another word: the word *the*.[6] This
the, in grammar, is recognized as the *article*. In our second example here, if we put the
two words together, we get *The Adam*. For some reason, this is different than just the first
example: *Adam*. What does this all mean?

When this particular article is added in Scripture, *Adam* seems to become emphatic
(which means one's "self," "this very," "this same" or "this same man Adam").[7] In other
words, *The Adam* easily stands for *one particular man*, whose name was *Adam*, a man set
apart from the others, him and him *alone*.[8] The word *Adam* without this article could,

then, easily stand for the rest of the Adamites, or *the group* Adam. Although it's not always protocol, it may help us to identify certain situations where God could be talking about the entire group of Adamites or singling out the one man, Adam.

What's So Special About this One Man?

There is more about this man.

> *And the LORD God said the angels who ministered before Him, Behold,* **Adam is sole on the earth,** *as* **I am sole** *in the heavens above; and it will be that they will arise from him* **who will know to discern between good and evil.**
> - *Targum Pseudo-Jonathan* III[9]

What a powerful verse, here. Apparently, God had something special planned for him. Adam was going to be formed at a *different* time, in a different way, and, yes, for a *different reason*. His main goal? Probably to help create an individual with a rock-solid moral structure, to be able to be a good example to others, and use this morality to help him do something so monumental as to run the Garden.

> *...God created Adam with own hand...*
> - *al-Tabari: The History of al-Tabari - Vol. I: General Introduction and From the Creation to the Flood* The Story of Adam 87[10]

> *And the LORD* **God** *formed man (Adam) of the dust of the ground, and* **breathed into his nostrils** *the breath of life;* **and man (Adam)** *became a living soul.*
> - *Gen.* 2:7 (KJV)

God Himself made the solitary Adam "a living soul." This was one reason Adam, as one man, was formed in a fairly special way. A couple of ancient Muslim authors also commented on this:

...he became... like potter's clay untouched by fire. When, after that... God blew the spirit into him...
> *- al-Tabari: The History of al-Tabari - Vol. I: General Introduction and From the Creation to the Flood* The Story of Adam 91[11]

...Adam... the most free and perfect of His creatures... the only one that was animated by His breath...
> *- Legends of the Mussulmans* Adam[12]

Let's look at more of what the Bible has to say.

In Our Image and Likeness...

*And God said, Let us make man in our **image**, after our likeness...*
> *- Gen.* 1:26 (KJV)

So, what is this *image* of God? This has been a hot button in times past, all the way up to today. There has almost always been *one* interpretation of this, and it's deeply guarded by Christians ancient and modern. You hear so many quotes, today, such as: "Every one of us (i.e. since we are all from Adam) has this same general human form as God, since we are created in His image;" "We are like God in form (and probably a lot more);" etc. Does this mean that we have a similar *form* to how God looks, or is? Do we have five fingers and toes as He does, and two arms and legs? It's funny how these quotes seem to come up so often in Christian/Catholic rhetoric, but they don't really go and explain too much about it. What if it could mean something *more*? According to a number of ancient texts, it does.

In the Bible, the English word translated as *image* comes from the original Hebrew, meaning "to shade."[13] This word has also been used to describe a spirit of the supernatural, something ghost like, what have you. This word *image*, as well, could be defined as a "likeness" or "resemblance" of something. Adam seemed to have been fashioned in this same *image* as God, maybe in a similar *spiritual* appearance (or *outer* form), like God and his angels were said to possess.

*The Hebrew word for "image" in all these passages is tzelem... meaning "shadow"
or "**reflection**"... Human beings... are similar to their mastery of the spiritual and
physical dimensions of the Maker.*   (Quayle, 2005, p. 23-24)[14]

So, what "reflection," "shadow" or "shade" are we really referring to? In the New
Testament, we see the English word for *man* originates in the Greek *anthropos*, a word
which could also mean "countenance" or "man-faced."[15] Factoring all of these
possibilities in, and we'll see that Adam's "image of God" could actually have been a
similar *countenance* or *shine* as God.[16] God and His angels could have "glowed" or
"shined" brightly, as one would picture an angel to do. Adam, too, may have had the
ability to glow the same, with a similar *shade* of brightness reserved for those of the
heavenly host. Well, what difference might this all make? One interpretation follows
along what a lot of Christians, today, would want you to think. The other doesn't
necessarily give them that courtesy. One interpretation almost places us with an element
of the "divine" inherently in us. The other forces us to admit we are just human,
regardless of any spiritual "additions" that may have been temporarily granted to our
imperfect forefathers.

Could it actually be only that angelic "shine?" We recall already that people of ancient
times would, quite often, identify each other by the features of *their face*. Could Adam
have had that angelic brightness, or shine, to *his* face, as well as his entire body? When
someone would see Adam coming, they knew there was something significant about him.
Adam was a respectful leader, someone of influence and moral authority in their brave,
new world.

*When you were **brightly** created in the likeness of God's shape, when every dear
creature was told that it should come to do you reverence.*
                         - Saltair na Rann 1789-1796[17]

This "shine" will become more important to our story, as we proceed further.

"The Thinker"

*And God said, Let us make man in our image, after our **likeness**...*
                                        - Gen. 1:26 (KJV)

There is more to Adam, and his position. As we recall, probably the most important characteristic of Adam to understand, and use for an example, was regarding how he *thought*. If this was the case, then what could be this "likeness" of God? We already have an idea what the *image* truly is. The word *likeness* originated from Hebrew words that could mean "to be like," a "similitude," as well as an "imagination" or "thought." Could being "in the likeness of God," here, refer to one's decision to follow the righteous ways of God, or to think or imagine how one could make themselves more Godly?

...Adam (was)... said to have received the inestimable gift of intellect... (a) "reflective or intellectual life"...
                                        (Bristowe, 1950, p. 91-92)[18]

...and there was in the body of Adam the inspiration of a speaking spirit, unto the illumination of the eyes and the hearing of the ears.
                                        - Targum Pseudo-Jonathan II[19]

This could also be thought of as one going after the "heart" of another.

...Adam... was in the mind (or, thought) of God aforetime...
                                        - Bakhayla Mikael p. 8[20]

...the spirit came to Adam by way of his head.
        - al-Tabari: The History of al-Tabari - Vol. I: General Introduction and From the Creation to the Flood The Story of Adam 91[21]

Adam was even known, by some ancient sources, as the *Thinker* - the one who possessed a specific *style* of thought.[22] Maybe Adam often used his rationality, sensibility and consciousness. Maybe these thoughts were, then, considered akin to the thoughts of

God. Maybe these thoughts were also good to have, if one was supposed to the Garden of Eden.

*In Sanskrit literature the first man is called Manu or Menu... The fact that the word "Man" meant a **thinker** Professor Max Muller writes: "Man, a derivative root, means **to think**. From this we have the Sanskrit Manu, originally the thinker, then man." (Lectures. Vol I.p.425).*   (Bristowe, 1927, p. 16-17)[23]

*...he (God) created man in the **likeness** of his own form, and put into him eyes to see, and ears to hear, and heart to **reflect**, and **intellect** wherewith to **deliberate**.*
     - 2 Enoch (The Book of the Secrets of Enoch) 65:2[24]

From the following ancient text, Adam was given the opportunity to name all of the animals he was to head up. We'll see how his striving for the "likeness of God" could have had an effect on his decision-making:

*(Adam speaking to God...) And Thy will was that I should name them all, one by one, with a suitable name. But **Thou gavest me understanding and knowledge, and a pure heart and a right mind from Thee**, that I should name them **after Thine own mind** regarding the naming of them.*
     - First Book of Adam and Eve (The Conflict of Adam and
     Eve with Satan) 34:8[25]

Adam and his direct descendents seemed to retain this way of thinking the most, not anyone else, not even the other Adamites. The main reason his descendants kept on with his way of thinking is, probably, because he drove it into them.

*Remember, O Lord that... Thou hast fashioned Adam, our father, in the **likeness** of Thy glory; Thou didst breathe a breath of life into his nostrils and, with **understanding**, **knowledge** Thou didst give him... Thou didst make him to rule over the Garden of Eden which Thou didst plant...*
     - The Words of the Heavenly Lights (4Q504) Fr. 8 recto[26]

Next, the Garden was to be his job, his main position, and it took someone with a level head and probably a lot of patience to run it properly. So, many of the things one could easily take as "common sense" would probably need to be manifested here, for it to all go smoothly. Are these thoughts akin to God?

...And Also From Different Material

And the LORD God... took dust from the place of the house of the sanctuary, and from the four winds of the world, and mixed from all the waters of the world...
                                                                    - Targum Pseudo-Jonathan II[27]

The Bible states our physical bodies came from elements of this earth, that's fairly obvious. One reason the Adamites were so-named was, according to one ancient source, because they were thought to be those "of the ground," especially *red* ground.[28] The man *Adam*, however, was said to have a name which also signified "his own place of origin."[29] Following this train of logic, we could figure that this man, Adam, may have been unique because God brought him up from **one specific kind** of dirt, unlike the other Adamic individuals. The other human groups were probably brought up in much the same way as the Adamites. So, where does that leave *Adam*, and how did the way God brought him up make a difference? Let's see.

Adam was apparently brought up from a fine *dust*, the dust of some red-colored ground! Well, what's the significance of this dust? Again, we see that the formation of Adam was a single, significant formation, apart from all the others. This *dust* that Adam was made from was even, according to some, a form of clay:[30]

*Now, for what reason did God make Adam out of these four materials unless it were [to show] that everything which is in the world should be in **subordination** to him through them? He took a grain from the earth in order that everything in nature which is formed of earth should be subject unto him; and a drop of water in order that everything which is in the seas and rivers should be his; and a puff of air so that all kinds [of creatures] which fly in the air might be given unto him; and the heat of fire so that all the beings that **are fiery in nature**, and **the celestial hosts**, might be **his helpers**.*
                                                    - Cave of Treasures The Creation of Adam[31]

On top of it, we'll see that Adam - this man of dust - would be given dominion over those working in the Garden, and **even** over some of angelic souls in the Garden, as well! Now, how could this "man of dust" be allowed to work on such a high level, or on a plateau of authority even higher than angels? Dust does not seem like a very good substance to make a leader out of, would it? Gold maybe, but dust… no.

God's Favorite - Red and White Dust?

So, as we begin to follow the average man's train of thought (today), it's easy to start gathering some rather interesting assumptions about this whole concept of Adam. If God was to create something like a viceroy, or leader, of this Garden, wouldn't He have made Adam *glorious* in every way, and out of glorious, high-value materials? Also, there are those, by now, who might begin to think that God may "play favorites," like He did with Adam. Maybe God could be part-racist, now-a-days, because He decided to make a leader out of one group, compared to another. Who knows. Maybe God is even sexist in a way, because He chose to make a man the leader, not a woman. The list could go on and on.

Yet, there is plenty to dispel all of this. Following this same train of logic, if He really "plays favorites" then He probably should have created all of the human groups in some sort of order. He definitely should have formed His viceroy, Adam, first, since he was the "top of the food chain," and the workers of the Garden later on. Make sense? He, however, began to bring up the souls from the *Darkness* in a much different, and somewhat mystifying, order: He began with the angels, then began to formulate the groups of *Owph of the Air*, *Chay of the Field*, the *Behemah* and the *Adamites*. **Lastly**, He began work on creating *Adam* himself![32] So, if we think about it: He formed the worthy angels first; then the other human beings; and *lastly* Adam (and from *dust* on top of it)! By today's standards, it doesn't seem like how one would give more status to a man, or a group. But, again, there's a reason for this all.

We continue further by looking a little more into Adam's physical characteristics. The name *Adam*, as we've already postulated, comes directly from a Hebrew word that means "red earth." Going deeper, this Hebrew word also has roots which can mean "to be red," "to cause to show red" or be "ruddy."[33] So, now, we can diagnose another unique characteristic of this man:

> ...**reddish clay** *suggests the presence of iron oxide, which is the mineral that makes blood red and accounts for the red-faced countenance of blushing. The same root turns up in the Biblical Hebrew as "Admoni"... where the description is commonly interpreted as "red-haired" or "ruddy".*
> ("Wikipedia, the Free Encyclopedia, *Adam*", n. d., p. 5)[34]

The word *ruddy* can also mean the ability of one to *show red* in their face, such as one's ability *to blush*. The word *Adam*, also, could stand for an individual who was thought to be *fair*. Put them all together, and we see the definition of Adam's name might also be related to the fairness, or whiteness, of his skin.[35] Most know the ability to *blush* is evident in a lot of people in the Caucasian race. So, if one were making conclusions about it all, they may be able to conclude that Adam had fair skin, white skin, as well as rosy (or red) cheeks.[36]

Now, wait a minute. Is this only an assumption? Is there some kind of racial thing going on? Well, it's really not meant to go in any political direction (as we'll see), or sound "superior" in any way, but only in the direction of describing *one* man, and his story.

As we stated, the rest of the group Adam belonged to, the Adamites, weren't really talked about much at all. It was, in reality, the descendents of Adam himself who often seemed to strive after God, and were noted for it. The descendants of Adam who really seemed to hit the "big time," as most who read the Bible know, were the *Israelites*. We'll eventually see that Adam, and the Israelites, both occasionally fell by the wayside, in regards to following the correct moral pathways, so being a member of this family is absolutely no guarantee of moral cohesiveness.

Further investigating into Adam's physical make-up, and we, next, understand that it shouldn't take a lot to understand that Israelites, as the descendants of Adam, should have had a similar complexion. There's actually a verse in the Bible which describes some of the Israeli people as "...purer than snow, they were whiter than milk, they were more ruddy in body than rubies (Lam. 4:7)." Ezra, in the Bible, also had the ability to *blush*

(Ezra 9:6). Solomon, son of the famous Jewish king David, was also said to have had a lover. His lover, the Queen of Sheba, described him as:

My beloved is white and ruddy, the chiefest among ten thousand.
                                    - *Song of Sol.* 5:10 (KJV)

Noah, another descendent of Adam, was described in this way:

And his body was white as snow and red as the blooming of a rose…
                                    - *1 Enoch* 106:2[37]

"Well… so what?" One might ask. Does that mean, again, that God "plays favorites," just because the Israelites may be this same hue? Did God assign those with light skin as some sort of *superior* group, here? We'll soon see that this was, clearly, **not** the case.

The Bible does state that human beings were made "a little lower than the angels (Psa. 8:5)." So, if this was really the case, one would naturally assume things like: God should have created the higher, angelic beings *first*; **with Adam *next*** (because he was a little lower than the angels); followed by the rest of the people. That all seems logical. Yet, as we know, it's not this way.

Also, if Adam was really fashioned for his *greatness* over people, then why wouldn't God have fashioned Adam out of the *best* material on earth? Those other groups of human beings, including the Adamites, were said to have been formed out of solid ground, yet **Adam** was formed out of plain old *dust*. We even can see that *dust*, to the ancients, was not a very worthy material to form something, none-the-less Adam! Dust was, in the past, often considered a material of very *low* quality.[38] The Hebrew meaning for *dust* (in Gen. 2) not only stands for "dry earth," but also "ashes," "debris," even "rubbish." Psa. 104:29 also seems to express dust as the ***lowness*** *and fragility of human nature*.[39] Interesting. The Bible sometimes even uses *dust* and ***dung*** interchangeably![40] So much for these assumptions. Yet, why the *choice* of dust? It really doesn't sound too practical, if God wanted a "picture-perfect" example of His man Adam.

The logic behind it all is simple: *humility*. The birth of Jesus Christ - the savior of the world - took place in a *manger*, or even a *cave*, and, again, not in some wonderful palace. We see **humility**, again, in how God wanted to make His point, here. It all doesn't fit well in what a number would, today, define as thoughts of "supremacy," or "superiority."

Gen. 2:

8 *And the LORD God planted a garden eastward in Eden; and there he put the man whom he had formed.*

15 *And the LORD God took the man, and put him into the garden of Eden to **dress it** and **to keep it**.*

We also see, in the above, that God didn't appoint Adam to sit on some **throne**. He didn't appoint him to be some dictator. God apportioned Adam to be *the leader of a garden* - lead **farmer**.[41] Now we know how really God works. He loves all people who want to follow Him, not just a select few. And, if you really want to try and make sense of it all, you really need to follow His ways, and not necessarily the ways of the world may tell you.

Now, with all of this said and done, and our understanding how God would use things such as *humility* in these particular ways, we might also need to understand that *someone* was needed to run the Garden of Eden. Somebody had to do it. Everybody can't run it at once. It'd simply be a case of "too many cooks spoil the broth." There is organization to every cosmos. There has to be, really, or there would be chaos. There's even hierarchy in the angels of the supernatural! So, why would this world be any different?

And, to top it all off, if one really considers all of the horrible things that resulted from the Fall of **Adam** and Eve, we really shouldn't be too happy with the viceroy Adam, overall. After all, Adam, an *Adamite*, did seem to help muck up everything for the rest of the human race. Even with this unique creation, he *was* a major factor in helping usher sin into the world. Not to say that other members of these other human groups may not have done the same thing, that's really not the point. What we're getting to is this: it seems clear that we are all human. No one has that "divine spark" imbedded within each one of us. We can reach a higher plane, each and every one of us, if we look to Him for guidance. God wants *everyone* to come into His fold, if they so *want* to. That is the true kicker.

Don't fall for all of the smoke and mirrors. It's simply that everyone has their own lot in life, and needs to fulfill it. Some were to make more money. Some were to be taller. Whatever. When it all boils down to is this: all of us - even Adam - is the same on Judgment Day. One's devotion to God while on earth, and willingness to accept Him in how He decides things, is what *really* should matter!

Ultimately, we've already stated the most *important* thing in it all (regarding Adam and his descendents): beyond everything else that can be worked up in order to muddy the waters of our understanding, we *do* know that it is the *choices* one makes (even Adam), and the choices our descendents make, which will help set the sails for understanding true right, true wrong, and what's next in our spiritual future:

> *...and it will be that they will arise from him* **who <u>will</u> <u>know</u> to discern between good and evil***.*
> — *Targum Pseudo-Jonathan* III[42]

The Seventh Day, and All Was Good (At Least Temporarily)

<u>Gen. 1</u>:
28 *And God blessed them, and God said unto them, Be fruitful, and multiply, and replenish the earth, and subdue it.*
31 *And God saw every thing that he had made, and, behold, it was very good. And the evening and the morning were the sixth day.*

<u>Gen. 2</u>:
1 *Thus the heavens and the earth were finished, and all the* **host** *of them.*

Moving forward, we've already postulated that there were a *host* of angels already brought up, and around the earth, slightly before the time of Adam's formation. The Hebrew word for *host*, in the above, most probably included these angels, as well.[43] A number of ancient sources also stated that *Adam* was given control over a number of those angelic beings. And, as we'll see, one lowly man's authority over these angels would soon be a major problem to the whole layout of this ancient Garden, a problem which would eventually affect the entire world God refashioned.

At the end of the Six-Day Creation God was apparently satisfied with His attempt to replenish the earth. Our current world was ready to go, with Adam, the angels, human beings and even humans with angelic-like qualities in the mixture. Our organized, functional *world* was now in order. There was a new harmony to the cosmos. As we recall:

> *Disposed he the wild races of the beasts,*
> *And to us mortals made subordinate*
> *All cattle; the God-formed one (**Adam**) made chief*
> *Of all things; and subordinate to man*
> *He put all variegated forms of life,*
> *And things that are **incomprehensible**.*
> *   - Sibylline Oracles* 2nd Fr. 13-8[44]

The incomprehensible agents in the Garden, here, were no doubt those of a mystical, supernatural nature.

Yet, everyone had a purpose. It all just seemed to work as it should. Angels had roles. The people of those different groups probably had some kind of role, somewhere. Each knew his or her place in the community, and keeping the Garden functioning.[45] But, this of course would not last for too long.

One Man to Manage… or Mismanage

With so much going on, the moral position that Adam held was probably something that a majority of the working order around would have looked up to. The pressure was on, and he did his best. But, there was more on the horizon.

Gen. 2:
5 …and there was not a man to till the ground.
*7 And the LORD God formed man (**Adam**) of the dust of the ground…*

God, though, may have thought He had His man. With Adam now on the scene, we'll now discover one *more* reason why the Garden really needed a "manager" of sorts: our world, even back in this early time, wasn't exactly perfect. It wasn't exactly free and clear of potential problems. Even though the world of our Six-Day Creation was made to be **very** *good*, it wasn't perfect. There were still things to figure out in the Garden, and egos to deal with.

First off, we see:

As Dr. Kitto writes: "To dress and keep the Garden of Eden, Adam not only required the necessary implements, but also the knowledge of operations for insuring future produce, the use of water and the various trainings of the plants and trees."
(Bristowe, 1927, p. 29)[46]

As with any garden, there was *some* work to be done. Even though it wasn't too hard, *a little* human effort was needed, there. People had to do something for their sustenance:[47]

...in spite of all this, man obtains his food in toil and trouble.
- Chronicles of Jerahmeel 6:14[48]

Understanding what our world looks like *now*, we probably can guess this fragile working environment (under Adam) wasn't going to last. The next question that may naturally arise is: if the world was fashioned so wonderfully under God, and it was made *very good*, then how *could* anything go wrong? What would have happened to Adam, which allowed for the destruction of this entire organized cosmos?

We'll now see that there were sentient beings, since the beginning of this world, who resented Adam's position of authority here, and even wanted to dispel him from it. The days of Adam presiding over a working cosmos such as this would soon be on a sliding scale, *downward*. The era of our world remaining "very good" (as in Gen. 1:31) was soon about to end.

Chapter 5

Adam and the Angels:
Dissension in the Garden

*And God saw every thing... and, behold, it **was** very good.*
                                             - Gen. 1:31 (KJV)

We'll now discover that, because *some* inhabitants were about to utilize their own "free will," tensions were about to rise. There would be those who had a problem with the way things were - a problem with Adam's authority. There would soon be "trouble in Paradise."

The first major accomplishment after the Six-Day Creation was, obviously, the Garden of Eden. The word *Eden* may relate to words such as "delight," "pleasure," as well as "paradise."[1] It may have even had a mountain close to it, the "gateway" mount to God Himself.[2] Possibly being created on the Third Day, the Garden was truly a beautiful place, where everything seemed to go well, there was no pain, and everyone seemed to be happy.

The word *Eden*, however, could also be equated with a "plain" or plot of "uncultivated land." From this, we may be able to gather that the Garden was located on an open, uncultivated plain. The meaning of a similar word *Edin* (in ancient Akkadian myth) is "steppe" or "terrace."[3] If this *Edin* could be the same as the Biblical *Eden*, then the Bible's Garden could have actually been a raised (or stepped) agricultural plot of land, or stepped terrace. Some ancient sources even said the Garden was a **walled enclosure**.[4] Why might this be so significant? Let's see.

According to one ancient source, Eve proclaimed:

*God set us to **guard** the Garden...*
                                             - Penitence of our Forefather Adam [44]17.3[5]

An interesting question that may naturally follow: if the world was created *very good*, then why would the Garden need to be placed on a stepped plateau, or even need to have surrounding walls? *Who* or what would individuals in the Garden really need protection from?[6]

The Fall of Angels… Before Our World

Around this time, there could have been at least three groups of angels in the vicinity of Adam, all of whom who had "fallen from grace." These highly-esteemed angels would rebel against God, and eventually be *demoted* from their once-lofty positions. What would have been their driving force? It would stem from the use of their own *free will*.[7] The first couple of occurrences could have taken place right around the time God created Adam. The third probably occurred around a thousand years later. There was trouble brewing, continually over time, on account of these angels.

Beyond these three, there might have even been a dissension of angels *before* the reformation of our current world! The prophet Jeremiah speaks of something very interesting:

<u>Jer. 4</u>:
24 *I beheld the mountains, and, lo, they trembled, and all the hills moved lightly.*
25 *I beheld, and, lo, there was no man, and all the **Fowl** (or birds) **of the Air** (or, the heavens) were fled.*
(in retranslation)

Could these tragic events be providing us a hint to the destruction of our previous world? And, if so, could there have been an angelic group, or group similar to the *Fowl of the Air*, before our current world who had *fled*? Maybe some of these angels or angel-like beings *fled* the destruction of the previous world in some way - taken down to the Darkness, or possibly even (somehow) "chased" away by God, and allowed to escape somewhere.[8] Who knows? We do know that a good deal of angels or spiritual *birds* (i.e. *owph*) may have been brought back into our current world by God, at the era of the Six-Day Creation.

There were angels, all around our atmosphere, whose role it was to "help out" or, otherwise, make sure the world was a better place... assisting whomever God said they should. That was their role. Instead, as we'll see, a number of these angels helped turn the working world in the *opposite* direction. What happened, and why?

Leader of the First Group?

Looking further into the Bible, and we may have names of at least two angelic groups who could have even existed, prior to our present world's formation:

Job 38:
1 *Then the LORD answered Job out of the whirlwind, and said...*
4 *Where wast thou when I laid the foundations of the earth? declare, if thou hast understanding...*
7 *When the **morning stars** sang together, and all the **sons of God** shouted for joy?*

Job 1:
6 *Now there was a day when the **sons of God** came to present themselves before the Lord, and **Satan** came also among them.*

Here, we see the *Morning Stars* and the *Sons of God*. These *Sons of God* are in both of the above verses, so it's fairly easy to associate them as one group. Let's, first, concentrate a little more on these *Morning Stars*. We recall, there was probably angels of *light* created on the First Day. Could this *light* be these *Morning Stars*?

What about the famous archangel Satan (or Lucifer)? Could he have, at one time, possibly been a leader of this angelic *light*? Or, was he a Son of God (as it seems he may have been associated with, in the above)? The Bible does say that Satan did appear as an angel of *light* (II Cor. 11:14), but he was also thought of as a *Son of the Morning* (in Isa. 14:12). We are simply not sure.

*And when he (Satan) was in the heavens, in the realms of **light**, he knew naught of darkness.*
        - First Book of Adam and Eve (The Conflict of Adam and Eve with Satan) 13:4[9]

At least, we know that Satan probably had sway over some groups of angels, in some way.[10] Whomever Satan was in charge of, and whatever group he was from, he apparently would be among the *first* who would want to dissent from Adam's position in the Garden. It only makes sense. But, why? What, in the onset, could have happened to allow him, to allow him to feel this way?

Former Ruler of the World?

*(God speaking) Adam has life on earth, and I created a garden in Eden in the east... I made the heavens open to him, that he should see the angels singing the song of victory, and the gloomless **light**; And he was continuously in paradise, and the devil understood that I **wanted to create another world**, because Adam was lord on earth, to rule and control it. The devil is the evil spirit of the lower places... and he understood his condemnation and the sin which **he had sinned before**...*
- *2 Enoch (The Book of the Secrets of Enoch)* 31:1-5[11]

Just who was this *devil*? Was it Satan, or was it someone else? A lot of us may assumed so, in the past. But, with a little esoteric knowledge of what may have happened before, it may now make more sense. Apparently, for whatever reason, this *devil* may have actually been brought down from heaven, and set into the world *before* our own. God may have directed *him* (believe it or not) to run some things on the earth... and it all didn't work out.[12] As we recall from our chapter on the *Gap Theory*, evil probably did not begin in the time of Adam. It was probably present *before* the foundation of our world! That's why God had to destroy it. So, another question which may naturally arise: just who or what might have brought on this previous world's destruction, and why?

According to ancient sources, including Mormon thought, God intended the angel *Sammael* (or *Satan*) to actually rule this previous world. He was once in a lofty position, sent down from his official position in heaven (watching over God's throne) to rule over this all. According to some, he was also, at one time, an overseer and musician of God's heavenly court. What a lofty position. We don't know if he was satisfied or dissatisfied with his new assignment on earth, but something went horribly wrong with his dominion down here. Apparently, as a punishment, this angel then *lost* his position as world ruler, and was also *not* able to ascend back into his former, heavenly abode. We have some ancient commentaries which seem to support this:

> *...he belonged to the **remnant** of the jinn (angels) who **were on earth**. They shed blood and caused corruption on it.*
> > *- al-Tabari: The History of al-Tabari - Vol. I: General Introduction and From the Creation to the Flood The Story of Iblis 84 (also 81)*[13]

> *...**they** cast the world into ruins, were themselves **driven** from the **world in ruin**...*
> > *- Genesis Rabbah 26:7*[14]

> ***Before** the Lord God [created] earth, he created the nine divisions of angels for the service of his divinity. Now the wicked Sadael and Beliar were the heads of the divisions of Satan; they were adorn gloriously, and were higher than all the angels and all the divisions of the angels... But the detestable Satan did not want to bless God and was arrogant in his heart... And the Lord God commanded the... great Gabriel, and the terrible Michael, and nine divisions of the angels, and they fall upon Sadael and all his attendants, smote them, and cast them down like hail from a cloud.*
> > *- Armenian Apocryphal Adam Literature Transgression 1-4*[15]

Apparently, Sammael (or Satan) rebelled, and his punishment was then laid out before him.[16] Even Jesus spoke of the Adversary as "Prince of this World" (John 16:30). Could this be because Satan might have once ruled over the world?[17]

> *...before Adam, the jinn (i.e. angels) were on the earth. God sent Iblis to act among them as judge. He did so conscientiously for a thousand years, so that he eventually was called "arbiter." God called him thus and reveled to him His name. At that, he became filled with haughtiness. He became self-important and caused terror, hostility, and hatred among those to whom God had sent him as arbiter. This is assumed to have caused them to fight so bitterly on earth for two thousand years that their horses waded in the blood of (those killed). They continued. This is (meant by) God's word: "Were We wearied by the first creation? No! Rather they are in uncertainty about a new creation (at the end of the world)," and (by) the statement of the angels: "Will You place on (earth) one who will cause corruption on it and shed blood?" At that, God sent a fire that consumed them. They continued. When Iblis saw the punishment that had descended upon his people, he ascended to heaven. He stayed with the angels worshiping God in heaven as zealously as did no other creature.*
> > *- al-Tabari: The History of al-Tabari - Vol. I: General Introduction and From the Creation to the Flood The Story of Adam 85-86*[18]

So, just who is this *Iblis*? Was he Satan, or another angel? Apparently, whomever he was, he seemed to have been around before the formation of our present world. So, to "let the cat out of the bag" a little early here, let's discover how there may actually have been **two** separate angelic beings around this time who became corrupt. These two leaders may have been mentioned throughout ancient texts, yet both were thought of as this same "devil." Sammael (or Satan), obviously, was one of them. The other will become more apparent, as time goes on. But, for now, the important thing to remember is that there could have been *more than one* angelic leader who went rouge back then.

Also, whatever really may have happened before our present era, whatever might have brought on the previous world's destruction, we do know that it all would have been engineered by God Himself. God had to do it, as a judgment against a world of wrongdoers. Apparently, as we see in the above, Iblis (whomever he might be) really felt afraid of God's wrath, and tried to do whatever he could possibly do to save his own skin. Assuredly, if God was a forgiving God (which He is), then punishment were made to fit the crime.

Now, to get to the nitty-gritty of what brought on all of this dissension, let's begin to put all of the pieces together.

The Angel's Replacement

*Certain of the angels having fallen, God made **men**, that they might take **their vacated places**.* (Baring-Gould, 1881, p. 21)[19]

*...Which to those rebel angels prohibited return... he stopped their service... **In their room** he created **mankind**... May He give them strength, never to neglect his world.* (Bristowe, 1950, p. 39)[20]

The above authors seem to follow the ancient presumption that, through the Six-Day Creation, mankind was created (at least in part) to *fill the void* left by the dissension of a number of ungrateful, fallen angels![21] And this dissention event, apparently, began *even before* the formation of our current world. One man then, in particular, was to be ushered in, and along with this, this would usher in a lot of problems as well:

*And God the beneficent, because of **Satan's arrogance**, created earthen **Adam** to fill the place of the fallen angels.*
- Armenian Apocryphal Adam Literature Transgression 1[22]

Adam, himself, may have also been formed to replace the authority of these highest angels on earth, at the time. It seems obvious that any angels who might have been "in charge" at this present time would have felt a little taken back by it all, and may have even wanted to get back some of their own dignity and worthiness, at least in their eyes.

*When Iblis saw the punishment that had descended... he ascended to heaven. He stayed with the angels worshiping God in heaven as zealously as did no other creature. He **continued to do so, until** God created **Adam**...*
- al-Tabari: The History of al-Tabari - Vol. I: General Introduction and From the Creation to the Flood The Story of Adam 86[23]

Adam's Dominion Questioned

*When the Holy One, blessed be He (i.e. God), desired to create man, He said to the angels, "Let us make man in our image..." He wanted to make him a leader over all the angels above, so that **he might govern** all the angels and **they would be under his rule**...*
- Zohar Beresheet A20[24]

*God... made **him** ruler over all the earth and of all the jinn (i.e. angels)...*
- al-Tabari: The History of al-Tabari - Vol. I: General Introduction and From the Creation to the Flood The First House on Earth 130[25]

Soon before the formation of humanity, God went to his accompanying angels (possibly, the *light*) and said, "Let us make man in our image" (Gen. 1:26). So, on top of this, God wanted these angels to understand one more thing about His final formulation - Adam:

*Just as all of you praise Me in the heights of heaven so he (**Adam**) professes My Unity on earth...*
- Pirke deR. Eliezer XIII[26]

God have *Adam* a crown of glory and honor, even over these surrounding angels.[27] He was to be the new viceroy of God on this earth:[28]

*...**Adam** walked about the Garden of Eden like one of the ministering angels.*
                                        - Chronicles of Jerahmeel 6:13[29]

According to one source, he was even given knowledge of the angels! According to the book *The Traditions of the Jews*, some of the upper angels in heaven were not even permitted to know some of this information Adam was privy to. And, Adam also took some of these 'upper secrets' and wrote down in his own, special book.[30] A number of these angels quickly began to gripe about how this whole thing was going down. And, as things began to progress, God was to advance Adam's position even further:

*And again, when he (God) bringeth in the firstbegotten into the world, he saith, And let all the **angels** of God worship him.*   *- Heb.* 1:6 (KJV)

In the original Hebrew, the word *worship* (in the above) stands for paying *homage* to, or showing *reverence* to. Adam was not to be worshiped as a god, but to be respected as the new leader. There's a difference, at least in God's eyes.

We may already know (via Psa. 8:5) that man was made a *little* lower than the angels. And, these angels, as lofty as they once were, were not very excited about recognizing Adam as the leading authority on earth. In consequence, Adam actually felt very honored, and remained totally humbled by it all.[31] As we know, this was because it was *God's* way.

*The animals all came to bow down to Adam and worship him, **Adam directed them** to all worship **God**, as ruler of the earth.*   (Baring-Gould, 1881, p. 26)[32]

Adam probably held himself to a standard such as the following:

*Do not rejoice that the **spirits submit to you**, but rejoice that your names are written in Heaven.*   - *Luke* 20:20 (KJV)

This helped solidified the authority and confidence God had in Adam. And, because of this, it becomes fairly easy to assume that certain angels received, as their punishment, a *lower* angelic "rank," or position in the heavens, and ended up only a few spiritual steps above Adam.[33] And, even with this, God wanted them to still bow down, and show reverence. This point would begin to upset some of the angels (the leading ones, especially) to the extreme, and they became even more spiteful. The rest of the angels weren't angry, and didn't complain. But the "top dogs," and a few others, would no longer have any of it. Their subjection to a being that they deemed *inferior* was more than a number could handle.

Adam has so much inherent glory and power the angels quaked and were dismayed, and prayed to God to remove this overwhelming, vast presence which he had made...
(Baring-Gould, 1881, p. 26)[34]

There would soon be a significant migration of angels *away* from this present, reorganized world. They just could not accept *Adam* position of rule over them. This would, again, result in God demoting these angels to *fall* further in their heavenly hierarchy, or rank. And, in consequence, the world as Adam inherited it was about to change.

A Major Problem - Free Will

*(God) gave **angels** the perfection of a created nature... He gave them **freedom**.*
(Baring-Gould, 1881, p. 15)[35]

So, it seems, because of these angels - and their *free will* - the working order of our world was about to be open to outside influences. This Garden of Eden, the wonderful place that it was, may have also needed to be *elevated*, and even secured with *walls*, for this very reason.

The Angel of Will

We'll now discover that there were angels in the Garden who's purpose may have been to give the area an atmosphere of harmony and solace, due to their singing abilities.[36] Satan, once the high musician and guardian of God's throne, could have even used some of his musical talent, and other talents, in the Garden, as well. Here, in the Bible, we see this about him:

Ezek. 28:

12 *...Thus saith the Lord GOD; Thou sealest up the sun, full of wisdom, and perfect in beauty.*

13 *Thou hast been in **Eden** the garden of God... the workmanship of thy **tabrets** and of **thy pipes** was prepared in thee in the day that thou wast created.*

14 *Thou art the anointed cherub that **covereth**; and I have set thee so: thou wast upon the holy mountain of God; thou hast walked up and down in the midst of the stones of fire.*

15 *Thou wast perfect in thy ways from the day that thou wast created, till **iniquity** was found in thee.*

16 *By the multitude of thy merchandise they have filled the midst of thee with violence, and thou hast sinned: therefore I will cast thee as profane **out of the mountain of God**: and I will destroy thee, O covering cherub, from the midst of the stones of fire.*

Regardless of how some of these angels may have once felt about Adam, regardless, even, of how hard some of them might have tried to get back into God's good graces, they must have done *some* wrong things in the process. They must have been a little excessive, in showing God how upset they were. And, because of this, *some* kind of response (by God) had to be on the horizon. In the above set of verses, we also see that it was around the time of the Garden of Eden that the Satan (or the devil) was to have *another* falling out. Through his rebellion, he was about to lose any position of authority he once maintained in this world of Adam, and was *further* demoted.

Envy of the Devil

*And the ministering Angels came down and rejoic'd before him (the man)... But when Sammael descended, and saw the glory that Adam was plac'd in, and the ministering Angels serving him at his Wedding, he **envied** him.*

(Eisenmenger, 1748, p. 195)[37]

*Through the devil's **envy** death **entered the world**, and those who are on his side suffer it.*   *- Wisd. 2:24*[38]

It was now that God told the angels of the earth to "bow yourselves" down in reverence to Adam, and this also was directed at Satan.[39] Interestingly enough, the first "racist" of our new world may not be considered the white Adam. It may not have been the Adamites, nor any other human being around. It was actually the **devil**.

The devil, Satan, whatever you might call him, was once an angel considered so "high up" in heavenly rank that he wasn't even considered able to manifest as a being on this earth! In other words, he was such a "big deal" in the heavenly realm that the material he was made out of wasn't even the same as what other angels were made out of. True heavenly angels seem to have composed of, primarily, a divine "**fire**" if you will.[40] But, the "lower" angels - those closer to all that's going on around the earth - were often made out of materials were *closer* to the earth, or *closer* to our "flesh and blood." The reason for this was, of course, to allow them the ability to manifest themselves into a human-like form, if altogether necessary.

From this, it seems that, even in the supernatural, we have "higher" and "lower" beings, "superior" and "inferior." The beings thought of as "higher" were made out of material that seemed to also help define their "rank." A divine *fire*, it seems, was one of the "highest" elements an angel could be made out of.

*And the Jinn (i.e. angel) race, We had created **before**, from the **fire** of a scorching wind.*   *- The Qur'an* 015:027[41]

The ensigns of Sammael and all his princes, and all his lords, have the resemblance of a red fire...   (Eisenmenger, 1748, p. 192)[42]

Adam, as we recall, was fashioned from lowly *dust*, a substance that, at the time, was of very little significance. So, as if it wasn't enough to be demoted to a lower position in this world, Satan - an angel of fire - was now ordered to *prostrate* himself before some man made out of dust. How humiliating to him. He was around longer; he was stronger. He was even thought, as we know, to have dominated the previous world for a time. Why should this son of fire have to bow to a son of clay?[43] It was at this point the devil spoke up:

> *And when the prince of the lower order of angels saw what great majesty had been given unto Adam, he was jealous of him from that day, and he did not wish to worship him. And he said unto his hosts, "Ye shall not worship him, and ye shall not praise him with the angels. It is meet that ye should worship me, because I am fire and spirit; and not that I should worship a thing of dust, which hath been fashioned of **fine dust**"...* - *Cave of Treasures* The Revolt of Satan, and the Battle in Heaven[44]

Satan actually thought the *opposite* should occur, that man should be bowing down to *him* instead.[45] But, because God created Adam after His own image and likeness, He wanted Adam to be the new *light* of the world, and bring forth human children who would become earthly representations of this "light." Some of the actual angels of *light*, however, had other ideas.[46] Very envious and scornful, the pride and free will of the devil (and other angels) allowed certain thoughts to spiral downward, even further:[47]

> *...and God the Lord spake: "Here is Adam. I have made thee in our image and likeness." And Michael (the angel) went out and called all the angels saying: "Worship the image of God as the Lord God hath commanded." And... he (Satan talking) called me and... I said to him... "I will not worship an inferior and younger being (than I). I am his senior in the Creation, before he was made was I already made. It is his duty to worship me." When the angels, who were under me, heard this, they refused to worship him. And Michael said... "if thou wilt not worship him, the Lord God will be wrath with thee." And I said, "If He be wrath with me, **I will set my seat above the stars of heaven** and **will be like the Highest**."*
> - *Vita Adae Et Evae* 13:2-15:3[48]

A lot of similarities exist between this account and the Book of Isaiah:

<u>Isa. 14:</u>

12 *How art thou fallen from heaven, O Lucifer (a.k.a. Satan), son of the morning!*
how art thou cut down to the ground, which didst weaken the nations!

13 *For thou hast said in thine heart, I will ascend into heaven, I will exalt my* **throne**
above the stars of God: I will sit also upon the mount of the congregation, in the
sides of the north:

14 *I will ascend above the heights of the clouds; I will be like the most High.*

God responded to the devil's rebellion:

And his name was called "Sâṯânâ" (i.e. Satan) because he turned aside [from the
right way]... (he) would not render obedience to God, and of his own free will he
asserted his independence and separated himself from God. But he was swept away
out of heaven and fell, and the fall of himself and of all his company from heaven took
place... And the apparel of their **glorious state** *was stripped off them...*
　　　　- Cave of Treasures The Revolt of Satan, and the Battle in Heaven[49]

The devil, now, lost even more of his previous, angelic "estate:"

(God speaking) But the wicked Satan who continued not in **his first estate**, *nor kept*
his faith... though I had created him... so that I hurled him down...
　　　　- First Book of Adam and Eve (The Conflict of Adam and
　　　　Eve with Satan) 6:7[50]

Once having a great countenance of *light*, Satan (the devil), and more and more of his

accomplices, were about to *further* lose what they once had.

O Adam, so long as the good angel was obedient to Me, a bright **light** *rested on him*
and on his hosts. But when he transgressed My commandment, I deprived him of that
bright nature, and he became dark... he transgressed, and I made him fall from
heaven upon the earth; and it was this darkness that came upon him.
　　　　- First Book of Adam and Eve (The Conflict of Adam and
　　　　Eve with Satan) 13:2-5[51]

In one interesting ancient interpretation, Satan actually explains to Adam, in detail, his

own position:

Satan also wept loudly and said to Adam. "All my arrogance and sorrow came to pass because of you; for, because of you I went forth from my dwelling; and because of you I was alienated from the throne of the cherubs… You did nothing to me, but I came to this measure because of you, on the day on which you were created"… Then Michael summoned all the angels… He called me and said, "You too, bow down to Adam." I said "Go away, Michael! I shall not bow down to him who is posterior to me… Thereupon, God became angry with me and commanded to expel us from our dwelling and to cast me and my angels, who were in agreement with me, to the earth; and **you** *were at the same time in the Garden… I had gone forth from the dwelling of* **light"**…   *- Penitence of our Forefather Adam 12.1-16.2*[52]

Another Punishment - Not to be Allowed in the Garden

God cast him (Satan?) out what had been before an angel of the earth, and keeper of terrestrial things, and **a guardian of Paradise**.
                                  (Baring-Gould, 1881, p. 18)[53]

In consequence of his arrogance, Satan was no longer admitted into the Garden of Eden, as before.[54] Now, the walls around the Garden apparently provided some sort of "spiritual" blockage against undesirables. Satan was even made to feel *fear* while in Adam's presence.[55] Although he now had these restrictions, Satan *still* maintained a lot of power. This led him to, desperately, look for a way to break this cycle of Adam's authority.

So, with this all, let's look more into one of the two angels involved in this insurrection. Why do we need to know information about such a negative character? As they say: "know thy enemy." We need to know just what we're up against, like Adam needed to.

Samma-el

Satan, actually, had a former name: **Sammael**.[56] Something happened in this powerful angel's mind to, possibly, lead him in the *opposite* direction of God, and His ways. It is, for numerous reasons, important to know just who this Sammael is, so that we can understand just what Adam was up against, and the numerous things we are up against today, and it's a lot.

Once thought to be among the highest-ranking angels, he also seemed to have many other obscure names, or avatars.[57] He was known as the *End of all Flesh*, the *Dog*, as well as the *Strange God*.[58] The name *Sammael* also means *The Blind One* or *Poison of God*.[59] The interesting meaning behind the names are (probably): the poison represents the *poison* of information, knowledge, or whatever else helping end a man's life and livelihood; he *blinds* all of those who get seduced by his ways. These attributes will, assuredly, become so important to us and our discussion, later on.

Also, in ancient times, he was known as the *angel of desolation, destruction* and *death*.[60] We don't know, for sure, if these titles came about from something he was associated with in the past. Maybe *he* was the one appointed to carry out some of the most horrible duties of the previous world, such as bringing about death and destruction. We're not sure.

Yet, the name most of us know him under today is, of course, *Satan*. Under this title, he eventually would be allowed to *accuse* human beings in front of God - the official "prosecutor" of God's court, if you will.[61] This is also where we get a couple meanings of the word *devil*: "slanderer," "malignant accuser," etc.[62] Any of these negative angels (or spirits) could be thought of as *devil*, however, because it also refers to an all-around, moral deviant. It doesn't have to just be Sammael.

Finally, Sammael is also known as the *Leviathan*:

*In that day the LORD with his sore and great and strong sword shall punish leviathan the piercing serpent, even leviathan that **crooked serpent**; and he shall slay the dragon that [is] in the **sea**.*   - *Isa.* 27:1 (KJV)

He (Satan) is call'd Leviathan. In the Treatise entitled Emek hammeleck, we have the following passage ... "And Gabriel shall hereafter hunt the Leviathan, that is, Sammael; as it is said 'Canst thou draw out Leviathan with a hook?'"
(Eisenmenger, 1748, p. 189)[63]

Leviathan has long been paired with the *sea*. Why? Does the leviathan live in a physical sea, or something? Or could this, once again, be considered something more *spiritual*, or supernatural? We know the *sea* could also represent the *Sea* of the supernatural. Could this be the *sea* that the leviathan "swims in?"

And, when the Bible talks about "fishes" of the *Sea*, could that also be some esoteric meaning for these supernatural angels?

> *The "fish being" idea also doubtless relates to the Shining Ones (angelic and/or other beings) arriving out of the waters of **the great Deluge**, or Deluges recorded in the myths of many different **cultures**.* (Gardiner and Osborn, 2006, p. 145)[64]

> *(The pagan fish/sea god) Oannes is the emblem of priestly, esoteric wisdom; he comes out **from the sea**, because the "great **deep**," the water, typifies... the secret doctrine.* (M.P. Blavatsky, n.d.)[65]

> *The fish-man was one of the esoteric symbols of the initiate in that ancient culture [Babylon]. No doubt it was taught that the man or woman who had so developed themselves as to have free **access** to **the Spiritual world** could be regarded as being **dual**. Such people would be regarded as being equally content to walk on the Earthly plane or **swim** in the **watery**.* (David Ovason, n.d.)[66]

According to the *Gesenius' Lexicon*, the Hebrew origins of the translated word *fish*, in the Bible, could *indeed* stand for something more, here. It comes from the Hebrew root *dagah*, which could associate with words such as "to multiply," to "increase" and to "cover:"[67] What, then, could this signify?

> *...to cover (like... to cover over; hence to be dark)... this verb is applied to multitude and plenty covering over everything (compare... a **great company**... a **great multitude**...).* ("Gesenius' Lexicon - *dagah*", n. d., p. 1)[68]

Could this be the *multitude* of angels in the supernatural? Again, it is really important that we look at the original Hebrew words for Bible verses, here. It only makes sense that, sometimes, the *fish* of the *Sea* could actually refer to the great **company** of angelic souls within it. We also see that:

*...where a god dies, that is, ceases to exist in human form, his life passes into the **waters** where he is buried; and this again is merely a theory to bring the **divine water** or the divine **fish** into harmony with anthropomorphic ideas.*

(Mackenzie, 1915, p. 28)[69]

It's obvious that Sammael was concerned about Adam, and didn't like the fact that God allowed Adam to have dominion over even the *fish* (or angels) all around him.[70] The *Zohar* has a very interesting comment, in regards to this description of *fish*, in Gen. 1:26:

*... "and let them have dominion over the fish of the sea"... meaning the ministers in the sea from the sphere of the **serpent**...*   *- Zohar* Mishpatim 18[71]

Now we know the reason Satan was also known as the *Leviathan*: he was once the leader of a great **company** (or *sea*) of angelic souls! It really wouldn't be a big deal if he just ruled over salmon or trout. Since Adam was allowed to have authority over even these *fish*, Sammael must have taken this as a reason to bring his grievances to *other* groups of angelic individuals around him, as well.

*...the wicked Sammael (Satan) made a covenant with all the **upper gods** (i.e. angels?) against his Lord, because the Holy and Blessed God had said to Adam and Eve, "And have dominion over the **fish of the Sea**." How can I prompt them that they sin, and be driven out before me? Then came he with all his **hosts**...*

(Eisenmenger, 1748, p. 193)[72]

The Allies of Satan's Cause

We've already seen that:

*It is written... "and let them have dominion over the fish of the sea" (Beresheet 1:26), meaning the **ministers** of the sea from the **sphere** of the serpent...*

- Zohar Mishpatim 18[73]

Satan began to recruit angels, angels under his "sphere," to work towards his new cause. One source stated he probably had 130 die-hard angelic ministers of authority behind him.[74] Interestingly enough, these allies were, according to one ancient source, called his *shells*, or *barks*. Why? The reason is example:

> ...*the princes encompass his throne as a **shell** surrounds its fruit.*
> (Eisenmenger, 1748, p. 187)[75]

His ministers soon become totally devoted to their leader in thought and deed.[76] The first fall of the angels, as noted in the Bible, could have possibly involved these higher angels of *fire*, who were now devoted to Sammael's cause. But, God was watching. Things don't get by Him! Their allegiance caused God to have to do what He had do - to *demote* entire groups.

The Second Wave of Envious Ones

Other groups of angels would, soon after, begin to show their dissidence as well, and follow in Sammael's footsteps. But, a second group of angels here would, possibly, be somewhat different. They would not be those *heavenly* angels, who came from above (like Satan). No, these would be a *lower* order of angelic beings, closer to human beings. We'll now see how grumblings also began to take place between lower classes of angels and their human manager. The complaints of this class would be made public through one of the first tasks that the Garden's new manager - Adam - was to be engaged in. There would, as a result of this, also be something else set up: a competition, to decide "who was who." Let's see what all of this means.

Competition for a Help-Mate

Adam, as we know, was assigned the job of dressing and keeping the Garden, the top manager of this whole process. One of the first responsibilities Adam had was to "name" practically every living being around him, animal *and* human being. It also seems that Adam was fairly lonely throughout this era of time, possibly because he saw a number of human beings around him with significant others. But, this manager had a huge job to do with the Garden, and not a lot of time to spend looking around for someone he could mate with. God noticed this, and, during this whole "naming" process, probably thought it might also be a good idea to bring a number of women around, in front of him, allowing him to subtly find a **mate**.[77]

> *And Adam gave names to every animal, **and** to the birds of the heaven, and to every beast of the open field. But for Adam, **no partner** was found like himself.*
> *- Genizah Manuscripts Gen. 2:20*[78]

The Bible mentions practically the same thing:

<u>Gen. 2:</u>
18 *And the LORD God said, It is not good that the man should be alone; I will make him an **help meet** for him.*
19 *And out of the ground the LORD God formed every Chay (Beast) of the Field, and every Owph (Fowl) of the Air; and brought them unto Adam to see what he would call them: and whatsoever Adam called **every living soul** (a.k.a. "creature"), that was the name thereof.*
20 *And Adam gave names to all Behemah, and to the Owph (Fowl) of the Air, and to every Chay (Beast) of the Field; but for Adam there was not found **an help meet** for him.*
        (in retranslation)

You'll notice, in the above, that Adam gave "names" to members of these pre-Adamite groups, as well. We are not sure why he needed to give them names, however. Maybe they all truly didn't have any. Maybe he was actually giving them titles, or working "names," to give them individual roles in the Garden. We simply don't know. He may have even been giving members of the animal kingdom their names, which were brought before him by God. We're not sure.

But, interestingly, this does seem to support the postulation that the human *Owph of the Air*, the *Chay of the Field*, and *Behemah* groups might indeed be human beings, not animals. Why would God only need to bring a group of *animals* in front of Adam, to help him choose a help meet (or mate)? Adam assuredly wasn't into bestiality.

Also, in the above, we see that Gen. 2:19 stated: "out of the ground the LORD God formed…" The way this was translated might not be entirely correct. Again, as we look into the original *Hebrew* here, we'll again find the answer. We know that God formed the *Chay of the Field* in Gen. 1:24 and *Owph of the Air* in Gen. 1:21. And, they were at two different times. So, it makes no sense, in the above, for God to form them "out of the ground" again, if they already were already there! What could the Bible *really* be saying here?

The original Hebrew word for *ground*, here, could also mean "a specific plot of land" or even "the whole inhabited earth." The English word *formed* could also originate in a Hebrew word which means to "plan," to be "predetermined" or "pre-ordained."[79] Put it all together, with these other Hebrew meanings, and this all seems to make sense:

Gen. 2:
19 *And* **on one specific plot of land** *the LORD God* **pre-ordained to have** *every Chay (Beast) of the Field, and every Owph (Fowl) of the Air brought down unto Adam to see what he would call them: and whatsoever Adam called every living* **soul** *(a.k.a.* **creature***), that was the name thereof.*
20 *And Adam gave names to all Behemah (Cattle), and to the Owph (Fowl) of the Air, and to every Chay (Beast) of the Field; but for Adam there was not found* **an help meet** *for him.*
    (in retranslation)

Now, we see that a particular plot of land was actually chosen for them all to come to - a "meeting" place if you will, possibly in a near-by field.

We also notice, in the above, that those with a *soul* came in front of Adam (i.e. the Hebrew word *nephesh*, again). Again, we see that this word translated into the English as *creature*, probably because the translators assumed these would all be animals. As we've already surmised, however, those who have the living soul, or *nephesh*, probably signified those living, *human* creatures (because human beings are the only ones with a soul).

So, now it was time for Adam to allow *human* workers to pass by him, to give them their names, titles, working assignments or whatever he felt they may have needed. Subtly, of course, he was also looking for a female to match his liking.

*What is that which is said in Genesis 2:23, Bone of my Bone, and Flesh of my Flesh. This Passage teaches us, that he (Adam) had coition with **beasts** (the other groups maybe?), both wild and tame, of every Kind; but his Mind could not be satisfied 'till he cohabited with **Eve**... 'Tis said by Some of the Sages, That the first Man had carnal Knowledge of all **Animals** (i.e. humans?), but could not be induc'd to chuse (choose) any one of them to be **his Wife**.* (Eisenmenger, 1748, p. 22)[80]

Maybe he tried to play house with some of these other people. And, even though the ones before him could have worked to some degree, he could still have been looking for the "perfect" woman. Who knows. Maybe he ultimately wanted a woman who thought exactly like him, had the same interests, whatever. In the Bible, it seems that Adam had grown a bit weary over time, because he didn't yet have the woman he always wanted. As some of us may recall (in the Bible), Adam made a statement, regarding the instant Eve came into being. He said something in the nature of Eve being "bones of his bones" and "flesh of his flesh." Since Eve was said to have been formed directly from Adam himself, it's pretty logical to assume that she was just like him.

Incidentally, an astute eye would, in the above, notice that we only have members of three different pre-Adamite groups here. What about the *Remes (Creeping Thing) that Creepeth*? Why didn't God bring them in front of Adam also, at this time? Maybe it was because they didn't work directly in the Garden of Eden, or didn't have roles like the others. We're not sure. Another possibility might be that Adam already **had** a mate from one of these *Remes*, and it didn't work out. We don't know for sure. Why didn't Adam also choose a wife from one of the other *Adamites* around him, as well? Same reasons maybe.

We *could* assume that Adam had one woman in his life before Eve, and it didn't work out. This was fairly commonplace, in ancient literature. And, this woman's *name* was also fairly obvious:

Lilith - Woman Left Out

*...and the first Eve - that is, **Lilith** - found him (Adam)...*
- Chronicles of Jerahmeel 23:1[81]

Speaking of relationships that don't work, there is a mountain of ancient evidence that suggests Adam could have even been in a sexual relationship with, or married to, one named *Lilith*. It could even have been at this time that Adam thought he had the perfect mate. The Bible might even allude to all of this, as well:

*Why had not God created Eve at the same time that He created Adam? Moreover, when Eve finally was created, why did Adam say, "**This time** [in some translations, "This **at last**"] bone of bones and flesh of my flesh"... (Gen. 2:23). To ancient interpreters, both questions seemed to suggest that Eve was not Adam's first mate...*
(Kugel, 1997, p. 113)[82]

According to a number of ancient sources, *Lilith* was his first help meet, or wife![83] Some sources stated that she was even created out of this same dust (or mud, clay, etc.) as Adam.[84] Possibly, because she was formed out of this same material, Adam may have assumed she would make a suitable mate. After all, they were so close. There are other sources, however, that claim Lilith was formed from a slightly *different* mixture than Adam, allowing her to, possibly, treat Adam. and their situation a little differently.[85]

Although Adam may have wanted it all to work, he also may have wanted her to understand her role as wife, and his as husband, and she wasn't going to have any part of it. Apparently, it seemed that Adam as the "head of the household" was too much for her to follow along with.[86] Why? Was Adam being mean, or was it something else? So, we see that, regardless of both being of the same dust, or something similar, they just didn't get along. Similarities do not assure success, however. But, what if Lilith also had some of the same thoughts as Sammael and other fallen angels?

In one example of her dissention, Lilith didn't want to lie under Adam, during sex. She thought: since she was so close in composition to Adam, physically, she figured that she wasn't the one who always had to lie underneath him.[87] She wanted to be on the same

level as Adam it seemed, and be "on top" of Adam whenever she felt like it. It's understandable that, today, many women may agree with these assumptions. But, back then, there was a hierarchy to a lot of things. Adam, then, complained to God, and Lilith ran away from it all. She, then, abandoned her position here, and would continually leave the Garden, when she felt like it. Even though God may have brought her back to Adam a number of times, she kept doing the same, and wouldn't budge in her position. She may have even consorted with other human, or angelic, beings around her. Eventually, Lilith was ousted, for good.

> *...(after Lilith) became proud and a vexation to her husband, God expelled her from paradise.* (Baring-Gould, 1881, p. 34)[88]

Eve, as most probably know, was created directly from Adam's *rib*. Another woman now came on the scene. And, for whatever reason, she was more compatible with Adam:

> *...when he (Adam) saw the woman fashioned from his rib, "This is now bone of my bone, and flesh of my flesh," which is as much as to say, Now God has given me a wife and companion, suitable for me, taken from my bone and flesh, but **the other wife** he gave me was not of my bone and flesh, and therefore not a suitable companion and wife for me.* (Baring-Gould, 1881, p. 34)[89]

Another Reason for this "Naming of the Animals"

Adam had now found the mate he was looking for. But, beyond even the naming or title-assigning of people here, beyond Adam subtly looking for a help meet, there was **one more** reason for this whole "naming of the animals." According to ancient sources, there were angels now around Adam who openly began to *challenge* his knowledge and understanding of the world he now lived in. Challenging him in these ways became a major indicator, at least in their minds, of his lack of authority, and ability, to run the entire Garden of Eden.

According to one source, "The according qualities with which Adam was blessed... aroused the **envy** of the angels."[90]

*The angels then began to envy him (Adam), saying, "Indeed, God will now **love him** more than He does us; if we can entice him to sin he will be destroyed from the earth."* - *Chronicles of Jerahmeel* 22:1[91]

These angels, as well, thought they were superior in most *every* way; and they, from their very make-up, considered themselves so much more knowledgeable. They did not want God to love this man as much as He did. Naturally, all of this would prompt them to continually challenge Adam's intellect.[92]

The following Bible verses seem to give more insight on *this* angelic dissension - strait from their own mouths:

Psa. 8:
3 *When I consider thy heavens, the work of thy fingers, the moon and the stars, which thou hast ordained;*
4 *What is **man**, that thou art mindful of him? and the son of man, that thou visitest **him**?*
5 *For thou hast made him a little lower than the angels, and hast **crowned him with glory and honour**.*
6 *Thou madest him to have **dominion over the works of thy hands**; thou hast put all things under his feet...*

Through their continual complaints, God may have eventually allowed them time to prove themselves. Now, this "naming" of every human being would also become a **test**, a dual between the angels and Adam. Whomever achieved this task *better* would, naturally, be considered more knowledgeable about the situation around them, and, by default, be worthy enough to be in this top position of authority.

The Dissidence of those "Of Old"

As we recall, a good number of angels around the world (at the time) were probably *brought up* from the previous world. Apparently, it seems that God may have allowed these angels memory and knowledge of the previous world, unlike mankind. Could this be the world the Bible refers to as the world "**of old**?" Why do these words keep coming up, throughout Scripture? So, if the angels easily understood "how the world worked" before the Six-Day Creation they would have understood *all* the negative aspects to it, as well! They knew what compromised both sides. And, in their minds, this may have given them fuel by which they considered to be an "upper hand." They were now going to show Adam who was boss, here. The competition was about to begin.

Angel Vs. Adam

God set up the contest: whomever could name *all* of the human beings (and even animals) placed in front of them would be deemed to be the more capable being. The loser had to submit to the winner's authority. This should settle it, once and for all.[93] Back and forth, Adam and the angels attempted to "name" each animal. Adam ended up accomplishing every task.[94] The angels tried, but could not finish it all. God, according to one source, may have even *prompted* Adam a little, to help him win.[95] After all, the angels were already trying to use knowledge of the previous world against him! Whatever the circumstances, Adam accomplished this feat, and was declared the victor. This was actually the way God wanted it from the beginning. But, this result also served to show that Adam was, actually, the more capable of the two, at least to these grumbling angels.

> *Then God said to the angels, "Were you not saying, What is man, that Thou shouldst remember him? Now his **wisdom** is greater than yours!"*
> *- Chronicles of Jerahmeel* 22:1[96]

When the angels failed in this endeavor, they were taken back.[97] And yet, instead of reconciling with their defeat, everything seemed to get worse. They doubled-down. They, then, allowed their free will and pride to get the better of them.

Angels to Burn

At this time, the angels became so angry and envious that it was so hard, if not impossible, for them to bow down in any way. Ultimately, their inner rage turned into thoughts of revenge.

We recall that, according to a number of sources, there were at least *two* distinct groups of angels who wanted to take action against Adam now. Immediately, God was going to put a stop to any of their advances. Another ancient source stated that some of these angels even tried to consume the Adam with fire. But, the protecting hand of God was going to stop them in their tracks. He, then, allowed Adam to go about his business - unscathed.

As a punishment, God addressed these angels, again, and eliminated the "glow" (or *image*) these angelic beings may have once had. He even *burnt up* some of them.[98] God would not let any group of rebellious angels stop His plans for Adam on this earth:

> *God created some (angelic) creatures and said: "Prostrate yourselves before Adam!" They replied: We shall not do that... He set a fire to consume them. He then created other creatures... They refused, and God sent a fire to consume them.*
> *- al-Tabari: The History of al-Tabari - Vol. I: General Introduction and From the Creation to the Flood The Story of Iblis 84*[99]

> *At the time the Holy One, blessed be He... said to them: Would ye advise me to create a man? And they asked Him: What will be his deeds? And He related before them such and such. They explained before Him: Lord of the Universe, what is the mortal, that Thou rememberest him, and the son of men, that Thou thinkest of him? [Ps. vii. 5]. He then put His little finger among them and they were all **burnt**. And the same was with the second coetus.* - *Babylonian Talmud* Sandhedrin, Chap. XI[100]

An interesting thing to note, here: the punishment God dished out to them seemed to be an ironic *outward* reflection of their *inner*, overly-passionate thoughts (their *fiery* thoughts).[101] They were burnt, or darkened, on the *outside* as a result of all the darkness they may have felt on the *inside*.

The Era of the "Fallen Ones" - Now Known as Nephilim

As if their demotion, even their loss of *image*, wasn't enough, many of these angels were now given a new title: **the "Nephilim"** (or the "Fallen Ones").

*How, you may well ask, can they (the Nephilim) subsist in this world? Rabbi Chiya said that they are among those referred to as "**Birds which fly upon the earth**."*
- *Zohar* Beresheet B69[102]

Again, we see a reference to *birds* or *fowl* as having some sort of angelic connection. These "fallen" angels were so-named because, through their attempts to bring the organized world of Adam down, they, *themselves*, fell down![103]

*...those angels wanted to denounce him. They asked the Holy One, blessed be He (God), "What is man, that you are mindful of him" (Tehilim 8:5), **for he is bound to sin** before you? Why, therefore, do you want us to be under him? The Holy One, blessed be He (God), replied, **If you were down below on earth like he**, you would sin more than he does.*
- *Zohar* Beresheet A20[104]

We recall that Sammael (or Satan) and his heavenly angels were probably made out of a divine *fire*. And, with their demotion, they still weren't considered "low" enough to be close in form to human beings, or be able to transform themselves into human form. These lower angels, however, probably could, and *had*![105]

Once with angelic qualities way above the average, terrestrial man, they now lost so much of that. They were *physically* demoted, to possess almost of the same attributes as human beings, and not much more![106] This was ultimate humiliation, at least in their minds.

*And these, as we have discussed, appear to men in the form of human beings. And how, you may ask, do they transform themselves from the shape of an angel to that of human beings? As we have learned, they can transform themselves into all kinds of shapes, and when they come down into this world, they clothe themselves with **the garments of earth's atmosphere** and **take on human form**.*
- *Zohar* Beresheet B69[107]

Yes, their demotion, or *loss of "estate,"* was a mortal blow to these Nephilim, on so many levels.

*...there are heretical accounts which suggest that when angels sin they "clothe themselves with the corruptibility **of the flesh**."*   (Godwin, 1990, p. 86)[108]

This assuredly made them less powerful than before, and even more resentful. The Nephilim wanted Adam to go down *even* faster now! So, with all of this in mind, let's take a look at a couple of Nephilim leaders, and what they did to further expedite their own cases against Adam, and all of mankind.

Azza, Uzza, and Azazel

A few prominent angelic leaders of the day were named *Azza, Uzza* and *Azazel*.[109] According to the *Third Book of Enoch*, certain top angels openly complained about Adam. Two of them, Azazel and Azza, ended up being notorious for their outbursts of total dissatisfaction (Azazel was even synonymous with the so-called "scapegoat" of the Bible, in Lev. 16:8).

Azazel, though, would have quite an interesting story about him: according to one source, even *before* the beginning of our Six-Day Creation, Azazel was disagreeing with God. Apparently, God *already* made the decision of who would be His up-and-coming people (i.e. Israel), and that Adam would be their ultimate patriarch. Azazel already knew of this, and made a prediction about the future. He told God that Adam's future descendents could eventually fall, and believed they would not turn out to be as great of a nation as God set them up to be. God, however, didn't falter. He continued on with His creation, and fashioned Adam, anyway. According to another ancient source, Azazel was even told by God to go fetch the dust He was going to use for Adam - probably in response to all of his constant bickering!

So, this angel, and fifty-or-so of his fellow *Nephilim* (or *fallen*) angels, were now made to take on new roles in the Garden. They, for their insolence, would be demoted to mid-level "managers" of the Garden of Eden![110] Worse than that, to them, they all felt the "sting" of taking on the general role of a human being, and, assuredly, even looking like them! To them, it was a step backwards, into the spiritual "gutter."

As they began to assume their new roles, they, then, began to cry out: "If we do not take counsel against this man so that he sin before his Creator, then we will not prevail against him!"[111] So, this became their new rallying cry. It became their new goal - to make Adam fall at any price.

Azazel, then, was considered the lead angel of the Nephilim, and possibly many more individuals around him, whomever wanted to join them. This angel played a very sinister role in the construct of dissention that was about to be set. He actually began to speak to human beings with a *forked* tongue. And yes, he probably strolled around the Garden proudly, under *another*, infamous name!

We've mentioned earlier that Sammael (or Satan) may not have been the **only** *leader* of angelic dissidents at this time. Azazel, another angel, was demoted to a terrestrial angel - one who could walk amongst Adam, Eve, and the whole earth. One could only guess who this *other*, largely-problematic leader might have been at this time, but it's not very hard. He was, indeed, someone that most of us have probably heard of, but weren't taught too much about. Yes, now it's time to learn who the *other half* of this whole "conspiracy of *devils*" really was.

Chapter 6

The Spoiler of the Garden

*And with guile **I** cheated thy (Adam's) wife and caused thee to be expelled through her (doing) from thy joy and luxury, as **I** have been driven out of my glory.*
- *Vita Adae Et Evae* 16:4[1]

Enter One of the Most Infamous Dissidents of Them All!

Adam was placed in the Garden as manager, leader, and even prophet over the land. Assuredly, he was supposed to be an example of God's "image" and "likeness" throughout the Garden - to show others around him proper ways to think and act.[2] Eve, now formed directly from Adam's rib, was there to accompany him. At least at first, they were seemingly the perfect couple.

Adam and Eve, of course, were both allowed entry into this "paradise on earth." Others, as we've also postulated, may *not* have been. According to one ancient source, some groups of people, such as the *Chay of the Field* and *Behemah*, were not only assigned to help work in and around the garden, but to help *guard* it.[3] Now, who or what they would have to guard it *from* would be an interesting concept for us to ponder. According to one ancient source, *The Book of the Cave of Treasures*, "in it (the Garden) dwelt the souls of the **righteous**. The souls of sinners dwelt in a deep place, outside Eden."[4] So, apparently, the walls were designed to keep out any of those who may not have been too righteous. Only a limited few of these fallen angels (i.e. the Nephilim) were probably allowed in. Sammael, Lilith and the others who openly despised Adam were definitely not allowed in. But, there was *one* leading angel allowed limited access to the Garden, one who seemed to "slip between the cracks," here. And, this one possibly was able to do something about that pesky little man named Adam, if he so-wanted.

This angel, along with Sammael, probably lost a lot of what he once had, because of this world's formation, and of Adam. This angel also may have decided to go into a "pact" with Sammael himself, in order to bring the man down.

Although the aforementioned angels, Azazel and Azza, were both well-known angels throughout a number of ancient texts, the former could have been this particular angel. As a mid-level "manager" of the Garden, he could have also been one of the most infamous characters of Biblical history - the *Serpent*!

The Garden's Serpent - A Fallen Angel?

*Before that time it (the serpent) had legs like other animals and according to one rabbinic tradition was **like a man** in appearance, standing upright on two legs. Therefore, the man representations of the temptation which depict the serpent as a snake curled round the Tree of Knowledge are really based on a **misunderstanding** of the scriptural text.* (Goldstein, 1933, p. 4)[5]

Many, today, concluded that this Serpent was nothing more than an animal - a talking snake, if you will. As we look deeper into ancient, alternate sources however, including *the Bible*, we see evidence that this Serpent may actually represent something more. If we think about it, how could an *animal* deceive Eve so horribly? How could a lowly snake turn the entire world of the Garden upside down, unless there was something *more* to him? One portion of an ancient Babylonian hymn - the *Penitential Hymn* - goes as such:

13. *Which to those **rebel angels** prohibited return*
14. *he (God) stopped their service, and sent them to the gods who were his enemies*
15. *In their room he created mankind.*
16. *The first (Adam) who received life, dwelt along with him.*
17. *May he give them strength, never to neglect his word,*
18. *Following the **serpent's** voice...*[6]

According to what so *many* of us have been taught in the past, a winding, slithery animal convinced Eve to disobey God, and she listened to him! A snake talked to her. Yet, we'll now see that it's quite possible this Serpent was a fallen **angelic being**, an angel sentenced to be more and more human. He was reduced in rank or stature, but still able to inflict some damage, here, if allowed. Yet, we're often told that this Serpent was nothing but a "modified" animal we see today, at best. How could a small reptile be able to *talk* to Eve in the first place? It doesn't even have any vocal cords. And, if he managed to, Eve really didn't seem very *surprised* that an animal would be able to strike up a conversation with her. It also says *nothing* about God removing this Serpent's vocal cords in the Bible. So, how could he have spoken, or even had the intelligence and rationality to engage in a conversation to fool someone, unless he was *more* than only an animal?

According to one ancient source, the Serpent was considered a *beast*, just like the *Chay of the Field* and the *Behemah*.[7] But, why? Could this be another example of how the word *beast* was apparently mistranslated into an animal, what it was, in fact, *human* (or *angelic*, in this case)?

As we've postulated, there were *Chay of the Field* and *Behemah* around the Garden, possibly to help out in the fields, help with the domestication of animals, or whatever other type of gardening project needed. The Bible even states the *Chay of the Field* and *Behemah* could have had something in common with this Serpent.

> *Now the serpent was more **subtil** than any **Beast (i.e. Chay?) of the Field** which the LORD God had made...*   *- Gen.* 3:1 (KJV)

Could this imply that the *Serpent* was, either associated with these people in some way, or a mid-level *manager* over them, more probably?[8] We really don't know for sure. Yet, in the Bible, we discover the word *beast* could also be used as an angelic being (c.f. Rev. 6:1). Put it all together, and we see that the Serpent could be just *below* Adam's position of authority in the Garden, which would give him a full capacity to talk, eat or breathe, just like any other human being.[9]

An Angel - in Serpent Form?

> *So it appears there were three distinct orders of **angels** in the lower echelons. At the top were the seven Archangel chiefs, who were known as **the aristocratic two-eyed serpents**...*   (Godwin, 1990, p. 71)[10]

We recall that Sammael (or Satan) was also known to be the *Leviathan* of the *Sea*. In the Talmud, however, this same Leviathan was known as the "strait or upright **Serpent**" or "crooked **serpent**."[11] Could this also default to become a description of the Garden's *Serpent*, as well? What if this Sammael and the Serpent had some similarities (as we'll soon see *how*, below)? Could this Serpent have actually *resembled* a common serpent in some ways, while on his terrestrial stay? What's it all about?

Characteristics of This Serpent

Now that we understand this Serpent could have taken on human form, we may want to find out if there a reason behind why these terrestrial angels were called *serpents*. Could these angelic beings have *serpentine-like* features one could see? From the preponderance of the ancient written evidence, the answer would probably be *no*… and *yes*. What that means is: some ancient sources stated the Serpent had human-like extremities, such as hands and feet.[12] Another holy text of the ancient *Zoroastrian* faith, for example, cited that the evil spirit - the father of the *daevas* (i.e. demons) - was *serpent-like*, and with legs.[13] Another text said that he ate *food*, just like any other human being would.[14] The same aforementioned *Zoroastrian* spirit was even said to have possessed the male *sex organ*. The talk of serpents flourished all over ancient pagan mythology and religion. So, all of this seems to provide evidence for the terrestrial, serpent angels to look similar to human beings, but maybe a little different too.

On the other extreme, there are also a number of ancient descriptions of human-like beings having *serpentine* characteristics, with these characteristics especially evident *in their face*.[15] But, there is a caveat: these humanoid beings were described as just coming out of the supernatural realm!

These humanoids were said to have shined like a bright *star*, much like how one would picture an appearing angel (if they allowed themselves to be visible in this world).[16] Another source stated that these serpents had *brilliant*, pale-white skin.[17] Still another source stated that some angels had "serpentine" features to their face, even though they had the overall shape and image of a man.

What it all boils down to is this: it seems that, the *more* these beings head towards living life as a terrestrial being on earth, the *more* human they will probably look! It's fairly simple. They were called serpent beings because, in their original supernatural form, they have serpentine features! These serpentine beings, in their original supernatural abode, would probably have serpentine features, especially in their face.

We've already alluded to those angels, such as the Serpent and the Nephilim, who were of a "lower" class then Sammael and his heavenly angels, for example. And these "lower-classed" angels could be able to manifest themselves into, more or less, an exact clone of human-like beings (given it was their place to do so). Heading back into their *original* appearance (as a *spiritual* being) would also bring them into showing their *true*, serpentine "colors."

To support this, let's look at a couple of ancient written texts. They may provide a few of curious examples of how serpents of the supernatural (fallen *and unfallen*) could temporarily have manifested themselves to people on earth, *and* what they might have looked like at the time!

"The Cloak of Feathers"

The following quote comes from the ancient work, *The Second Book of Enoch*: a couple of large, shining angels, even identified as having *wings*, were able to manifest themselves in front of a human being.

> *And there appeared to me two **men**, exceedingly big, so that I never saw such on earth; their **faces were shining like the sun**... with **clothing** and singing of various kinds in appearance purple, their **wings** were brighter than gold...*
> *- 2 Enoch (The Book of the Secrets of Enoch)* 1:6[18]

It appears that these angels looked *somewhat* like a man, but the observers knew they were something more. These angels (in the above) were also said to be wearing some type of purple *cloak*, and appeared to have *wings*. What could all of this mean?

There were other angelic beings, from other ancient works, who were said to have worn *winged* cloaks when appearing to humans.[19] One source describes angels as being "clothed like **birds**, with *wings* for garments."[20] Another account records angels as wearing *feathered* cloaks. Could this all be a part of the reason why so many angels are, so often, depicted as having "wings?" Or, could this "wing" be just a symbol of what would be an angelic "bird," rising up to the heavens? Maybe, to the human eye, the witnessing of an angelic being wearing a *feathered* cloak might appear as if it had some connection to bird *wings*. We are not sure.

Another ancient work, *The Testament of Amram*, stated some other interesting things. *Amram*, the father of Moses, apparently had a dream, or vision, one night.[21] In his description, he described an angel who looked like a *serpent*, and was also wearing a cloak:

> *His looks were frightening [like those of a **vip]er**, and his [ga]rm[en]ts were multi-coloured and he was extremely dark... And afterwards I looked and behold... by his appearance and his **face** was like that of an **adder**...*
> - *The Testament of Amram (4Q544)* f #1[22]

Interestingly enough, the description of *this* particular angel seems to be a lot darker, possibly more macabre. And, it's also interesting that this serpentine angel had a face shaped like an *adder* (or *viper*). There have even been a number of ancient figurines found which possessed *these same* facial characteristics! They were located in the ancient land of *Ubaid* (a part of ancient Mesopotamia) and *Jarmo* (in ancient Iraqi Kurdistan).[23] Could these figurines have been an accurate description of these serpentine angels, ones who were able to manifest themselves to ancient people of the world?

Maybe some of these angels who were able to manifest come from *above*. Their heavenly origins might explain why they were so brilliant, pleasant-looking, whatever. The same for the other side: maybe some came from *below*. And their evil-looking, frightening appearances might just be a reflection of the *Darkness* they originated from!

The Dragon

There is another ancient symbol, known throughout mythologies of old: *the dragon.* The Serpent of the Garden, according to some ancient sources, was also considered to be a *dragon.*[24] Well, just what is this *dragon*? Why was he called that? The Bible also makes mention of the "great dragon" (in Rev. 12:3, 12:9), as well as a *"fiery,* flying serpent" (in Isa. 30:6).[25] We'll soon discover a good deal more about *why* a Serpent may have been referred to as "fiery." It's more than one might think. For simplicity sake, however, we will introduce it as such: the word *fiery,* in the Bible, could also be likened to how one holds a strongly *emotion* or *passion* over something. It's not just supernatural composition, or their makeup. That, reportedly, was how certain angelic beings were: very **emotional** and **passionate**. In this case, they were emotional and passionate about their whole situation with Adam, and wholly bent on change in the Garden. More often than not, this "fiery" reference deals with personality - how "fired" up, emotionally, a person or angel could get!

So, as we begin to link this "fiery" dragon with the Serpent, we'll soon discover that the Bible also has an apparent correlation between the two:

*In that day the LORD with his sore and great and strong sword shall punish leviathan the piercing **serpent**, even leviathan that crooked **serpent**; and he shall slay the **dragon** that is in the sea.*   *- Isa.* 27:1 (KJV)

*And he laid hold on the **dragon**, that old **serpent**, which is the **Devil**...*   *- Rev.* 20:2 (KJV)

It seems that, in some ways, they are almost equal. Also, if we look at Rev. 12:9, it says this "old Serpent" was a *he,* not an animal. Could these serpentine angels, especially the *Serpent* himself, be the origin of so many mythological stories about a divine *serpent,* a *"bird-man"* or a *dragon*?

What is important to understand here is that these serpentine angels might have looked more serpentine in their original, spirit form. If they were righteous, and from heaven, they may have beautiful, slightly serpentine features. If they come from the *Darkness,* they again might have serpentine features, but very ghastly and ugly. If and when they are forced to be more and more *human*, and live on our terrestrial world, either will look more and more human. Fairly simple.

We also take away from this that: *all* serpents in the spiritual world are not necessarily *evil*, just the ones who turned away from God, and go on to follow other pathways, and other angels. So, it's also important to look into the *thoughts* and *attitudes* of these angels we well, and not just what they look like on the outside, to understand what they're really all about, and the reason people describe them as they do.

So, let's now look into some of these thought-attributes of angels, especially this Serpent, and gather more insight into what all may have *really* gone on in the Garden of Eden.

Nachash - His Biblical Name

*He is called... the old serpent... the erect serpent, or else only **Nachasch**, i.e. serpent.*   (Eisenmenger, 1748, p. 187-9)[26]

If we substitute the original Hebrew word for *serpent* into Gen. 3:1, we have:

*Now **Nachash** was more subtil than any beast of the field which the LORD God had made...*   - *Gen.* 3:1 (in retranslation)

As we see, the Serpent seems to go by multiple names, even *in the Bible*. The word *Nachash* could be a descriptive title of the Serpent, in relation to how this individual may have *thought*, or even *related* to others. The word *Nachash* has also been associated with a "whisperer," "magician," "enchanter," or even "hypnotist."[27] One reason for Nachash's association with the Serpent (in these ways) might lie in his *verbal* approach to Eve, and how he worked to verbally manipulate her.

The above verse states that Nachash was more "subtil" (or subtle) than most anyone around him. Could he have at least acted a lot like a typical *serpent* of our animal world would have, in this respect? As a predator, would he begin by slithering his way up to his prey (Eve), wanting to find ways to catch her off guard?

We now see that the word *Nachash* could also be associated with the Arabic word *Chanas* or *khanasa*, meaning, "he departed, drew off, lay hid, seduced or slunk away."[28] Again, Nachash, by acting in these mysterious ways, probably hid his true intentions from Eve at the start, at least until he had an opportunity to "strike." Real snakes, in their own right, aren't particularly clever overall, but they do seem to have a good ability to sneak up on their prey, and strike… quite well!

We also recall that one of the meanings of *Nachash* is an "enchanter." Was the Serpent able to seduce human beings, at least in part, by using soft-spoken, enchanting words? Let's look a little more in this mysterious and cunning angelic creature, and some of the characteristics that made him such a formidable enemy to Adam, Eve, and the working order of the world.

The Fiery Seraphim

In *The Companion Bible*, we find an interesting interpretation of the word *Nachash*:

*In Genesis 3 we have neither allegory, myth, legend, nor fable, but literal historical facts set forth, and emphasized by the use of certain Figures of speech… All the confusion of thought and conflicting exegesis have arisen from taking literally what is expressed by Figures, or from taking figuratively what is literal… Hence, in Chaldee it (Nachash) means brass or copper, because of its **shining**… In the same way Saraph, in Isaiah 6:2, 6, means a burning one, and, because the serpents mentioned in Num. 21 were burning, in the poison of their bite, they were called Saraphim, or Seraphs… Nachash is thus used as being interchangeable with **Saraph**. Now, if Saraph is used of a serpent because its bite was burning, and is also used of a celestial or spirit being (a burning one), why should not Nachash be used of a serpent because its appearance was shining, and be also used of a **celestial or spirit-being** (a shining one)… The Nachash, or serpent, who beguiled Eve (II Cor. 11:3) is spoken of as "an **angel** of light" in v. 14. Have we not, in this, a clear intimation that it was not a snake, but a **glorious shining being**, apparently an **angel**, to whom Eve paid such great deference, acknowledging him as one who seemed to possess superior knowledge, and who was evidently a being of a superior knowledge, and who was evidently a being of a superior (not an inferior) order?* - *The Companion Bible* Appx. 19[29]

The title *Nachash* could also mean a "shining one."[30] From the above, we clearly see that *Nachash* might have also been a shining being at a time - a *Seraph*, or *Seraphim*. We also see, in the above, that a *Seraph* represents a high-ranking angel with human attributes.[31] Could the Serpent once have been one of these glorious *Seraph*, now demoted to work in the Garden?[32]

A few other literary works describe the Seraphim:

The Seraphim are identical with the Chalkadri... and, probably, also with the "serpents" of I Enoch...
                    - 3 Enoch (The Hebrew Book of Enoch) 26:8 (notes)[33]

...the Seraphim are more identified with the serpent or dragon than any other angelic order.   (Godwin, 1990, p. 25)[34]

Another literary work describes the *Seraphim* as very tall angels, with six wings: one pair for "flying;" another pair for covering their eyes in front of God; and another pair for covering their "feet" (i.e. their *genitalia*).[35] Yes, it's interesting to see that these angels were also said to have *phalli*:

*Now the angels have **phalli**, hearken unto [Isaiah 6:2 and Ezekiel 1:12] the prophet, who saith, 'With two of their wings they covered their faces, with two others they covered their feet, with two others they covered their hands, and with two others they covered their **phalli***'...   - Bakhayla Mikael p. 17[36]

Could they, also, work like phalli would in human beings?

Along with this attribute, these Seraphim could also have been considered passionate angels. Looking deeper into the name, we notice the word *Seraphim* could either come from the word *seraph* (meaning "to burn") or a noun *seraph* (meaning "fiery, flying serpent").[37] The *Seraph* was considered a "fiery, flying **serpent**" in the Bible a number of times (e.g. Num. 21:8, Deut. 8:15, Isa. 14:29 & 30:6). Could these heavenly *Seraphim* also represent an angel who's was very passionate and emotionally vibrant?

Many More Titles

Beyond *Nachash*, we've already postulated the Serpent may have other names. We've already mentioned the angel *Azazel*. One ancient source, *The Apocalypse of Abraham* (in verses 23:7-12, 14:5-6, and 31:5), stated that the tempter of the Garden was a serpent, or dragon. And, the same was described as "having hands and feet like a man's, on his back… wings." All of this seems to fit into our theory about how the Serpent was, actually, a Seraphim at one time. On top of this, this same *Apocalypse of Abraham* solidifies one more name of the Serpent:

> *…this is Adam… this is Eve. And he who is between them is the impiety of their behavior unto perdition, **Azazel** himself.*
> *- Apocalypse of Abraham* 23:11-12[38]

According to another source, the above was considered that *old Serpent*, or **Seducer** *of Mankind*.[39] But, why *this* name?

Strong… In Rebellion

The word *Azazel*, itself, means the "strong one of God" or "of whom God strengthened."[40] Azazel once may have been considered a mighty warrior of God's resolve. But, now, after his fall, he was considered the one who became "belligerent towards God," or one strong in his rebellion.[41] These became the name's *new* definitions. Why go one way, and then another? It may show us that, at one time, this angel could have ranked fairly high in God's service, until something negative happened. This was a lot like Sammael, as we notice. Was it because of Adam? And, also, was it possibly because this angel had some authority over the previous world, and lost it?

According to other sources, this Serpent was also known as the angel *Gadriel*, *Gadreel*, or *Katriel*.[42] The word *Gadriel* itself means, "God is my helper." But, again, it could also take on a negative tone, such as "he intrigued or revolted."[43]

Azazel and Gadriel *do* both seem to possess similarities, as well as with Nachash himself. Gadriel was said to have had hands and feet, with six wings on each side of his back. Azazel had much of the same.[44] Gadriel was known for teaching men how to create tools, weapons of war, and how to kill people in an effective manner.[45] Azazel was known for showing mankind how to forge metals and create articles of war, such as swords, knives, shields, and breastplates. Most importantly, Azazel and Gadriel both were known for one other thing - the angel who *led Eve astray*.[46]

So, from what we can surmise now, Nachash, Azazel and Gadriel were all probably one in the same - the fallen Seraphim now thought of collectively as the *Serpent*. And, from this, it seems a lot more probable that there was more to this vengeful, man-hating being than just a slithering (and, *somehow*, talking) animal.

Thoughts of the Serpent

Now that we've established the Serpent could probably have been a Serpentine angel (who lost his former, angelic estate), we have to ask ourselves: what *thoughts* could have been behind such a move away from God? How could he do something so drastic, to allow him to lose so much?[47] There a number of possible answers to this.

Let's delve more into the Serpent's thought-patterns, and motivations.

Adam was upright and straightforward, it being said of him, "Behold, Adam is one of us" (Gen. 3:22), as **one of the ministering angels***... Adam reclined in the Garden of Eden, while ministering angels, hovering over him, roasted flesh and strained wine for him.*
                                                                                (Goldin, 1929, p. 20)[48]

A lowly *man* as one of the angels? Surely, certain *emotions* would begin to "fire up" in this angelic being:

But when the **Serpent** *came and saw the Honour that was done them he cast an* **envious** *eye upon them, and was full of* **Passion** *and Spite against them.*
                                                                                (Eisenmenger, 1748, p. 196)[49]

*Had **envy** not wormed its way into his (the serpent's) soul, he... would have lived happily with Adam and Eve... it was precisely his **wisdom** that led to his undoing.*
(Frankel, 1989, p. 28)[50]

Had the Serpent not been cursed, he would have been a great benefit to man...
(Jung, 1974, p. 69)[51]

We now discover a couple of major emotions behind the Serpent's thoughts. One commentary stated that the Serpent could have actually started his whole dissension with a statement such as the following:

***I** will... be king of the whole earth: I will walk with my body erect, and eat of all the **dainties** of the world.*   (Eisenmenger, 1748, p. 198)[52]

The word *dainty*, in the above, comes from an archaic Middle English word meaning "high-esteem," "dignity" or "worth."[53] It could also stand for "fastidiousness," "scornful," "despising," "arrogant" or even as "having high and often capricious standards." In other words, the Serpent began to be proud and arrogant in his own thoughts. He wanted to go after royal luxuries of this world, and thought he was entitled to them.[54] Sound familiar? It'll start to make sense later.

The Serpent also had the ability to capitalize on these *subtle* thoughts, in order to help him carry out deceptive purposes in the future.[55]

*The word **subtle** does not mean clever as we think of it in English. The Hebrew word, **aruwm**, could be cunning in an evil sense, but most scholars, such as Ferrar Fenton, define the word as "more impudent:" as a person who does **not know his place** or **station** in life. You might also define it as "cock" or lacking in modesty. So, if you mix immodest, cocky, contemptuous, cunning and impudent into one Hebrew word, then you can imagine what "subtle" means in this verse.*
("Star Wars, Lesson Seven", n. d.)[56]

As one may guess, his arrogance and cockiness could had led to the downfall of his previous, angelic estate:

*His name was Azazil. He was one of the most **zealous** and **knowledgeable** of the angels. That led him to **haughtiness**.*
                        - al-Tabari: The History of al-Tabari - Vol. I: General Introduction and
                        From the Creation to the Flood The Story of Iblis 83[57]

Another interpretation of Gen. 3:1 substitutes the word "*subtle*" with:

*...the serpent... He Who Waits in Ambush was more **smooth-tonged** / **slier** than any other life in the field...*   (Halevi, 1997, p. 166)[58]

*And the serpent was the **shrewdest** of all the beasts of the open field...*
                        - Genizah Manuscripts Gen. 3:1[59]

Adding further to our argument here, the word *shrewd* could also stand for one acting "mischievous," "abusive," or even "dangerous."[60] In other words, the knowledge of this Serpent could, eventually, become a dangerous thing to other individuals around him. To top it off, he, quite likely, had also contained knowledge of our world *of old* - the previous world. With all of this, he, as with other angels, could have used all of this knowledge as a means to his own ends. Where does this all lead?

A Knowledge of Their Past

If you've been there before, you have the "upper hand" over any new recruit, and this includes the entire human race. Another of the more sinister meanings of *Nachash* is, "to acquire knowledge through **experience**."[61] How long could this Serpent have been around, to gather such an arsenal of knowledge and experience? It seems obvious he didn't just jump on the scene around the time that Adam was formed. Since we've postulated this Serpent could have even had an understanding of the world before our own (the "world *of old*"), he also could have known what *brought it all down*, and how to manipulate people who lived during these times, as well.

In a number of ancient works (even the Bible), the Serpent and Sammael/Satan were *both* considered the **old** Serpent (the Serpent *of old*). Could it be because they both lived in this world?[62] And, what about Sammael/Satan? He was in the same boat, in so many ways. What part could *he* have had in the Serpent's up-and-coming attempt to dethrone mankind?

The Serpent's Crusade - To Corrupt Adam

Iblis (the Serpent?) said to angels Don't be afraid of that one Adam for I sold, and he is hollow. When I am given authority over him, I shall **ruin him**.
> - al-Tabari: The History of al-Tabari - Vol. I: General Introduction and From the Creation to the Flood The Story of Adam 91[63]

From the written evidence, we now can see how the Serpent was probably, once, a high-ranking angel. He has so many different names and titles. Yet, so many of us were taught that the Serpent of Gen. 3 was actually **Satan** himself. Was this true? Yes, in a way.

As already postulated, the Serpent was lowered in both position and rank. Satan (and some of his fellow angels of fire) also rebelled, and were lowered in position and rank. Certain angels were lowered into terrestrial angels, to serve out their sentence on earth, such as the Nephilim. And, since Sammael (or Satan) and his angels were made out of a pure, angelic *fire*, they could not do the same. How could Sammael actually be this Serpent?

Well, we know that the Serpent and other angelic serpents *could* be in the Garden. And, if both of them were on the pathway to upstart Adam, why couldn't they, somehow, join forces?

Two Sides of the Same Plot

As previously stated, there may have been *walls* around the Garden of Eden, to keep certain undesirables (such as Sammael/Satan) out. Since they were only spirit, they could not influence Adam and Eve in any way (at least as long as the two were "spiritually-protected" within Eden's wall). The Serpent, however, was in a different position.

We see:

*Azazil (a.k.a. Azazel)... was one of the dwellers and **cultivators** on earth.*
- *al-Tabari: The History of al-Tabari - Vol. I: General Introduction and From the Creation to the Flood The Story of Iblis 83*[64]

Certain angels had access to the Garden, and could make a difference.

*The jinn were dwellers of the earth from **among the angels**.*
- *al-Tabari: The History of al-Tabari - Vol. I: General Introduction and From the Creation to the Flood The Story of Iblis 83*[65]

*They were called jinn because they were **the keepers of Paradise**... Iblis (the Serpent?) was a keeper (of Paradise).*
- *al-Tabari: The History of al-Tabari - Vol. I: General Introduction and From the Creation to the Flood The Story of Iblis 80*[66]

This, subtly, became the Serpent *and* Sammael's golden opportunity.

*And God said unto Adam, "See Satan's love for thee, who pretended to give thee the Godhead and greatness; and, behold, he burns thee with fire, and seeks to **destroy thee** from off the earth."*
- *First Book of Adam and Eve (The Conflict of Adam and Eve with Satan) 46:4*[67]

Almost all the dissenters around Adam had this same thought: "If we do not take counsel against this man so that he sin before his Creator, we cannot prevail against him."[68] If they were able to corrupt man, they thought that this would actually negate *their* own current positions in the world! It's like calling "fowl" to God, and making him get their old positions back. After all, if Adam wasn't what God thought he was, naturally, He should get rid of them, and put things back to where they belong. It would help them to recover the power that they once lost. so, they set out to be elevated back to the positions they once had…. by hook or crook.

Some ancient sources state that *this* was around the time Sammael (Satan) approached the Serpent (Nachash, Azazel, or Gadriel), and a conversation arose:

*...the devil (Satan) told the serpent, "I (hear) that you are wiser than all the animals (human beings?)... for Adam gives food to all the animals (human beings?), thus **also to you**. When then all the animals (i.e. human beings?) come **to bow down** before Adam from day to day and from morning to morning, every day, you **also** come to bow down. **You were created <u>before</u> him**... and you bow down before this little one! And why do you eat (food) inferior to Adam's and his spouse's and not the good fruit of paradise? But come and hearken to me so that we may have Adam expelled from the wall of paradise just as **we are outside**. Perhaps we can re-enter somehow to paradise"... "Be a sheath for me and I will speak to the woman through your mouth a word by which we will trick (them)."*   - *Book of Adam* [44]16.3a-16.4[69]

Interestingly, in the above, we also seem to have more ancient evidence that there were other ancient people on earth, besides Adam. It also seems clear that the so-called "animals," in the above, were not really animals at all! What kind of animal feels the obligation to *bow down* to anyone?

Now, going back to our story, we see that, upon Sammael's proposal, the Serpent found that this would be useful, and agreed to allow him to help out. Sammael then (symbolically) *rode* atop of the Serpent, as one would don a horse. What that means is this: Satan was probably given permission to *possess* the Serpent, and speak (and act) through his own body.[70] He now found a door into this Garden area, via the Serpent's mouth![71] And, it is for this reason that a variety of sources (including scholars of the Bible) would be right, assuming Sammael (or Satan) and the Serpent were **identical**, or that Satan was the *only* Serpent.[72] They worked together, here. But, as we really know, there could have been *two* individuals here, both working on Adam's destruction.[73]

Together, in this way, they waited for an opportunity to undermine Adam and Eve, in whatever way possible, all in order to deceive them, and gain control of "their" world, once again.

Another version of this same account, above, is as follows:

*...the devil (Satan) went to Adam's lot, where the male creatures were... And the devil spake to the serpent saying, "Rise up, come to me and I will tell thee a word whereby thou mayst have profit." And he arose and came to him. And the devil saith to him: "I hear that thou art wiser than all the beasts, and I have come to counsel thee. Why dost thou eat of Adam's **tares** and not of paradise? Rise up and we will cause him to be cast out of paradise, even as we were cast out through him." The serpent saith to him, "I fear lest the Lord be wroth with me." The devil saith to him:*

*"Fear not, only be my vessel and I will speak through thy mouth words to deceive him." And instantly he hung himself from the wall of paradise, and when the angels ascended to worship God, then Satan appeared in the form of an angel and sang hymns like the angels... And I (Eve speaking) bent over the wall and saw him, like **an angel**. But he saith to me... "What are thou doing in paradise?" And I said to him. 'God set us to guard and to eat of it.' The devil answered **through** the mouth **of the serpent**... "Follow me."*   - Apocalypse of Moses / Apocalypsis Mosis 16:1-18:6[74]

A Twisted Conversation With Eve

Interestingly enough, one ancient source cites that the time set for Eve's seduction was, in actuality, some sort of twisted *remembrance* of what may have happened earlier, to Sammael:

*...some say that... Satan was deposed from his degree... on the sixth day, when he envied Adam, who was created in the image of God... but in that sixth hour of the sixth day, when he was cast out, he **approached to seduce**...*
    - Barhebraeus Gen. 3:1-4[75]

The stage was set. One afternoon, Eve was all alone. In some sick act of remembrance, the Serpent arose at this time, and went over to confront her. He was going to use every trick up his proverbial sleeve to deceive this newly-formed woman. As we recall, this Serpent was probably endowed with gifts of knowledge, and even the understanding of our previous world. The Serpent's ability, here, allowed him to verbally pounce all over Eve's newly-developed ways of looking at the world. He had the ability to encourage her to think *twice* about what God, or Adam, might have told her. He always seemed to have the right things to say, injecting the potential for insecurity into almost every thought Eve could have drummed up. This would enable the Serpent to badger Eve with questions such as, "Yea, hath God said (in Gen. 3:1)," and quickly make her *doubt* even God!

Let's discover how the Serpent used his sneakiness, his worldly knowledge, and one other method of manipulation - a poignant technique that, after it was "all said and done," allowed for the contamination of the **entire world**, from that point on! What could do all this? It would, eventually, become a common practice between individuals in our post-Fall world, a practice known simply as *fornication*.[76]

Chapter 7

Fornication
With the "Other Side"

*...(Sammael/Satan) did not change his intelligence as far as (his) understanding of righteous and sinful things. And he understood **his condemnation** and the sin which **he had sinned before**, therefore he conceived thought against Adam, in such form he **entered** and **seduced** Eva (i.e. Eve)...*
                        - 2 Enoch (The Book of the Secrets of Enoch) 31:5[1]

Things in our world were about to become much more *complex*. The Serpent had knowledge of the world *before* our own. Sammael/Satan did *too*. They both felt the need to bring down Adam in any way possible. Now, we'll see there could have been a little more to the techniques they used, besides their verbal manifestations of envy, anger and hatred:

*He (the Serpent) saw Adam and Eve, in blissful ignorance of shame, happy in their love, and he became jealous and envious... (A) main purpose, however, of the Serpent is not the death of Adam, but **the possession** of his widow Eve. Because he saw their **joys of love**, he **lusted** after Eve.*   (Jung, 1974, p. 68-69)[2]

Wow. It seems like the closer to human beings that angels become, the more passions, desires, or even physical "needs" an angel desires! There was no doubt about it: the terrestrial Serpent was *male*, and Sammael knew it. According to ancient sources, this angel-turned-human now began to experience *sexual* passions, as well.[3] Satan could have finalized the contract between he and the Serpent by allowing this angel to, underhandedly, slither his way into setting up another contract: one allowing him to subsist on the richest, most luscious "food" in the garden - Eve *herself!*[4]

*(The historian) Philo regards the serpent as a symbol of pleasure, including **sexual** lust.*   (McClausland, 1872, p. 130)[5]

With more and more human passions coming to him, there was one more "fact of life" the Serpent may have had to deal with: *women*. Interestingly, the Bible mentions the Serpent right *after* the following verse, "And they **were both naked**, the man and his wife, and were not ashamed (Gen. 2:25)." Could it be that the Serpent noticed Adam and Eve both naked, and began to desire her *as well*? The couple (Adam and Eve) seemed to enjoy a wonderful paradise. Maybe another thought that entered the Serpent's mind at this time was: "**I** will destroy Adam and *marry* Eve, and truly rule."[6]

If we also think about it, if the Serpent was an animal - an ordinary reptile - he probably would not have had *any* desire, sexually, for Eve. Only a *man*, or a human-like individual, would have sexual desires for a woman.[7] All of this may sound completely contrary to Biblical teaching, here; but, as we'll see, Scripture may begin to give us hints towards this all being a reality! Layered within the verses of Genesis and Revelation, there could be a number of obscure bits of information we never really contemplated before. Could this be an example of a story element that may have been obscured, or translated in a different way, to make it sound more like something else? And, if so… *why*? As we'll see, there could, in actuality, be a lot more to this temptation of Eve, and other stories, than many of us may have assumed.

One ancient source seems to make a comparison: the author (of the below) compares a woman to *Eve's* actions, all the way back in the Garden.

*(A heroic mother expressing principles to her children)… "**I** was a pure virgin and did not go outside my father's house; but I guarded the rib from which woman (Eve) was made. No **seducer** corrupted me… nor did the Destroyer, the deceitful **serpent**, defile the purity of **my virginity**."* - 4 Maccabees 18:7-8[8]

In other words, this woman did not allow herself to be sexually corrupted, as Eve did. Well, does that mean Eve was actually *sexually* exploited, here? And, if so, this may throw an entirely new light on this whole temptation event in the Garden. And, as we'll also see, the ramifications of this *one* act would affect the Serpent, Eve, and even Adam, for the rest of their lives. Let's move further.

The "Soft Target?"

What about this "seduction" of Eve? Did anything of this magnitude *really* happen? Most of us were not taught this. We were taught the Serpent only used slimy *words* to seduce Eve. Regardless, the Serpent may have considered Eve to be an "easier target" for his manipulation. We know he set out to use anything at his disposal, to achieve his nefarious goals. The Serpent may have assumed, from his experience in the world before, that a typical woman may be more prone to *listen to all creatures* (including terrestrial angels), and even have more compassion towards them.[9] This may help him, in his quest.

According to one ancient source, the Serpent / Sammael assumed that Adam would, probably, have been a little more hardheaded.[10] And, since Sammael also knew the Serpent was *male*, he probably counted on there being some type of sexual tension between the two. This, of course, would further help work to the Serpent's advantage.

Because of all these attributes, the Serpent probably solidified his belief in Eve being the best target for this seduction. Now, he (they) needed to, somehow, find some way in. Their target was now in scope.

When a conversation arose between the two, Eve informed the Serpent of the one (and only) *law* that they had: they were *not* to eat of the fruit of one tree. This tree, of course, was the *Tree of the Knowledge of Good and Evil*. One of the Serpent's acts of trickery may have revolved around Eve's perceptions of motherhood, and having children. Apparently, Eve understood this possibility was coming for her, and longed to have children *right away*. So, armed with this information, the Serpent tried to convince her that this tree actually *allowed* a greater chance for her fertility![11] With her sudden interest, the Serpent was on his way to twist any perceptions she already had about the tree, and her situation.

Another twist the Serpent used involved Eve's authority in the Garden. Again, in the following quotes, please try to picture "beasts" and "animals" (below) as actual, *human beings* (we recall that early translators, here, may often have assumed certain words should be translated as "beasts" or "animals").

Anyhow, Eve speaking:

*...while I was guarding my own portion (of paradise)... the devil came to Adam's portion. And there were **beasts** there... for the Lord had also divided the **beasts** between us. All (that were) male He had given to Adam, and all (that were) female, He had given to me. **And we each had fed our own ones**.*

- Book of Adam [44]15:3-4[12]

Apparently, Adam, not only helped oversee the cultivation of the Garden, but he (and Eve) also helped redistribute the food that was brought in. According to one ancient source, the Serpent made it known to Eve: "I am distressed for you, for you are like the animals... but I, I do not desire your ignorance" (*The Book of Adam* [44]18.1). In other words, the Serpent said that Eve really didn't act like a manager at all, but more like one of the hired personnel.[13] He said this to undermine Eve's power and authority, and subtly set out to show her how much wisdom and experience *he* already had in this world. Ultimately, this eventually was to show Eve how she should actually be looking up to *him*, and *his* superior intellect, rather than going with her own assumptions.

Then, the Serpent accosted Eve with the famous words, "Yea, hath God said?" In other words, he said something like, "What? Who are you putting your faith in here, regarding this tree? God or (knowledgeable) me? No. You are actually being hood-winked by God, really. Don't you see that? The fruit of this tree does not actually cause death, it gives you the opposite. It brings forth *life*, and can help bring you life (i.e. the potential for children). It also helps to confer **wisdom**, not punishment. You're such a fool. God is doing this on purpose - keeping you in a perpetual state of ignorant bliss."[14]

Although it wasn't really like that at all, and God clearly warned Eve that *death* would result from the eating this fruit, the Serpent kept trying to convince her that the *opposite* of almost everything God said was true. God's "death," here, would actually give her immortality, if she only partook of it.[15] There is a great deal of worldly knowledge to be gained also. She could maintain a better way of life now, if only she had sense enough to do it the Serpent's way!

A rationale the Serpent also used was to try to convince Eve that, since she and Adam were created *last*, God may, next, want to create *other* beings superior to them. So, she'd better act fast, if she didn't want to be left behind. And, with the Serpent's coaxing, she may have, then, concluded that: if only she ate of the fruit, then maybe *she* could become more like God himself, and be able to create new worlds. A lot of this "god-like" potential knowledge and ability left Eve curious, and, as any human might be, in want. She may have even thought this was a chance to gain what the Serpent (non-verbally) claimed to be "enlightenment."

Most of us know there was *some* ancient knowledge actually hidden from Adam and Eve by God, but it was for a very good reason: the misuse of it could actually help lead one towards their own death or destruction. Adam and Eve did know that some knowledge was intentionally hidden from them, but may not have realized the veracity of why it had to be, why it was for their own good. The Serpent knew this also, and played on it the best he could.

The Serpent / Sammael would use all he (they) could, to disrupt the apple cart. They use a number of tricks like this today. Their big attempt is to try and preach the *opposite* as the true ways to go. They play on our desires to look "behind the curtain," to be curious, and want to know *more* than, perhaps, what God thinks we should. The Serpent wants us to seek our own "enlightenment," apart from God. He also capitalized on Eve's *compassion* and *human* tendencies to want to advance herself, as long as it's without the help of God.

Assuredly, God already knew there were potential problems looming within this conversation between the Serpent and Eve:

*Then I commanded thee concerning the tree, that thou eat not thereof. Yet I knew that Satan, **who deceived himself**, would also deceive thee.*
- First Book of Adam and Eve (The Conflict of Adam and Eve with Satan) 13:16[16]

Eve now wanted to taste the fruit. And, in one final condition of her acceptance, the Serpent would allow Eve access to all of this wonderful "knowledge" and "power" if, and *only* if, *he* had one thing in return – she needs to give this same fruit to Adam, and have him eat.[17] Eve was still a little hesitant about jumping into this "opportunity." So, in order to cement the deal, the Serpent may have had one more trick up his sleeve.

Beguiled - Wholly Seduced?

As one ancient source stated, it was also at this time that "the woman was **inflamed** by the Serpent."[18] What could be the meaning of the word "inflamed," here? Let's take a good look at what the Bible said that happened:

*...And the woman said, The serpent **beguiled** me, and I did eat.*
- Gen. 3:13 (KJV)

Did the Bible totally *leave out* an important part of the story here, or could it, subtly, have left *clues* behind, for us to find? Could it have subtly hinted to *something else* which may have also been going on, here? What does the word *beguiled* mean? Could it mean a little *more* than just casual, verbal seduction?

If we look in the Bible, we see the way *beguiled* was implied in another verse, and how it could, actually, support our argument:

*...for I have espoused you to one husband, that I may present [you as] a chaste **virgin** to Christ. But I fear, lest by any means, as the serpent **beguiled** Eve through his subtilty, so your minds should be corrupted from the simplicity that is in Christ.*
- II Cor. 11:1-3 (KJV)

Paul, the writer of this verse, desired the reader to come to Christ as *untainted* as a **virgin**, unlike what happened between Eve and the Serpent. We also see that the Serpent reportedly *tainted* Eve. Could this mean that Eve was no longer a **virgin** after her exchange with him? Could he have *beguiled* her, or *wholly* seduced her (seduced her in *all* ways, even sexually)?[19]

*Possibly, the lure of a snake is unconsciously **sexual**.*
(Pember, 1975, p. 127)[20]

It's totally understandable why so many people have never heard of this possibility. It's very exposing (as we'll soon see). And, it's understandable why so many may want to automatically dismiss it - thank you "political correctness." Yet, as we'll soon see, the "closer to home" some things are the more *voracity* an evil force out there will react to it, and try to shut it up. So, just because so many may, today, "quickly discount" the possibility of sexuality going on, that doesn't mean it didn't happen. This very well may be accurate history. This, if discovered, would be *exposure* for sure, not only to Sammael and the Serpent, but so many more after them (as we'll see).

With all of this, we really should understand that: what these individuals (so often) fear the *worst* is what they (so often) scream the loudest against! It is what they, most rapidly, try to divert you from wanting to know, to question, or even want to investigate. So, judging by the level of resistance and aggressive-downplaying we already find today, a missing element of the Adam and Eve story as big as this should, naturally, be worth a much greater look, and a much deeper level of investigation.

And, even if this extra element might sound a little outrageous at first, or even impossible to the ears of some, there *are* a good number of ancient and modern works that actually allude to *sex* as part of this whole seduction process:[21]

*(Eve speaking)... And he (the serpent) put upon the fruit which he gave me to eat the poison of his wickedness, that is, of his **desire**, for desire is the head (another version: has root and origin) of all sin.*   - Schatzhohle III[22]

*The Serpent was envious of Adam, on account of Eve. And having **polluted** her, he inveigled her to eat of the forbidden fruit.*   (Eisenmenger, 1748, p. 21)[23]

...the serpent had intercourse with Eve and injected filth into her...
                                                    - Zohar Pekudei 21[24]

*The **Talmud** tells us how the serpent in the Garden of Eden had sexual relations with Eve and injects its filth into her, which affected all her descendants.*
                                                    (Unterman, 1991, p. 150)[25]

Even ancient *pagan* texts, some with similarities to this story, point to a sexual encounter between a serpent and their "Eve-like" character:

*In a story preserved in the prologue of Gilgamesh, Enkidu and the Underworld, the goddess Inanna (i.e. Eve?) gains knowledge of **sex** by descending to earth and eating from various plants and fruits. She transplants the huluppu tree from the Euphrates to her own garden, but a wicked serpent made its nest amongst the roots of the tree. This tale **connects** the serpent to the garden, and with the presence of Inanna, the **theme of sexuality**.* ("Wikipedia, *Eve*", n. d., p. 4)[26]

At the time the Serpent seduced Eve with subtle words, he could have easily started working on her on *another* level! He began to caress her, touched her in certain areas, and, ultimately, began to provide her with more knowledge about her body than she probably ever knew! Now engaged in an act of coition - within their newfound, sexual frenzy - Eve probably gave in, and agreed to eat the fruit of the Tree of Knowledge. And, with the pact they made previously, Eve also had to fulfill her promise to the Serpent: to give the fruit to *Adam*, as well, and make him eat. The Serpent got what he wanted on so many levels. And, from this point on, the rest of the story is much the same as it was in the Bible.

After she bit into the fruit, she *instantly* saw the Serpent's true colors. The Angel of Death (i.e. Sammael/Satan) also begun to show himself to Eve, which really shocked her. It was also the time she realized she made a *great* mistake. This fallen angel now helped bring death into Eve's world, not life. He destroyed her authority over the Garden, not enhanced it. And, ultimately, she had to go do the same thing to Adam.

Interestingly enough, the name *Azazel* (i.e. the Serpent) was also known as the angel of death and destruction.[27] Doesn't this further help to confirm that he and Satan were *both* the Biblical "Serpent," here?

The "Evil Inclination" Planted

What else could have happened, at the time of their sexual union? According to many ancient sources, upon completion of their coition, the Serpent injected his so-called "**evil inclination**" into Eve. This "evil inclination" seems to represent a supernatural type of "poison" or "disease" of sorts. It was also thought of as the Serpent's *filth*: representing a "built in" desire for evil and destruction inside people; a tendency to be "beast-like" (as far as morality); or a tendency to follow the ways of the "other side." People would carry on these negative thoughts along with them for the rest of their lives, often hidden in the darkest, most remote corners of the mind, waiting for their time to come to the surface, and strike.

Although eating the fruit *did* allow Eve to gain the knowledge (or discernment) of good and evil, she also acquired *other* carnal (or "worldly," "animal-like," etc.) thoughts and desires. These thoughts, when they persistently come out of an individual, will help negatively affect, not only the individual, but the entire human species.[28] That's what the Serpent always wanted.

The Poison of Lust

> *(Eve speaking)... (and) he went and poured upon the fruit the poison of his wickedness, which is **lust**, the **root and beginning of every sin**, and he bent the branch on the earth and I took of the fruit and I ate.*
> - *Apocalypse of Moses / Apocalypsis Mosis* 19:3[29]

On top of this all, Eve began to develop other desires internally - especially *lustful* desires. What exactly is this *lust*, according to the Bible? One ancient source stated that *Azazel* (the Serpent) would, eventually, be known as the angel who taught women how to enjoy *sexual* pleasures, and engage in acts of sexual promiscuity.[30] He also would be known for teaching women how to use makeup, and how to wear all kinds of costly stones (to make themselves look more sexually attractive to men). Interestingly, all of these *do* seem to involve sex.

> *And the whole earth has been corrupted through the works that were taught by Azazel: to him **ascribe all sin**.* - *1 Enoch* 10:8[31]

And, Eve's newfound knowledge, here, may have also given her enough ammunition to fulfill her promise to the Serpent: to seduce Adam. She needed to "finish the deal," which would ultimately help spread the Serpent's "evil inclination" to the rest of the world's populous. Eventually, he would also work on ways to spread his ideologies and corrupt belief-systems to every human being he could.

Beastliness Incarnate

*(The Serpent) goes in unto Eve and infests her with **lasciviousness**… in spite of all his superiority to his fellow beasts, he left some **beastliness** in Eve…*

(Jung, 1974, p. 76)[32]

Lasciviousness is one example of this Biblical **lust**.[33] These desires are not just sexual, they could also represent one's intent to *take* something of this world, and use it to help make them *equal* to God, or even *above*. Sex, often, could be used in this way: if a person feels coitus is part of their route to achieving a "god-like" state, they, then, may continually desire to engage in it from then on, and as much as possible, thus making the *true* ways to reach God obsolete.

This one act between the Serpent and Eve already seemed to have laid the groundwork for so much *more* corruption - political and religious - to come, as we'll see.

Come One, Come All

Eve may have felt somewhat good, at least during their sexual exchange. She may have had a temporary feeling of euphoria. But, after it was all over, she quickly began to feel *guilt*, shame for allowing herself to have taken this particular route. In fact, she soon began to feel very despondent, terrible. Eve even lost that *image* of God (i.e. that supernatural "glow," or shine) that she and Adam once had. Now, she began to see how she altered the present order of things, and endangered everyone and everything.

Because of these negativities, she - with her newfound "evil inclination" - did not want to be alone in her shame. She knew she had to seduce Adam, as well. It was necessary, now. So, beyond having to honor the Serpent's request, this also became a necessity for her not to suffer all of those negative feelings by herself.[34] She was created from Adam. If she was going to falter, and live life as a fallen being, she wanted to do it *with* Adam. If she was going to die, then he was going to die with her. It only seemed fair, and natural. Also, if she could help it, she didn't want Adam to have a chance with any other woman around.[35] She probably couldn't stomach it, if he did. And, she probably also knew about Lilith, and her former relationship with Adam. All of these thoughts would be almost too much for almost anyone to handle on their own, in her mind.

One ancient source stated that Eve may have even started giving the fruit of the Tree of Knowledge to other people and animals around her. Hoping to bring most everything and everyone to the same level she was, it really didn't pan out too well for her, in the end. It only served to make her feel worse:

> *...I have sinned before your **elect angels**... I have sinned before the generations of the heavens. I have sinned before the **birds (Owph?) of the heavens**. I have sinned before the **beasts (Chay?) of the earth**. I have sinned against you, God, by my greed, against **all your creatures** (i.e. people?).*   - Book of Adam [45]32.2[36]

Animals, as we know, really don't care about who may have morally sinned against them! The above, again, has to represent people. Animals, for the most part, care about eating, or being eaten. And, it's also interesting to see how she mentions two groups of living beings here: the *Owph (Fowl) of the Air* and *Chay (Beasts) of the Field*. Could this, as well, further support that these were actually two groups of *people*, living at the time of the Garden of Eden?

Continuing on, we'll discover that, in regards to Eve's newfound sadness, the Serpent had a comment to make:

> *Then the beast (the Serpent / Sammael) replied to her and told Eve, "It is not from our greed(iness) that your discontent and your weeping come, but your discontent and your weeping come from your own greed(iness), for at the beginning of creation, it was you who harkened to the beast, the serpent. How did you dare open your mouth and eat of the tree of which God had commanded you not to eat?"*
>   - Book of Adam [38]11.1-[38]11.2[37]

It's sad, but true. Eve harkened to a beast (i.e. an angel?), or leader of them, and not God. Now it was time to pay the price. When she first encountered Adam, he quickly began to perceive that something was wrong:

*He (Adam) had thought… a **beast** had entered paradise…*
- Book of Adam [44]21.2[38]

He knew that something evil had just happened. He wasn't quite sure what. Did one of these *Chay (Beasts) of the Field*, or a *leader* of them, do something they weren't supposed to? Or, was is more like: did someone do something that wasn't exactly savory (and acted like a "beast" might)?[39] Adam probably summed up what happened to Eve. He probably figured out that she may have done something with the Serpent, and, initially, didn't want anything to do with that. Eve tearfully pleaded with Adam. She could have even tried to seduce him sexually, the same way the Serpent tried to seduce her. Adam, however, had a lot of feelings for Eve. He, then, debated for almost three hours on what to do.

In the end, Adam eventually made the decision: "Eve, I love you. I would rather die with you than outlive you… God could never console me with another woman equaling your loveliness!" He then gave in, and ate the forbidden fruit. Another ancient account shows Eve coming to Adam *without* her heavenly splendor (or "image" of God). And, when Adam asked why, she refused to tell him until he ate of the forbidden fruit.[40]

So, even though he knew he was about to do something wrong, Adam's rationale was simple: it was to show his *love* for Eve. Yet, it may sound somewhat noble by today's standards, but, of course, it was **disobedient**. He should have obeyed his Lord, and not do what might have sounded *good* at the time. He was just as wrong as Eve was, in this case. He should have not allowed any *other* interpretation, including his *own*, to dominate God's direction on right and wrong, here.

These two exchanges (between the Serpent and Eve and between Eve and Adam) would give rise to something else disastrously going on: ***fornication***.

Fornication and Adultery

*But thou... pouredst out thy **fornications** on every one that passed by... How weak is thine heart, saith the Lord God, seeing thou doest all these things, the work of an imperious whorish woman... But as a wife that committeth **adultery**, which taketh stranger instead of her husband! They give gifts to all whores: but thou givest thy gifts to all thy lovers, and hirest them... Wherefore, O Harlot, hear the word of the LORD... (because) thy filthiness was poured out, and thy nakedness discovered through thy whoredoms with thy lovers...*   *- Ezek. 16:15-36 (KJV)*

Both Adam and Eve, according to a number of ancient sources, were seduced by sexual seduction, here. Both were given seductive rhetoric, as well. And, eventually, both gave into the seduction, which cost them dearly. And, regardless, Adam and Eve both *chose* their own destiny. The woman chose her destiny by allowing the Serpent to have his way with her, and wanting to follow his pathway. The man, also, chose to follow the woman's pathway. He, in a sense, did the same thing!

We have an interesting quote, in regards to understanding this whole thing:

*That tree was from the tree of knowledge of good and evil (Gen. 2:9, 17). Upon eating from the tree, Eve was aware of what she had done. She now had the **knowledge** of evil and she was aware that she had sinned against God. In that knowledge, and having fallen, she then offered the fruit from the tree to Adam. Adam was not deceived (I Tim 2:14). He knew when he saw Eve that she **had** sinned, because she had lost the spiritual glow that results from being in close spiritual harmony with God. Moses had this same glow when he came down from Sinai (Ex 34:29-30). Adam **elected** to eat the fruit, knowing what he was doing. His **love** for Eve (whom he knew had sinned) was greater than his love of God. This is a tactic used time and again by Satan. The downfall of God's people **is frequently through the temptations of godless women** (see Numbers 25:1-9)... The same basic scenario is being **repeated after the Garden of Eden**, only on a larger scale. **There is a wholesale abandonment of God and his righteous ways for women known to be in sin**. This is what God calls **fornication**, not referring only to a sexual sin, but the sin of mixing the righteous with the wicked, truth with evil. (One example of this is the word fornication as attributed to the **harlot church** in Rev 17:4 and 18:3). This sin was so prevalent, and so blatant, a rejection of God that it could not be allowed to continue indefinitely.*   ("There Were Giants on the earth... The Nephilim", n. d., p. 2)[41]

This is another important way to define *fornication*. This definition of *fornication* seems to go way beyond "sex outside of marriage." It often doesn't relate to sex at all, but *intent*: Eve, trying to *change* Adam's mind through manipulation and seduction, constitutes fornication. And, in this definition, fornication was committed in this case. The two went beyond some innate, even occasional, drive for sex, and used this experience for other ways. She used it to help seduce him, and bring him down.

The Serpent "screwed over" Eve with fornication, as well. He also mixed sex's original purpose with something *evil*, and used it as a means to his own end. It also *disparages* the other individual in the process. This, as a whole, makes the above definition of fornication what it is.

Actually, this type of fornication occurred throughout the Bible, even though many may, today, not want to recognize it as such. They get stuck on the sexual aspect of it, and how sex could be used for it. Regardless, it happened between Sampson and Delilah. It happened between David and Bathsheba, and so many others.[42] Again, it wasn't the physical act of *sex* as the problem, but *the way it was used*, and *what one (or both) participant thought they were getting out of it*. So, through it, a lot of men and women were turned away from their original desire or purpose, and turned to another way. This is also a reason why the act of *sex* gained such a bad reputation, over the years.

> *For so long as he (Adam) was by himself, as accorded with such solitude, he went on growing like to the world and like God... But when woman too had been made... love enters in... and this desire likewise engendered **bodily pleasure**, that pleasure which is the beginning of wrongs and violation of law, the pleasure for the sake of which men bring on themselves the life of mortality and wretchedness in lieu of that of immortality and bliss.*
> - *Works of Philo Judaeus* On the Creation 151-152 (also 165-166)[43]

Doing what he thought was the "right thing" (at least on a humanistic level) clearly wasn't for Adam, in the end. The two brought on a lot of negativity to our world, by their choices.

In the same vein of fornication, *adultery* is not only defined as any person having sex outside the bonds of marriage, but one particular person (usually a woman) having sexual relations with someone *other* than her husband. Well, what's the big deal with that, here?

What's the difference between the above and what we've always been taught? And, why bring it up - what relevance might this have to what happened in the Garden of Eden?

*Indeed, every act of sexual intercourse which has occurred between those **unlike** one another is **adultery**.* - Gospel of Philip[44]

Interestingly enough, certain thoughts about adultery could have also originated in the Garden of Eden: Eve reached out, and had sexual relations with someone other than Adam. Eve also may have very well had sex with a terrestrial, angelic being, one *unlike* her. We're not talking about mixing different groups of pre-Adamite people, or mixing Adamites with anyone else, or anything like that. These human-to-human mixtures are not the problem. We're talking about a human being mating with one of the terrestrial *angelic* beings. This represents like and *unlike*. And, as we'll soon see, *this* manner of mixing - human with someone "not-exactly" human - was greatly *abhorred* by God in the past, and still is. This was what made adultery such a bad word. More on this, later.

The Loss of Adam's Angelic-Like State

Now, the time of Adam's temptation had come and gone. He failed miserably.[45] Adam would have continued being God's representative to the world if he only resisted, but he didn't. After he fell, everything and everyone around him also fell. The whole world - epitomized in the Garden - would never be the same. The Angel of Death showed his true colors to Eve, and what death was all about. And, on top of it, Eve showed Adam what a fallen world, and the Evil Inclination, were all about. Sammael / the Serpent were both victorious.

Adam would never be able to return to this former state, and this included his once-brilliant *image*, or countenance, that God gave him.[46]

*And on thee, O Adam, while in My garden and obedient to Me, did that **bright light** rest also. But when I heard of thy transgression, I **deprived** thee of **that bright light**.*
- First Book of Adam and Eve (The Conflict of Adam and Eve with Satan) 13:6-7[47]

Now Adam, Eve and everyone around them would become familiar with the concepts of pain, death, and all the sadness that would go along with it.[48] The *Chay of the Field*, the *Behemah* and *Owph of the Air* probably began to think twice about their roles in the Garden. Their leader, Adam, made a huge error. Why would they want to respect Adam and Eve anymore, or care about whatever service they may have performed in the Garden of Eden? Even members of the animal kingdom were beginning to be less controllable, and a lot more savage overall, for the curse of the Fall also extended to them. Maybe even the *Owph (Fowl) of the Air* - those with certain angelic qualities - lost some of the what they had. All were affected. All suffered. Anyone who had something even remotely to do with the Garden probably found themselves without their former purpose.[49]

Animals, as we mentioned, truly became "wild," and a number began to live without order. Some became aggressive, even hungry for blood. A few ancient sources stated that both animals and humans now had their teeth "turned on edge" (i.e. sharpened) because of the Fall, which signified the beginning of what some would call the "law of the jungle." Battles for superiority and survival began to take place everywhere. Even human beings began to act *wild*, or *uncivilized*:

*And the **beasts** (angels?, humans?) of whom you ruled shall rise up against you. You shall be weakened because you have not kept my commandments.*
- Book of Adam [44]24.4[50]

Negative elements to our world were sprouting up all over, even beyond the animal kingdom. Thorns and thistles were beginning to grow all over the place, and infect the plant kingdom. The world was no longer *very good*.

Adam, because of these changes, probably felt the worst out of everyone. The following ancient verse, coming from a work loosely known as "The Cry of Adam," described how totally despondent he felt for his actions (please notice how he also seems to mention the *Owph of the Air*, the *Chay of the Field*, and the *Behemah*):

> *O **birds (Fowl?) of the heavens**, come down to me and see my weeping!*
> *O **beasts (Chay?)**, see me who am tormented!*
> *O **wild animals (i.e. Behemah?)**, look at me, who am ashamed!*
> *Have pity on me, who was once your lord, sovereign, and king, but am*
> *now equal to you, **but more unworthy!***
>   - *Armenian Apocryphal Adam Literature* Repentance 20[51]

Assuredly, Eve and other women began to question their roles with the men of their lives. Whatever might have gone on before the Fall is now different. Not only did Adam lose the authority over human beings and animals, he probably lost the respect of Eve, as well.

The Serpent and his fellow angels - the Nephilim - felt so vindicated! They also felt they were able to break away from *their* assigned roles in the Garden. All was changing, including this. According to Heb. 2:5, our future world will *no longer* be under the dominion of angels. Logically, if this is going to be the case, then one could easily assume that, now, they have a supernatural "dominion" over our world. But, before the Fall, it's easy to assume the opposite was probably true - *man* had dominion over the angels of this world.

We have another interesting quote:

> *Woe for the loss of a great servant. For had not the **serpent** been cursed, every*
> *Israelite would have had two valuable serpents... to bring him costly gems,*
> *precious stones and pearls. Moreover, one would have fastened a thong under its tail,*
> *with which it would bring forth earth for his garden and waste land...*
>   - *Babylonian Talmud* Sanhedrin 59a[52]

As we see in the above source, people may have had two serpentine angels - angelic servants - to aid them in their everyday life, possibly helping with much of their work at hand... that is, if Adam didn't fall. After the Fall, mankind had to resort to stubborn mules and beasts of burden to help them with more difficult tasks. All of this newfound chaos was exactly what the Serpent / Sammael wanted.

*And the woman said, "It is the serpent who instructed me." And he (God) cursed the serpent, and called him "**devil**."*   *- Testimony of Truth*[53]

Hence, the ways of our present, evil world had begun.

The Curses Pronounced - On Adam

*Then the Lord became angry at them, and said to Adam, "Because you have done this, and you did not listen to my counsel, but hastily listened to **your wife's** counsel, thorns will spring forth to you in place of this immortal plant."*
                    - Armenian Apocryphal Adam Literature Transgression 41[54]

God, no doubt, was very, *very* angry. And, the time had now come for all of those involved to pay the price for their disobedience. The punishments began to be dealt out - they had to - to Adam, Eve *and* the Serpent.

Gen. 3:
17 *And unto Adam he said, Because thou hast hearkened unto the voice **of thy wife**, and hast eaten of the **tree**, of which I commanded thee, saying, Thou shalt not eat of it: cursed is the ground for thy sake; in sorrow shalt thou eat of it all the days of thy life;*
18 *Thorns also and thistles shall it bring forth to thee; and thou shalt eat the herb of the field;*
19 *In the sweat of thy face shalt thou eat bread, till thou return unto the ground; for out of it wast thou taken: for dust thou art, and unto dust shalt thou return.*

Adam was given a few curses, by God, for his disobedience. Interestingly enough, they all seemed to have to do with *working the ground*, probably because that was once his major responsibility. Adam ate of a forbidden tree in the Garden, so now the ground was forbidden from staying truly bountiful, and easy to manage.

Another punishment of Adam was that he, now, had to work by "the sweat of his brow."[55] If we think about it, it may be logical to assume that, before this time, Adam *didn't* have to work too hard (obviously, it wouldn't really be much of a punishment if he did). But, again, *why* didn't he have to? It only makes sense to assume that, probably, there were more people around him, to help him out.[56] Who manages a huge garden by themselves and never once needs to sweat?

Also, Adam was now ordered to eat the foods of the field (Gen. 3:18), such as wheat, and not the wonderful fruits of paradise he was once used to.

> *For the next seven days, they could find nothing fit to eat, only food for cattle and wild beasts.* (Frankel, 1989, p. 32)[57]

For Adam, the thoughts of having to do such dirty work, without *quickly* achieving a satisfying sustenance, began to make Adam *shiver* with stress and nervousness:[58]

> *"(God said)... and thou shalt eat the herb of the field." When Adam heard that the Holy One blessed be He told him "And thou shalt eat the herb of the field," his limbs trembled. He said before Him: "Lord of the Universe! Shall I and my cattle eat in one crib?" The Holy One blessed be He replied: "Considering that thy limbs **trembled** (at the thought), thou shalt eat bread in the sweat of thy brow."* (Jung, 1974, p. 75)[59]

Through this fear, Adam began to show God how much he respected Him (in regards to his punishments). He seemed deeply concerned about what he did wrong, and inner turmoil began to manifest all over his outer body. God noticed his uneasiness, and began to show mercy on him. After this, Adam calmed down, and ended up being more at ease with God's overall judgment.[60]

The Serpent, and his reactions, were a different story, however.

Curses on the Serpent

*...whoever sets his eyes on that which is not his is not granted what he seeks and what he possesses is taken from him. We thus find it with the primeval **serpent** [in the Garden of Eden] which set its eyes on that which was not proper for it; what it sought was not granted to it and what it possessed was taken from it. The Holy One, blessed be He (i.e. God), said: I declared: Let it be **king** over every animal and beast; but now, Cursed art thou above all cattle and above every beast of the field.*
                                                    - Babylonian Talmud Sotah 9a-9b[61]

The reason a lot of people may have believed that this Serpent was an actual *animal* may revolve around a couple of curses that God placed on him. We have:

*And the LORD God said unto the serpent, Because thou hast done this, thou art cursed above all cattle (Behemah?), and above every beast (Chay?) of the Field; **upon thy belly** shalt thou go, and **dust shalt thou eat** all the days of thy life...*
                                                    - Gen. 3:14 (KJV)

We see, here, that the Serpent was made to crawl *on its belly*, and also *eat dust*. The form of a modern *snake* seems to have been his end result, due to these curses, right? Well, our response to that is this: what the Bible says, for the most part, could be taken *literally*. The above verse, however, doesn't necessarily point towards having a literal meaning, however - one of the few *exceptions* out there. The reason for this being different is simple: people then, as today, had their own ways of saying things. These two above phrases actually could be known as ancient Hebrew *idioms*, *methods of thought*, or *figures of speech* - commonly thought of as *Hebraisms*.

In ancient Israel, the terms "upon thy belly" and "dust shalt thou eat" were often used as figurative expressions of *degradation*. It makes sense here. What sort of animal goes around, anyhow, and eats *dust*? Let's see how these figures of speech could actually work into our story, here.

After his fornication with Eve, the Serpent - Sammael's vessel - was not going to escape without any punishment. He did not have *total* victory, here! He was already "demoted" once before, by God. And, now, it's time for more. While in this "demoted" status, the Serpent still walked about with an erect, cocky posture. He still thought he was "top dog," and wanted all of the "dainties" of the world for himself. Now, he was about to lose all of that. Well, just what might these *dainties* have been? Once, the Serpent, as a "mid-level manager," could have had authority over anyone who had something to do with the Garden. Now, he would be considered **lower** than all of them! So, as we'll see, these curses probably weren't a manipulation of what he looked like *bodily*, but more of how he would think or feel.

Let's dig into this, a little deeper.

"Upon Thy Belly..."

"upon thy belly shalt thou go" - *a **Hebraism** (an idiom, figure of speech, etc.) for utter defeat... **humiliation**.*
- *The Companion Bible* Appx. 19[62]

First, we see that this above phrase is a *derogatory* term, aimed at the Serpent.[63] If we want to look at one example of this in the Bible, we see:

*Wherefore hidest thou thy face, and forgettest our affliction and our oppression? For our soul is bowed down to the dust: **our belly** cleaveth **unto the earth**.*
- *Psa.* 44:23-24 (KJV)

The Serpent and other serpentine angels would, now, have their "estates" lowered even further - with practically *no* more angelic qualities. They, as with any other human being, would also be destined to suffer "death" as we know it, living out the same lives as most any other human being out there. Yet, their punishments would go way beyond the physical, here.

Now, this "mid-level" manager of the Garden would have to suffer something he never really had before: feelings of human *defeat*; ultimate *humiliation*; and *low self-esteem*. His *mind* was also sentenced to feel extremely "low," all of the time, and continually be overwhelmed with feelings of **insecurity**. So, as we now see, his punishments extended to his *thoughts, feelings,* and *perceptions of self-worth*. But, with a worthy angel of the supernatural, this punishment becomes *so much* worse.

*"(God speaking) Thou has said, Thou wilt be king over the whole world: thou shalt therefore be cursed above all cattle. Thou hast said, Thou wilt walk with thy body **erect**; therefore upon thy belly shalt thou creep. Thou hast said, Thou wilst eat of all the dainties of the world; therefore **dust** shalt thou eat off the days of thy life."*

(Eisenmenger, 1748, p. 198)[64]

"...Dust Shalt Thou Eat"

"dust shalt thou eat" - *a **Hebraism** (an idiom, figure of speech, etc.) for constant, continuous **disappointment**, **failure**, and **mortification**.*
- *The Companion Bible* Appx. 19[65]

We recall, from Adam's formulation, that *dust* was not a very worthy substance to be created out of, or even behold. And, we recall that *dust* could have even been associated with dung or worthlessness - a sign of one's own *humility*.[66] Adam was fashioned from it, but Sammael / the Serpent were now about to *feel* like it.

We see some examples of this *"dust,"* throughout the Bible:

*...and his enemies shall **lick the dust**.*
- *Psa.* 72:9 (KJV)

*...they shall bow down to thee with their **face toward the earth**, and **lick up the dust**...*   - *Isa.* 49:23 (KJV)

A serpent doesn't eat dust, here; it only eats small animals. It eats meat. This also gives us further validity to his angelic origin, and not animal. The Bible must speak truth here; and, again, it *does*. Both seem to further validate that these statements were in reference to some *inner* degradation of the mind, not an outer, physical change to the Serpent's body.

But, there would be *some* outer changes to the Serpent, not necessarily the loss of his arms and legs:

*But he turned to the serpent (in great wrath) and said: "Since thou hast done this… thou shalt feed on **dust** all the days of thy life… There shall **not be left thee ear** nor **wing**, nor **one limb** of all that with which **thou dist ensnare** them in thy malice and causedst them to be cast out of paradise; and I will put enmity between thee and his seed"…*   *- Apocalypse of Moses / Apocalypsis Mosis* 26:1-4[67]

Possibly, this may refer to the loss of a few spiritual "gifts" (such as certain supernatural (hearing) "senses," or the ability to use his "wings" - to swiftly go back and forth into the supernatural). But, beyond this, he may have even lost some of the use of that *sexual organ* which helped to seduce Eve, as well! He may now have suffer, somewhat, with his coition. Who knows. How *appropriate*, however. How humiliating, as well.

The loss of his supernatural "senses" (such as this "hearing"), his swiftness, and his overall prowess would probably give him a good deal of "earthly" physical problems, as would happen with other mortal beings. He helped to create this fallen world, now was his time to lie in the bed he helped to build.

*(Sammael / the Serpent have)… slid from the upper height to the nether region… (as well, they) shalt chew **earthly** things.*
    - Barhebraeus Gen. 3:14[68]

…dark and noisome shall be the serpents dwelling.
(Baring-Gould, 1881, p. 43)[69]

Instead of having the "dainties" (i.e. "wonderful things") at his disposal, he quickly began to lose everything. And, if he did manage to father semi-human descendants or anything like that, they, too, would assuredly suffer some of the same issues that he had, *internally* and *externally*! The important thing to take away from all this is: the worst curse the Serpent had to face now was his feelings of low self-esteem, his misery, worthlessness, and self-torment. This mental anguish would stick with him for the rest of his life, here on earth.[70]

…what he (the serpent) desired was not given him, and what he possessed was taken from him.
    (Halevi, 1997, p. 204)[71]

*"(God speaking to the serpent)... they shall have healing and **thou** shalt have no healing."*   (Jung, 1974, p. 71)[72]

*Some of the angels by an act of free will obeyed the will of God, and in such obedience found perfect happiness; other angels by an act of free will rebelled against the will of God, and in such disobedience found **misery**.*
                                        (Baring-Gould, 1881, p. 16)[73]

Curses Upon Eve

*Thereupon God imposed punishment on Adam for yielding to a woman's counsel... Eve He punished by **childbirth** and **its attendant pains**, because she had **deluded** (deceived) Adam, even as the serpent had **beguiled** her.*
                                        - *Flavius Josephus* Jewish Antiquities 1:45-50[74]

Eve would have some punishments dished out to her, as well. Interestingly, we see that most of hers would involve **sex**. Could this be an ironic *response*, by God, to the act that she and the Serpent once participated in?

*Unto the woman He (God) said, **Multiplying**, I will **multiply thy affliction** by the **blood of thy virginity**...*   — *Targum Pseudo-Jonathan* III[75]

Possibly, she was no longer a virgin after this time. And, if that was true, the *bloodshed* coming out of her lower vaginal area may have begun to sport some specific significances to her situation. We'll see, from now on, that God often seems to distribute His punishments out to people, *measure for measure*.

And, in the Bible, we see that, with the following curses allotted to Eve:

- a greatly multiplied sorrow when she experiences pregnancy
- sorrow when she brings forth children   (Gen. 3:16)

Sorrow and pain, from this moment on, seemed to become a necessary element of human conception. Eve may have brought these sorrows upon herself, and womankind after her, because of the coition she was involved in. Once, she wanted to be *fruitful* by eating the Tree of Knowledge. Now, she'll suffer in her ability to multiply because of it.

From that point on, when a woman undertakes the responsibility of childbearing, especially at the point of giving birth, they'll probably suffer noticeable, sometimes almost *unbearable*, fits of anguish:

> *...and on that occasion you shall come near to losing your life from your great anguish and pains.*   (Halevi, 1997, p. 204)[76]

> *...your giving birth will be changed **into death**.*
> - *Armenian Apocryphal Adam Literature* Transgression[77]

When God punished Eve, He could have said something such as the following:

> *Since thou hast hearkened to the serpent... thou shalt be in throes of travail and intolerable agonies; thou <u>shalt</u> <u>bear</u> <u>children</u> in much **trembling** and in one hour thou shalt come to the birth... But thou shalt confess and say: "Lord, Lord, save me, I will turn no more to the **sin of the flesh**." And on this account, from thine own words I will judge thee, by reason of the enmity which the enemy **has planted in thee**.*
> - *Apocalypse of Moses / Apocalypsis Mosis* 25:1-4[78]

This says so much. The word *trembling*, in the above, could equate to one "with great sorrow."[79] It also says that: when a woman gives birth, she may often think or say something such as, "No more will I ever want to have sex again!" It's funny, but some ancient sources claim that, at the moment of childbirth, outbursts such as the above may actually signify a woman's own, subconscious attempt to make *atonement* for Eve's original sin, here.

On top of these, her coitus with the Serpent also brought her to the point where she may have no longer thought of herself as "innocent." She's all grown up now! Their act, according to one ancient source, then began to activate Eve's *menstrual* cycle (as well as establish menstrual cycles in all women since her). Again, certain punishments seemed to be dished out to Eve in an *ironic* way:[80]

*Now, you, Eve, as you **caused the tree to bleed**, you **will bleed** every new moon.*
- al-Tabari: The History of al-Tabari - Vol. I: General Introduction and
From the Creation to the Flood God's Testing of Adam 107[81]

Apparently, menstrual pains also seemed to now be another "side-effect" of her coitus in the Garden.

And, according to the Bible, a typical woman may now have:

...a desire to be with her husband again, or to her husband when she has travail, and he will rule over her.   *- Gen.* 3:16 (in retranslation)

What this may mean is: when Eve (and other women after her) gets in an argument with the man in her life, she may come off cynical or angry, at first. Then, she will be a little afraid. And, finally, she'll want to return to him. Why? Could this have relevance to the Garden? Could Eve, by her "going astray" with another male (as she did with the Serpent) have brought this curse upon her? Could this be a curse that will actually bring her thoughts to the point where she may want to *go back* with the same man she took issue with, or had problems with, before?

*(May you, Eve)... give birth to many fruits... and you will **harden your heart** in view of the great **combat** which the **serpent constituted** in you. (But may you) return at once to the same point, may you **bear your offspring** in hurt and return in pity to your husband...*   *- Book of Adam* [44]25.1-4[82]

Eve, and possibly a good number of women after her, was, then, cursed to become a lot more *emotional* about things than she ever was, originally:

*Eve shall be afflicted with variety of **strange affections**.*
(Baring-Gould, 1881, p. 43)[83]

Why did Eve seem to get "hit" harder, here, in regards to these curses? Apparently, one reason was, in part, because of her attitude at the time she faced God. She seemed to be a little less repentant than Adam was, for whatever reason. God did not like that, and took action. This led her further down the "totem pole" of degradation, as well as authority (between her and Adam). God, apparently, took this time of punishment very, very seriously. Adam became very afraid of his punishments, and showed it. Eve, however, may have been more preoccupied with her situation, how the Serpent "screwed" her over, and how cruel it was to be punished, when she did her best.

*And toward your husband will be your **turning**, and he will have dominion over you, whether to admit or find fault.*   - *Targum On Genesis* 3:16[84]

Interesting: the word *turning*, in the above, seems of special significance:

*Now, "turning" was the ordinary Hebrew word for repentance. So it must have seemed that the whole point of this verse (if we understood as "turning") was that Eve had been **unrepentant** when she was reproached by God in the openings words of Gen. 3:16... Unlike her husband, she showed no remorse. As a result, she was then **further** sentenced...*   (Kugel, 1998, p. 143)[85]

According to another source, the meaning of the word *Eve* could, sometimes, be equated to "a serpent."[86] Why? We see now, in the following ancient text, that God may have spoken this to Eve:

*The serpent was thy serpent, and **thou** wast Adam's serpent.*
     - *Genesis Rabbah* 23:2[87]

In other words, Eve actually was the same to Adam as what the Serpent was *to her*: a temptress, seducer, etc.[88] She wasn't exactly innocent in these acts of fornication. And, now, we see that there also seemed to be some merit to this assumption, in the Bible.

Adam - Not a Part of the Transgression

<u>I Tim. 2:</u>
14 *...Adam was not deceived, but the woman being deceived was **in the transgression.***
15 ***Not** withstanding she shall **be saved in childbearing**.*

Notice that the word "childbearing" seems to have been mentioned right after Eve was said to have been "in the transgression." Again, the two may be related in some way, or one could have been in consequence to the other. We're not sure. What we could get out of it is: the Serpent committed a *transgression* against Eve, by committing fornication with her. Eve, also, committed a transgression against Adam, in somewhat the same way. Adam, however, did not turn around and commit fornication with anyone else, though... the process stopped with him. We're not saying that men never commit fornication. It's just that, in the particular case of the Garden, the Serpent and the woman were both guilty of this act. And, this could be another reason why Eve had a little bit more to her punishments.

Eve, the verse also states, would eventually be *saved* from her transgressions in a certain way; because, through *her descendants*, one would be born that would become the savior of the world. This would be the one to "right the wrongs" committed in the Garden of Eden. And his name would be one most of us know already as *Jesus Christ*.[89] We will examine this concept in much more detail, later.

The Curse of Seed on the Earth

Also, regarding the above, could there have been **more than one** outcome to all of these sexual transgressions? If one of Eve's descendants would help bring on the savior of the world, could there be other descendants coming from all of this - maybe, one who was not exactly on the Lord's side? Could there have been a consequence to these actions which might actually be there to plague Adam, and all the rest of the people in the Garden, until the end of time?

*And Eve said to Adam: "Live thou, my Lord, to thee life is granted, since thou hast committed neither **the first** nor **the second error**. But I have erred and been led astray."* - Vita Adae Et Evae 18:1-2[90]

What was the first *and second* error, here? Obviously, she committed the "first error" by eating the forbidden fruit. Could a "second **error**" involve the results of her sex with this Serpent?

Interestingly enough, shortly after this above verse, we see:

*And she made there a booth, while she had in her **womb** offspring of three months old.* - Vita Adae Et Evae 18:3[91]

Well, what if something *did* come out of their sexual experience (beyond just regret)? What if she *knew* something already, and was beginning to prepare for it? What if she indeed was pregnant? And, how much would this complicate the rest of her world?

As we begin to dig deeper, ancient sources stated that Eve seemed to be *with child* some time after being seduced by the Serpent. It seems to be the same case, in the above. If a child was on the way, then what would have been the circumstances of *this* birth? And, if the Serpent was, possibly, the father, then what effect would this offspring have on the world to come?

Chapter 8

The Offspring

*(God, speaking to the **Serpent**)… And I will put enmity between thee and the woman, and between **thy seed** and her seed…*   *- Gen.* 3:15 (KJV)

The above prophecy was given by God, directly to the Serpent himself.

First off, what do we mean by "thy seed," here? Since God was talking to the Serpent, what kind of seed are we talking about… the seed of baby snakes? How could a little enmity (or hatred) between women and slimy, slithery serpents be of such importance, especially regarding what happened in the Garden of Eden? Makes no real sense, if we think about it. There are plenty of animals in our world that scare people. Why is this enmity so noteworthy here, and to be included by God? It seems to go way beyond one own irrational paranoia about snakes. So, if we agree that this situation may not really be about snakes, just what kind of "seed" are we referring to, then?

As we see, God was making this statement to the Serpent, right after the probable copulation between he and Eve. Maybe that coition would, now, set the stage for two individual **blood lines** to be born - the descendants of Adam and Eve **and** the descendants of Eve and the Serpent! If this was the case, then the above verse, actually, becomes a **focal point** of so much in the Bible, and this book! It'll be very important, as we progress.

It's quite possible Eve and the Serpent could have been able to spawn **offspring**, because of their action. And, if this did indeed happen, this particular offspring would be one able to be in conflict with Eve, and so many of her other descendants (as the verse stated). Could *this* be why the prophecy was important enough to be brought up here, at this time, by God? According to a number of ancient sources, *this* is exactly what happened: two separate bloodlines would come about, through Eve. Something big was on the horizon. Something monumental was about to unfold.

Through seduction, ancient sources tell us that the Serpent could even have tried, more than once, to have additional offspring with Eve, later on in life. He could have even tried to impregnate other women along the way! Yes, the Serpent obviously wanted to spread his seed around a lot during these early times. It makes total sense: if he was going further down, to live out the rest of his terrestrial life as a human-like being, why not make the best of it. As they say: there's *immortality* in one's descendants. Why not try? At least he had that going for him. It's now survival of the species, in any way possible! And, the less people who know about it overall, the better.

So, it would be through a number of these Serpent pregnancies, and pregnancies resulting from other terrestrial angels with human women, that entire groups of people would slowly come about. Collectively, these groups would be thought of (at least in ancient Jewish theology) as the *mixed multitudes*.

The one offspring who would directly spring from the Serpent and Eve, here, would be considered "patriarch" of all the mixed multitudes. It only makes sense. This individual would also go on to launch one of the most important struggles of our time - pitting one "side" against another![1] Just *who* this offspring may have been, and what effect he had on the whole world since, are the questions. Let's look more into this prophecy, just who "he" was, and what it may *really* mean to all of us, today.

The Head and Heel

> *...I will put enmity between thee and the woman, and between thy seed and her seed...*
>   - *Gen.* 3:15 (KJV)

Next, while proclaiming the above prophecy, God prophesied that a *savior* would eventually arise from one seed line, and stop the progression of the other, in an extreme way:

> *...it (the savior) shall **bruise** thy head, and thou shalt bruise his heel.*
>   - *Gen.* 3:15 (KJV)

This *savior*, as already stated, was to be *Jesus Christ*.[2] In another ancient text, we see God proclaimed to the Serpent:

*Let the precious cross **which my Son** will take upon the earth condemn you (the Serpent) because of the deceit by which you deceived Adam. But may you again be **crushed** and **broken** because of the evil of your heart. And I will set enmity between you and the offspring of the woman: she will lay in wait for your head and you will lay in wait for her heel until the day of judgment.*

- Book of Adam [44]26.3-4[3]

What this simply means is: Jesus would **crush**, or **break**, the "head" (i.e. the *power*) of the Serpent in so many ways, or break any *hold* the Serpent had over the world at the time. In the process of doing this, however, this particular individual would have his *own heel* bruised, signifying that Jesus would be sacrificed on the cross, and killed. But, he would rise again, and defeat (or crush) the power-structure that Sammael / the Serpent had, from the beginning on.[4]

Let's explain this in a little more detail. *Strong's Concordance* gives us a couple of Hebrew meanings for the English word *bruise*, here: to "snap at," to "overwhelm" or to "cover." So, another interpretation of this all might be that the seeds of the Serpent would, throughout the ages, continually try to snap "at the **heels** of Christ, groveling in the battle, while Christ, the Lion of Judah, snaps at the **head** of the serpent," crushing his skull.[5] The descendants of the Serpent - those with his blood - will, from this point of time on, continually try to inflict suffering on the bloodline of Adam. This would continue, all the way up to the time of Christ's birth. And yes, it wasn't just figuratively, not by a long shot. There were actual, *physical* births going on, with real bloodlines, here. It's not just one theology or philosophy defeating another on the cross (as most Christian theologians might try to make us believe, today). There's **nothing** in the Bible about this being any kind of metaphor.

With this also being actual seed lines, we'll discover how mixed, angelic descendants would, throughout history, continually work to compromise (even *destroy*) the Adamic seed line (i.e. the descendants of Adam and Eve). One major goal they have is: to stop baby Jesus from ever coming into existence. If they could prevent this seed from being passed on to him, they believed it, then, would destroy the savior's purposes here on earth, and save their own skins from this prophecy. It is war, here. But, in the end, most of us know what actually happened - the "Serpent-seeds" would be defeated. The savior *would* crush the power the Serpent (in *all* ways) by his own death, burial and resurrection.

> *...all Satan's plans and plots, policy and purposes, one day will be finally* **crushed** *and ended, never more to mar or hider the purposes of God.*
> — *The Companion Bible* Appx. 19[6]

It was a very powerful reason for Christ's existence!

To explain how Jesus accomplished this, we must first recall that the major punishment Adam and Eve inherited was *death*. And, through *Christ's* death, burial and resurrection, his would provide a substitute-sacrifice, for all mankind. This sacrifice would "snap" (or break) the Serpent's head. Through his resurrection, he also defeated the hold, or power, that *death* had upon the world. In this way, he snaps (in two) the world by which Adam and Eve helped to usher in. One verse says it well:

> *...as the children are partakers of flesh and blood, he (Jesus) also himself likewise took part of the same; that through* **death** *he might destroy him that had the power of death, that is, the* **devil***...*
> — *Heb.* 2:14 (KJV)

Jesus' unblemished sacrifice on the cross paved the way for the human existence to **make atonement**, again, with God. It took a perfect, substitute sacrifice. This was the nitty-gritty of it all.

There is more.

The Poison "Head"

> *...it (the savior) shall bruise thy* **head***...*
> — *Gen.* 3:15 (KJV)

If we think about it, the *head* of a snake is where his poison sac is. And, the *mouth* of a snake is the point where all the *poison* comes out![7] If we begin to follow this train of logic, we may begin to ask: how about the rest of the "mouths" out there? The *head* of most any animal is where *thought processes* occur. So, from this, could there be an interesting parallel to real "poison" coming out one's mouth and "ideological" poison? Looking at it another way: could this "head," symbolized in the above, be, in part, the *theologies, philosophies* and *schools of thought* pushed by the Serpent and his literal seeds?

*(God speaking to the serpent)… and the poison of death shall be **in thy mouth**…*
- Targum Pseudo-Jonathan III[8]

And, we'll also soon discover that those largely responsible for railroading Jesus to his execution may have, indeed, possessed actual *blood* of the Serpent, along with their promoting a certain *ideology* or *school of thought* to those around them. Both the power of these seed lines, and their ideologies, needed to be "crushed."

Adam to Jesus

One thing is for certain: the seed line of the "first Adam," here, was needed, in order to begin the framework for the rest of his descendants to be born… those leading to up the "last Adam," Jesus Christ:

I Cor. 15:
45 *And so it is written, The **first** man (**Adam**) was made a living soul; the **last Adam** was made a quickening spirit.*
47 *The first man is of the earth, earthy; the second man is the Lord from heaven.*

The original Greek word for *man*, in the above, is *anthropos*. It not only means *man*, but a *special* kind of man. It represents a man distinguished, "from beings of a different order."[9] In other words, it could have easily represented Adam, a slightly-different man because of his soul, given directly though God, Himself. And, after the Fall, his role on earth would be a little different, too: to pass on his special seed (and way of thinking) until the last "Adam" - Jesus Christ - took over the scene! No offense meant to any other human seed line out there, but Adam's seed, obviously, was needed to fulfill this prophecy. It just makes sense. Any other seed wasn't the apportioned one, here… simple.

The First Adam lived to die; The Second Adam died to live. Go, and imitate the penitence of the First Adam; Go, and celebrate the Goodness of the Second Adam.
(Alvarez, 1713)[10]

And, if we look at the genealogy of Jesus, we do seem to see a special significance to his seed line. His lineage, as noted in the Book of Luke (and also Matthew), begins with Jesus himself, and goes straight back to *Adam*. Let's take a look at how it's worded right near the end of it all:[11]

*…(we have Cainan being)… the son of Enos, which was the son of Seth, which was the son of Adam, which was **the son of God**.* - *Luke* 3:38 (KJV)

Adam's special circumstance, as a "son" of God here, helped to establish an important narrative in the Bible:

*This is the book **of the generations of Adam**. In the day that God created man, in the likeness of God made he him…* - *Gen.* 5:1 (KJV)

So, the Bible, among other things, seems to be the story of one particular man, Adam. The, then, goes down his family bloodline, eventually reaching the savior of the world. And, Adam was thought to be a "son" of God because, as we know, he had his soul formed directly by God. From then on, Adam was supposed to think and act in ways similar to his heavenly "Father" here, and pass it on. As they say, "Like father like son."

And, this also doesn't mean that any other bloodline in our world isn't important, or doesn't matter - it's just had to be that way, in this case, to fulfill prophecy! It makes sense to have Jesus come from the blood line of the one who helped cause all of this ruckus in the first place! We can't express this enough, because (as we'll see) there will be so many out there trying to refute this all, or somehow call it mean, wrong or unfair to say it was from Adam. They'll use whatever grounds they could to make their point. So, be careful Don't be fooled.

Also, although the wonderful *image* Adam once had would fade (i.e. the brilliant, angel-like *shine* God had given him), the special significance of his seed line would not, nor would the ways he looked at the world. His descendants, and these ways of Adam, *had* to survive, and continue on, if the prophecy of Gen. 3:15 was to be fulfilled:

(In regards to Jesus Christ, himself)... He (God) hath appointed heir of all things, by whom also he made the worlds; Who being in the brightness of his glory, and the express image of his person...   *- Heb. 1:2-3 (KJV)*

So, to allow for this fulfillment of prophecy, there quite often needed to be some manner of *separation* over time, between the seeds of Adam and seeds of the outside world. This was, of course, to *deter* any possible ways of compromise, or sabotage, to the line by the Serpent, and other fallen angels. If they were able to insert their own seeds into these people, then they no longer would wholly be of Adam. Seed compromised.

The Necessity for Untainted Seed

*By a profound principle of genetic science, discovered only recently, the blood line, or type, is determined through the **male**, or father, and thus the blood of Christ was technically, and truly, not tainted by the **curse of Adam** as it is in the rest of humanity, since Jesus did not have **an earthly father**. The **same sinless blood** was poured out at Calvary for all whom are redeemed in Christ. No other death could have accomplished the substitutionary atonement and the propitiation of His righteousness unto us.*   (Unruh, n. d.)[12]

Now, the **male** seed becomes important for this very reason. And, since Jesus was to be born of a virgin, he *could* not to have any Serpent's seed within him. God would not allow any type of adulteration.

*...in such form he (the serpent) entered and seduced Eva, but **did not touch** Adam...*
- 2 Enoch (The Book of the Secrets of Enoch) 31:5[13]

And, although those of Adam's seed were needed to carry out this task, they were by no means perfect people. There were those who were compromised.

But, as we recall:

*...Adam **was not deceived**, but the woman being deceived was in the transgression.*
- I Tim. 2:14 (KJV)

Interestingly enough, since Adam didn't participate in the major transgression of the Garden (i.e. fornication), he may not have been liable for as much pain and suffering as Eve and the Serpent. And, because of this rationale, Jewish law seemed to be a little more favorable to the *male*, overall. Not only was he to remain head of the family, the man was still expected to remain an example of God's moral code, here on earth.

Although this may not sound fair to some, we, again, are seeing how occurrences at the **Garden of Eden** could have been behind so many things people faced, throughout the centuries, and why men and women were treated so differently, in the past.

The Force of Separation

And, even though Adam was given a "lighter sentence," here, he wasn't very happy with what Eve did to him, overall. Angered by how things turned out, he made a fairly interesting but seemingly appropriate proclamation, based upon his point of view:

*And Adam called his wife's name Eve; because she was the **mother** of all living...*
- Gen. 3:20 (KJV)

This sounds like a compliment, at least at first. Adam said Eve would be the *matriarch* of all of mankind! Wow, what a comment... or was it? On top of it, we really need to contemplate: why would Adam be the least bit happy with Eve here, when (according to the Bible) he just got through blaming her for his role in the Fall? She helped to talk him into eating the fruit. He may have even discovered she had sex with someone else. Adam, assuredly, wasn't in the mood to compliment Eve. But, rather, he could have made a comment on this whole "seed line" prophecy God laid out!

The original Hebrew for *mother*, in the above, is the word *em*. It not only means "mother;" but (according to *Strong's Concordance*) it can also stand for "a point of departure or division." So, if we recall the prophecy of Gen. 3:15 (above), we do discover there was going to be a split, or division, of human descendants here. And, Eve, because of her unique position, was actually the focal point of this division! She had sex with the Serpent, and could have already been pregnant by him. She and Adam would, also, eventually have children. Adam probably identified her as the center, or *point of division*, for this very reason. She had one "foot" in his door and one "foot" in the Serpent's!

*And Adam called his wife's name Eve; because she was the **point of division** between all the living human beings...*   *- Gen.* 3:20 (in retranslation)

We also know that, from now on, the up-and-coming descendants of the Serpent - through Eve - would work to *separate* or *divide* themselves from Adam, or cause *division* in the descendants of Adam, working to corrupt anyone who may want to eventually think the same way Adam did. It's all about mental disruption, and the twisting of morals. As already stated, the "poison" coming out of the Serpent's head could be ideologies, or certain rhetoric, designed to manipulate the masses.[14] The descendants of the Serpent would indeed, over the years, *divide* others away from the ways of God.

Thoughts, *world views*, and specific *ways of thinking* truly can be used to divide people - no doubt about it. It's all around us, if we really look around. No wonder why one ancient source stated that the first offspring of Eve and the Serpent would be thought of as "the ***divider*** of the kingdom."[15] He would be the one who would work to being everyone, including those of Adam, in the direction of following *his* ways of the world, world views *he* subscribed to. So, to move on, let's learn a little more about just *who* this individual may have been.

Time to Leave the Garden

The LORD God sent him forth from the garden of Eden, to till the ground from whence he was taken.   *- Gen.* 3:23 (KJV)

After the Fall, Adam (and the rest of the human race) had to go to work, and work *hard* - no more lives of leisure, for most everyone. The time, also, was nigh for Adam and Eve to physically *leave* the Garden of Eden.[16] They could not stay.

As well, one pillar of this Genesis 3:15 Prophecy (also known as the *Protoevangelium)* was about to be established - the first descendant of Eve would soon be born. And, when God makes a prophecy it *has* to come true, and it is not to be interrupted. That's just the way a perfect God works. These two seed lines now have to start, and be at enmity to each other! Interestingly enough, Adam may have already had an idea that this all was about to occur.

According to one ancient source "the union of Adam and Eve was consummated **after** the expulsion from Paradise."[17] So, whether or not Adam and Eve copulated before they left the garden, it's still a great possibility that a third party - the *Serpent* - stepped into the middle of their relationship, and inserted himself. Quite possibly, a child of the Serpent may have already been in Eve's womb!

One ancient work describes how an angel approached Eve, and began to confide in her. He began instructing her how to correctly manage what may be growing inside of her:

*If you had not been brought help... you would have conceived such a thorn that you could not have rescued yourself from your sufferings. Rise up now and prepare yourself to **give birth to a child**.*   *- Book of Adam* 21.2[18]

To Eve's surprise, she now found out she was, indeed, with child. And, let's look at some reasons why *Adam* may have already been suspicions that this particular child, probably, was not his.

And Adam Knew Eve...

*And Adam **knew** Eve his wife; and she conceived...*
                                                   - Gen. 4:1 (KJV)

When one reads this Bible verse, it seems obvious that Adam *knew* (or had *sex* with) Eve, and their first offspring was *Cain* - it seems simple. And, to so many today, this is proof-positive that Adam was the father of Eve's first child... right? Possibly not.

We have some other interesting interpretations of this verse: many may have assumed that the word *knew*, in the above, means "to have sex with." And, we also know that the original language of the Bible was Hebrew, and there were people out there who translated these words according to what *they* thought it should say, or was *taught*. Yet, again, to find out what the original Hebrew may *really* be referring to, we need to dig a little deeper; and go beyond this realm of assumption.

The Hebrew original for *knew*, in the above, actually comes from *two* Hebrew words: *yada* and *eth*.[19] The word *yada* does mean, "to know (a person carnally)," but it can also mean to "recognize," "discern" or "acknowledge." The other word, *eth*, is untranslatable in English, but is rooted in a word that stands for "sign," a "distinguishing mark," or an "omen." Put them together, and we could have:

*And Adam eventually **acknowledged** the **distinguishing sign** that had come upon Eve...*   *- Gen.* 4:1 (in retranslation)

On top of it, the Hebrew word for *conceived*, in the above, could also represent one "with child." So, to top it all off, we have another way to retranslate this verse:

*And Adam eventually **acknowledged** the **distinguishing sign** that had come upon Eve; that she was **with child**, and realized she was about to give birth...*
                                        - Gen. 4:1 (in retranslation)

Wow. The Bible can't really state it much clearer than that. Adam *understood* that she was pregnant, and what it all meant to her, and him. We have other interpretations to further back this up:

*Adam knew his wife, not in the sexual sense, but knew **something about her**.*
(Kugel, 1997, p. 86)[20]

What is the meaning of "knew?" (He knew) that she had conceived.
- *Pirke deR. Eliezer* XXI[21]

Adam *knew* she was pregnant, by simply looking at her bulge. And, then, he went on to make a conclusion about it. Sounds a lot different than what the King James' translators tried to portray, as well as other translations… but, now we know *why*! There is a lot of information here, which could expose. Certain translators may have felt the need to follow tradition, or translate things according to how *they were taught*, or they didn't want any interpretations *other* than what the "establishment" at the time wanted them to put in. It could get quite complex, really.

Yet, we now see there could easily have been another interpretation of the word *knew*, here: "the time had come when Adam and Eve were expelled from the Garden, and Adam took his wife away from there, with the *knowledge* she was already pregnant. From there, they settled to the east of the Garden."[22]

The Serpent was able to drive a wedge in between Adam and Eve, by this insemination, and this baby would end up being someone they couldn't really ignore, or set aside. Interestingly enough, they also seemed to have gained a great amount of *cover* for it, over the years!

The Offspring of Amalek

*And Adam **knew** his wife, who had conceived by the angel **Sammael**, was pregnant…*
(Eisenmenger, 1748, p. 198)[23]

We already have a number of other names for the Serpent: Nachash, Gadriel, Azazel, etc. And, we know there are some other names for Sammael, as well: Satan, Lucifer, etc. Let's look at *one* more title the Serpent may have had, as well, and how it relates to the child he was instrumental in bringing forth.

The Hebrew word *El* is synonymous with the English word *God*.[24] As we recall, from earlier, some theorized that the *El-ohim* actually stands for "God and his angels." So, a "strange El," then, would probably represent an *El* (or, "a *god*") who came from a *strange* origin (a "fallen" one, fallen angel, etc.). And, we'll see that (in the below) other women, since Adam's time, would also unite sexually with fallen angels (or "strange El's"). Their unions began to form entire groups of "mixed multitudes," sometimes thought of as *strange* (because of the angelic-human mixture).

So, with all of this, we have yet another name for the Serpent:

*These are all mixed among Yisrael (Israel), but none of them is cursed as **Amalek**, who is the evil **Serpent**, a Strange El: The one who uncovers all nakedness in the world. This means that it… causes incest in the world. It is the murderer. From it, all murders in the world originate, and its spouse is the potion of death of idol-worship. So the three transgressions of idol-worship, incest and bloodshed derive from… Amalek, who **is the serpent** and another El. They are all related to the aspect of Samael, who has many different aspects, but they are not the same. Samael, who is from the side of the Serpent, is the most cursed of them all.*
- Zohar Beresheet A29

According to the above source, incest, murder and idol-worship all seems to have originated from the *Serpent* - a.k.a. **Amalek**. The descendents of Amalek would go on to form a significant group of "mixed multitudes," known as the **Amalekites**.

Interestingly enough, ancient sources state that these Amalekites *would* survive, and even thrive, throughout the ages. They would be present, up to the time of Israel, and far beyond. And, many of his descendants would be just as God predicted: continually at *enmity* with Adam, his descendants, and anyone who may choose to follow God's ways.

We also see (in the above) that *Amalek* was the origin of those who commit **murder**. Who, in the Bible, was famous for committing **murder**? Yes, this was also the same individual we accredit to being the Serpent's first son.

*Having been made pregnant by the **seed of the devil**... she brought forth a **son**.*
                                        - Tertullian On Patience 5:15[25]

*And I will put enmity between thee and the woman, and between the seed **of thy son**, and the seed of her sons...*   *- Targum Pseudo-Jonathan II*[26]

And, this all was the same person - the one the Bible names ***Cain***![27]

Cain

Could **the Serpent** really be the father of Cain, not Adam?[28]

*(Cain)... who, on account of the foulness of the **murder** which he had committed, has **nothing in him** resembling his father (or Adam, his presumptive father), either in **body or soul**.*
                    - Works of Philo Judaeus Questions and Answers on Genesis 1(81)[29]

Maybe the reason Cain did not resemble Adam in any way was obvious: Adam *was not* really his father!

Now afterward, she bore Cain - (the serpent's) son, begotten on Eve's "shadow," or physical body, by... (the serpent's) act of raping her... The posterity of Cain are therefore the offspring of devils.   *- The Reality of the Rulers*[30]

*The descendants of Kayin (Cain), after he (Kayin) was driven from the face of the earth, are **strange** creatures...*   *- Zohar Vayishlach 28*[31]

Again, in the above, we see the word *strange* was used. We know that this could represent one descended from a *strange* god, or fallen angel. In so many ways, we'll discover how the Serpent probably had *everything* to do with the birth of Cain, and not Adam - his presumptive father![32]

There have been other theories related to this whole concept: some accounts speculated that there could have even been an "infusion," of sorts, between the Serpent's seed and Adam's seed:

Samael begot the spirit, the soul of Cain, Adam became his bodily father…
(Jung, 1974, p. 79)[33]

Know then, Cain was form'd from the impurity, and that drop which the serpent injected into Eve: but as it was impossible, without the mixture of Adam's seed, for the spirit to cloath itself with a human body, and be brought forth into this world; so the seed of Adam furnish'd means for the cloathing it with a body.
(Eisenmenger, 1748, p. 197)[34]

It sounds much more simplistic, and sensical, to accept the possibility the terrestrial Serpent alone fathered Cain. Cain was only the Serpent's son, lock, stock and barrel. And, we'll also see that, from this point on, a number of angelic/human unions would produce offspring such as Cain, in vast numbers. The *Book of Enoch*, for example, mentions a **serpent** angel named *Taba'et* siring a mixed human offspring.[35] Whatever way Cain may have been conceived, he sure acted as though he had blood of *the Serpent*, as we'll see.

Let's look some more ancient evidence of Cain, and his origin.

Cain - A "Shining One"

*What is the meaning of the word "knew?" He knew that she had conceived. And she saw his likeness that it was **not** of the earthly beings…*   (Jung, 1974, p. 78)[36]

*…Cain was not of Adam's seed, **nor** after his likeness, nor after his image… The Pal. Targum to Gen 5:3 adds: "… Eve had borne Cain, who was not like to him" (i.e. Adam).*   - Pirke deR. Eliezer XXII[37]

Adam, as we've already postulated, had a shining, "angel-like" appearance before the Fall. After his sinned, however, he lost most of it. Cain, interestingly enough, was *born* with practically this same, brilliant countenance. The reason? He came out looking similar to other serpent *angels* of the Garden!

(Cain's) shape was not like that of other men.
(Eisenmenger, 1748, p. 197)[38]

*...And his **face** was not like that of other human beings, and all those who descend from him are called "Bene Elohim".*   (Jung, 1974, p. 78)[39]

As we've already stated, angels were once considered "stars," "luminaries" and "angels of light."[40] Angels, even those demoted to live their lives in this terrestrial world, may still have retained a degree of *countenance* to them, and were probably able to pass on this brilliant shine to their hybrid descendants (at least for a couple of generations). Now, it's pretty easy to see why baby Cain could have had a lot of the same:

*Cain's color was that of the **stars**.*
- Book of Adam 21.3a[41]

The Shocking Moment

Eve, as well, probably *knew* what the angels around her looked like. If she noticed baby Cain also had a bright countenance, she could have easily assumed a terrestrial angel may have planted seed in her, or something of the like. Let's look at her exclamation at this time, according to the Bible:[42]

Gen. 4:
1 *And Adam knew Eve his wife; and she conceived, and bare Cain, and said, I have gotten a man **from the LORD**.*
2 *And she again bare his brother Abel.*

Another translation has it as:

Gen. 4:
1 *And Adam knew Eve his wife; and she conceived, and bare Cain, and said, I have gotten a man **from an angel of the LORD**.*
2 *And she again bare his brother Abel.*
        - The Jerusalem Translation

Apparently, she may have thought she conceived Cain through the Lord, or through some angel of the Lord! If it came through fallen Adam, or any other man, it wouldn't have come out shining. That's for sure. Another source stated that Eve may have even been frightened of this child, and wanted to kill him.[43] The bright shine was truly shocking.

It also seems Cain wasn't the *only* baby born at this time. Eve, apparently, was also pregnant with another child (as we shall see)! Her other son, *Abel*, probably had a similar "angelic" brightness to him. Some sources state that both looked as though they were conceived by an angel.

If the two did come from a fallen angel, it's fairly easy to assume Eve wouldn't think *either* son had came from Adam. And, it's pretty obvious, from the above, *who* she may have believed her sons came from. Here's another variant of the above verse in Genesis:

> *And Adam knew his wife, who **had desired the Angel**; and she conceived, and bare Kain; and she said, I have acquired a man, **the angel of the Lord**.*
> *- Targum Pseudo-Jonathan IV*[44]

Who Cain was *really* from, and the ways he would want to follow (and try to convince others to follow), would really set the stage for some much in the past, and in this book! Let's see.

Gotten From the Lord?

We recall the verse:

> *And Adam knew Eve his wife; and she conceived, and bare Cain, and said, I have **gotten** a man from the LORD.*   *- Gen.* 4:1 (KJV)

Eve said, here, that she had *gotten* a man from the Lord. Now, from *whom* was he "gotten" for sure? Another interpretation of where she had "gotten" him from is, of course, you know who:

And Adam knew his wife, who had conceived by the angel Sammael, was pregnant, and bare Cain, whose resemblance was like the upper (Creatures) and not like the lower. And she said, I have **got the man, the angel of the Lord.**

(Eisenmenger, 1748, p. 198)[45]

Interestingly, a couple of alternate meanings of the name *Cain* are "**gotten,**" "acquired" and "possession."[46] What's the significance, here? Could this possibly give us further evidence that Cain was *acquired*, or *gotten*, by some other source, instead of Eve's mate? Interestingly enough, we also notice that Eve calls this newly-born son a *man*, not a child. A man, obviously, is a human being who's already grown up. Why not call him a "baby?"[47]

...this divinely begotten child could appropriately be called a **man** *(rather than a* "**baby**"*) because* **angels** *are* **frequently called "man"** *in the Bible (see Gen. 18:2, 32:24, and elsewhere). Thus, some ancient interpreters concluded that Cain had in fact been half-human, half-angelic creature begotten by the devil.*

(Kugel, 1997, p. 87)[48]

The "Promised Seed" - Already, in Her Lifetime?

...there has broken out another heresy also... that they magnify Cain **as if he** *had been conceived of some* **potent Virtue** *which operated in him...*
("The Gospel of Judas: Cain - Cainites - Kenite - Rechabites", n. d., p. 15)[49]

We recall the prophecy of Gen. 3:15, concerning the seeds of Eve and seeds of the Serpent. We recall it said: "it shall bruise thy head, and thou shalt bruise his heel...." In another side note here, we discover that, at the birth of Cain, Eve could have thought something else was going on. The reason she may have been so astonished by Cain's birth was because she thought it was also time for her *own* salvation. Because Cain had such as brilliant countenance, she may have believed that the time for salvation of the world was at hand - the "promised seed" of God was already there! And, with the Genesis 3:15 Prophecy already being fulfilled, she, maybe, could feel some reprieve from all of the misery building up inside her.

Maybe Eve was so upset about what happened at the Fall that she began to live in states of denial. Most likely, she probably knew who the real father was. Regardless, by looking her son's angelic *shine*, she may began to rationalize with herself: maybe this shine was a sign of *something "good."* Maybe Cain's birth, no matter the real circumstances of it, was something positive, "angelic," or "of God."

She literally may not have understood how those *of the darkness* could imitate any of those of the light, at least for a time! Maybe she was in such torment, after losing the paradise she enjoyed before, that she was just blinding herself to the truth, and what the shine of Cain really represented.

> *It may be well here to note that whenever the word 'Lord' is printed in our English Bibles in capitals, its Hebrew Equivalent is Jehovah - a term which marks the idea of the* **covenant** *God. Apparently she connected the birth of her son with* **the immediate fulfillment** *of the promise concerning the Seed...*
> ("The World Before the Flood and The History of the Patriarchs", n. d., p. 5-6)[50]

The word *covenant* means "promise." Maybe Cain was, at first, considered the "promised one," who would solve all the problems of this fallen world. Regardless of reality, here, Eve probably loved baby Cain very much, and would continued to love him, no matter how he may have turned out. That's the scary thing.

But, as we may assume, Cain's angelic appearance probably pointed him in *the opposite* direction of the prophesied "savior," here, because the terrestrial angels of the time were probably not very happy with God. They were angry, envious and bent on world destruction; and Cain was, at least partly, a member of this clan.

If she continued to perpetuate these seemingly-positive thoughts about Cain over time, what effect would this have on his ego? What if he actually began to feel as though he was someone special, because of his mom's treatment? What about his descendants? What if so many of them began to feel the same? The prophecy was extremely famous. No doubt, everyone knew a history of what went on in the Garden. What if Cain and his descendents began, over time, to accept *themselves* as the ones who were chosen? Although the Bible made it clear that the real savior would be born of a seed of *Adam*, maybe Cain and his descendants began to think the descendants of Adam were actually members of the "other side." The Serpent, probably, was perpetuating a great deal of cognitive dissidence, overall, and Eve undoubtedly could have helped his resolve by holding onto the opinions she did, intentionally or *unintentionally*.

Of course, a typical mother may want what's best for the child, regardless of who the father may be. And, most of the time, she'll always want to present her child in the best possible light. Any misconceived thoughts out there would assuredly complicate matters in Cain's mind, as well as the number of individuals after him.

If we think about it: if Cain's descendants began take on the view that *they* were the rightful ones in this whole argument, then that could usher in a whole "sibling rivalry," unlike the world had ever seen. It would continue to the end of time… each side thinking *they* were part of some "divine light!" Wow. If this actually came to fruition as we speculated, wouldn't it develop into a long, drawn-out battle of wills and ideology? Apparently, that's *exactly* what happened, and exactly what God said would happen (between the two seed lines). There would be great *enmity* between two groups of people, and two philosophies coming from each. And, of course, a majority of this dissention began with *Cain*.

Well, how about a few of these ideological *thoughts* of Cain's side? How do we differentiate them?

More About This "Possessor"

Cain, from the very beginning, was *notorious* to so many around him. We have written evidence, in the ancient *Book of Adam*, which, not only shows Cain as the son of the Serpent, but also shows that there were other people around at the time of his birth. Soon before Cain was to be born, Eve had a *midwife*: a woman used to assist her in the child's delivery.[51] This midwife, somehow, was able to sense some *real truths* about Cain, right from the get-go.

Soon after his birth, the lad began to mature, incredibly fast.

He fell into the hands of the midwife and (at once) he began to pluck up the grass, for in his mother's hut grass was planted.   - *Book of Adam* 21.3a[52]

Even as a baby, he got up, grabbed a blade of grass, and gave it to his mother! According to another ancient source, he was able to get up, and possibly even *walk*, not too long after his birth. All of this was miraculous for a baby - "angel-like."

Some interpreters apparently understood that the baby Cain was born with abilities well beyond his years. (Kugel, 1997, p. 85)[53]

Whatever the situation, here, these wondrous acts of baby Cain could have been a prelude to how good of a *farmer* he might actually be (and even *more*, as we soon shall see).[54] Let's look, for example, at that blade of grass he supposedly picked up, and gave to his mother: this "blade" could have been a type of *reed*, *stick* or *stalk*. Interestingly enough, a stick, according to some ancient texts, was the exact weapon Cain would use in the future, to commit murder![55]

So, once this midwife saw Cain grab the stalk, she quickly sensed that something was extremely negative about him, and his character. She made an interesting interpolation at this point, in regards to his future on this earth:

*The midwife replied to him (Cain) and told him, "God is just that he did not at all leave you in my hands. For, you are Cain, the perverse one, killer of the good, for you are the one **who plucks up** the fruit bearing tree, and **not** him who plants it. You are the bearer of **bitterness** and not of sweetness." And the power (an angel) told Adam, "Remain by Eve until she had done with the infant what I have taught her."*
                                                                    - Book of Adam 21:3b-21:3c[56]

Wow, an angel of the Lord actually had to come and intervene, here. What a story we have! The midwife was so set on what she sensed that an angel of God had to tell Adam to remain with Eve, and help watch over him. Now, why would God already have to take preventative measures for Cain? Maybe the midwife already understood what he was all about, and what kind of individual he was going to be like, in the future.

As we'll soon see, maybe there was good reason for her negative thoughts.

And Adam Begat...

We have another piece of Biblical "proof" that Cain's was of the **Serpent's** seed line. When we look to Biblical references regarding genealogy, for example, we often notice the words: "...and so-and-so *begat* so-and-so." The word *begat* simply stands for a male creating a son from his own seed. And, the Bible often states things in ways to *assure* the reader there will be no doubt to what it saying. In this case, the word *begat* often seems to assure those reading that a certain man actually became the father of someone else! It's interesting, though, that the word *begat* was first mentioned in the Bible - not with Cain or Abel - but with Adam's son *Seth* (in Gen. 5:3)! Nowhere in Scripture does it say that Adam *begat* either Cain or Abel!

Adam's son *Seth* was also the first son who, according to the Bible, looked *similar* to Adam when he was a baby (in Gen. 5:3)! These facts could easily lead us to believe that Cain and Abel were not actually *begat* by Adam at all, even in the Bible! And, if they weren't *begat* by Adam, then by *who*? The ancient, written evidence for a different ancestor of Cain may be coming more and more apparent, now.

Adam and Cain also seemed to be different, on a number of other levels:

...Adam (is) not (cursed), but the earth is cursed because of him, lest the curse should pass over upon the just who are of his seed, as from Cain, who was cursed, upon his seed. - Barhebraeus Gen. 3:17[57]

In other words, God wasn't exactly happy with this sexual situation between Eve and the Serpent, but, assuredly, understood that it wasn't Cain fault no responsibility he was in the situation he was. He wasn't even necessarily considered a "bad seed" because of the circumstances of his birth. The problem was where he took his life, and how he worked to bring so many along with him. We'll soon see more about it.

Also, looking at the curses dished out to Adam and (eventually to) Cain, we'll see another interesting anomaly: Adam's curse seemed to be a little different than whatever curse He would dish out to Cain, later on (in the next chapter). God seemed to have taken out His anger on the *ground* (by making the ground less workable), rather than taking it out on Adam's person. Cain, on the other hand, would be the opposite. God seemed to have taken out His anger on Cain's *person*, and his genes, rather than the ground itself. Why? We're not sure. Maybe it was Cain's attitude, or the way he handled the situation with God. Either way, this undoubtedly would be something that Cain (and his kind) would have to contend with, soon enough - and it would be a big deal.

So, he and his eventual generations would, from now on, have to contend with a number of *internal* issues, rather than just contend with a changed world around him (like Adam). Cain and his own would, now, probably find it a little bit *harder* to overcome the number of negative elements now present in our world. Life, through this, may end up being a bit harder for Cain and his descendents, if they did not concentrate more on what they were doing, or work harder to overcome that which ails them. God must have considered the act that Cain will do (to deserve his curse) much worse than what Adam did. Maybe it was something up the lines of murder.

Still, being of Cain's blood, or of his seed line, wasn't meant to be a death sentence to anyone. Even though God may have been very angry with Cain, even though He may not have wanted angels and human beings to mix, He's still a loving God, overall. And, as we'll see, these offspring could, as well, do right by God... if they only wanted to. Even Cain could have. It all depends on attitude. It depends on one's frame of mind, and what they want out of life. We'll eventually see how God knew there was just people in *all* groups, no matter their origins, and was willing to help out *anyone* (or any group) who made the conscious effort to follow His ways.

Speaking of this, we'll now see one such person, of this particular blood line, who made up his mind to *do* just that.

Twin Sons, Plus a Whole Lot More

*These folk recount another tale, according to which, they say, the **devil** came to Eve and united with her as a **man** with a woman and begot on her Cain **and Abel**... For, they say, **they** were physically begotten from the **devil's** sperm...*
- The Archontics According to St. Epiphanius 40.5.3-4[58]

As we see, the Serpent could have sired **Cain**... *as well as* **Abel**. Ancient sources tell us that, in early times, when human beings were born, they were often born as *twins*.[59] Could these two characters of the Bible also be twins, both sons of a fallen, angelic being?[60] We recall our Biblical reinterpretation:

Gen. 4:
1 *And Adam **eventually acknowledged the distinguishing sign** that had come upon Eve; that she **was with child**, and **realized** she was about to give birth to Cain, and, after the birth, she said, I have gotten a man through an angel of the LORD.*
(in retranslation)

If we notice, the next verse, immediately, follows with:

Gen. 4:
2 *And she **again** bare his brother Abel.*

The word *again*, in Hebrew, could easily signify, "without **adding** any further qualification as in the case of Cain."[61] In other words, the two births didn't need to be noted any differently because they **were not different**. They probably were one event.

The word *again*, here, could also mean to "add," "augment" or to "continue on." Does that mean Eve's birthing process was "added to," or "augmented," here, to allow her to also bare Abel? Interestingly, one ancient Jewish Rabbi stated:

*...as it is said, "And she conceived, and bare (**with**) Cain" (Genesis 4:1). At that hour she had an additional capacity for child-bearing (as it is said), "And she **continued** to bear his brother Abel" (ibid. 2).* - *Pirke deR. Eliezer XXI*[62]

In other words, Eve's labor was "augmented" or "continued" on.[63] Could they have come out of the womb, as twins?

Let's look at the above Bible verse again, inserting these other possible Hebrew meanings:

*And she **continued on** with the birthing process, and bore his brother Abel.*
- *Gen.* 4:2 (in retranslation)

Abel, obviously, would have been another offspring of Eve and the Serpent:

*No wonder that **Abel**… meant "serpent shining" and that Cain was thought to be of serpent descent… According to Hyde Clarke and C. Staniland Wake in Serpent and Siva Worship, Abel (Mbale) and Cain (Kane/can) are names given to elder and younger brothers. Abel resolves into **Ab** (Snake) and **El** (God/shining)…*
(Gardiner, 2006, p. 18)[64]

Next, according to the Bible, we'll see that in "the process of time" Cain and Abel were required to give an offering to God (Gen. 4:3). In other words, they were required to give God an offering once *they reached a certain age.* And, according to the Bible, it seems they both did their sacrifice on the same day![65] So, if they were required to sacrifice at a certain age, and they both did it on the same day, logic dictates that they were probably born on the same day! Makes sense. And, that's exactly what the Bible seems to state, here. There probably wouldn't have been any conflict between Cain and Abel if they were doing sacrifices on totally different days. This gives us reason enough to conclude that they were probably born together, on the same day, *and* from the same seed.

One Father - Different Attitudes

*Ialdabaoth… The first and chief ruler… Called… **Samael**
(a.k.a. Sammael or the serpent)…
Abel. A **just** son of Ialdabaoth and Eve.
Cain. An **unjust** son of Ialdabaoth and Eve.*
    - Secret Book According to John Mythic Char. II- III[66]

As we see, in the above, the two were of the same father. But, we also see that they didn't necessarily *act* the same. One ancient name for Cain was *Adiaphotos*, or "full of light." And, we know why: Cain had a bright countenance, or shine, from birth. Abel, on the other hand, was also known as *Amilabes*, or "well-minded."[67] Could it be that Abel, **even though** he was also a seed of the Serpent, still could have managed to be a just and worthy person?

Cain certainly wasn't the prophesized seed, neither was Abel (because they both had blood of the Serpent). Yet, the two seemed different, on so many levels:

*According to Dr. Keith Bertrand of the Department of Theriogenology. University of Georgia, the blood of the mother never mingles with her child, the blood of twins **do** intermingle. This it is possible that Abel might well have had some of the seed of Satan in him, and this may also be a reason why Almighty God saw so it that he did not produce any "questionable" Seed Line.*

("Star Wars - Lesson Eight", n. d., p. 4-5)[68]

Again, although Abel may have grown up a very righteous individual, there was a very obvious reason he couldn't carry on the seed of Adam to the savior. That doesn't mean he couldn't be in God's favor, however, and be accepted! Abel *chose* to do what was right. He utilized his *free will* to honor God in positive ways. That's the difference. Cain could have chose to follow God, as well. And, temporarily, he tried to, somewhat, but it all began to fall apart, real soon. One thing though: this gives us absolute *proof* that, no matter who you are - even a **son of the Serpent himself** - you can *choose* to follow a proper path, and go the right direction, if you want to! Life is like that: simple. Anyone could be in God's favor - if they really *want* to! This will all be so important, later on.

We'll soon see that, noticing Abel was rising in the ranks of God's favor, Cain began to go the other route, and have a sullen, bad attitude. And, as we'll see, he began to go *out* from the presence of the Lord, both symbolically *and literally*, to do things his *own* way.

...even by the same father, different kinds of seeds can come forth out of the same womb. It will either be a spiritual seed of God or a religious seed of the devil. One will believe every word and promise of God, the other will despise God's word and make His promises of none effect. The twins of Isaac and Rebekah (Jacob and Esau, for example) showed a type of what could come forth...

(Gan, n. d., p. 17)[69]

Differences would arise in their character: "Abel, a lover of righteousness; Cain, wholly intent upon possessing worldly things, and wholly intent on absorbing whatever he could around him."[70] As with the blade of grass Cain first wanted to possess (as a baby), he would continue on, trying to *possess* whatever "dainties" of this world he could get his hands on, just like his father.

The Spark of Evil

Most of us know, from the Bible, that Cain was labeled the first murderer. Let's look at how this murder could have occurred, and many of the facts that surrounded it. Let's also discover what may have gone on *inside* of Cain's mind, to allow such a dastardly deed to take place!

*After Adam and his wife sinned, and the serpent had intercourse with Eve and injected filth into her, Eve bore Cain. He had the shape from above and from below... Therefore, he was the first to bring **death** into the world, caused by his side, as he came from the filth of the serpent. The **nature of the serpent is to lurk** so **as to kill**, and his issue, Cain, **learned his ways**.* - *Zohar* Pekudei 21[71]

*Of the **mixed multitude** it is written: "Now the serpent was craftier than any beast of the field" (Beresheet 3:1). Here, "craftier" means to do **evil** more than all the other animals... the members of the mixed multitude are the children of **the primordial Serpent** (a.k.a. the serpent of "old") that seduced Chavah (Eve) by the tree of knowledge, so the mixed multitude is indeed the impurity that the Serpent injected into Chavah. From this impurity, which is considered the mixed multitude, **Kayin** (Cain) came forth and **slew** Hevel (Abel)...* - *Zohar* Beresheet A28[72]

Not only was Cain physically *different* than Adam, he began to turn out different in his *thoughts*, his *attitudes* and *world views*. Cain seemed to lean more towards much of the same *inner* personality traits as his father, the Serpent. The Serpent was cocky, imprudent, and self-absorbed. Cain began to think (and act) in these ways, as well. It's probably these same inner characteristics that allowed Cain to easily act on any improper thoughts that may have come into his mind! He didn't have self-restraint, as Abel probably did. These "serpent-like" rationales easily could have led him down some dark and unpredictable pathways, even into acts of violence.

> *Know then, that Cain was formed from the impurity… that drop which the serpent injected into Eve.* (Eisenmenger, 1748, p. 197)[73]

The Child Destined for Sorrow - Abel

We already know a few meanings of the name *Cain*. Abel's name has a few different meanings, himself: "breath;" "mist;" "nothingness;" even "fading away." They all seem appropriate for what, soon, was about to happen to him![74] And, according to many ancient sources, the major reason Cain would become so angry and spiteful towards his brother would be over a woman. She was just another element to our world that Cain, desperately, wanted to *possess*.

This woman, in fact, was believed to be one of Cain's own sisters. One ancient source stated that: when Adam looked at Cain's face (as a newborn), he instantly began to conclude that he would be ill-tempered, later on in life.[75] He just felt it. One of Cain's sisters, however, was very beautiful. To Adam, this one seemed to have a good-tempered face, as well. She must really have been really gorgeous, because she was even said to have looked like her mother Eve.[76]

The opposite was for Abel, however. Adam saw a good-tempered face on him. And, although Adam may not have been keen on sons marrying their own sisters, it was still permissible in the day. As a result, Adam began to realize there was a degree of attraction between the siblings, and began to find ways to unite each brother with a "similar" sister. He decided to put the two ill-tempered ones together, the same with the good-tempered. Yet, Cain wanted the beautiful, good-tempered sister for his own!

Any type of disagreement, here, could have helped Cain's inner thoughts to start bubbling over.[77] Somewhere in the back of his mind, Cain may have also begun to see this intention of Adam as some type of plot again him, to *disgrace* him even, or make him feel *inferior* to Abel. He may have even assumed that other people may be around him, plotting against him the same. These insecure, irrational perceptions could also begin to fuel his emotional *fire*.

Adam was trying to act as a "father" would, here. He did it for Eve. The least Cain could have done was obey him. Yet, Cain, as with the Serpent, would want things his *own* way, and not stop until he achieved them.[78] Adam, at least, tried to do what seemed right, and wanted to be fair to everybody. So, according to one ancient source, Adam even allowed Cain a chance to *prove* himself worthy of that sister, if that's what he wanted so bad. And, how he would prove it? It'd be through his up-and-coming sacrifice! Yes, if Cain's sacrifice proved to be satisfactory to God, then Adam might change his mind, and go against his original wishes. But, the kicker here is: the sacrifice had to be *good* - exactly what God wanted.

So, now, the time for sacrifice was upon them. Would Cain strive not to let Adam down, and go the same direction that his brother went (after God)? Or, would Cain find it better to *choose* after his own heart, and succumb to a lot of these negative, fiery thoughts beginning to build up in his mind?

Let's see how it all panned out, and what ways Cain *actually* decided to follow.

Chapter 9

The Cockatrice

*"...out of the **serpent's** root shall come forth a **cockatrice**."*
- Isa. 14:29 (KJV)

<u>a cockatrice (or basilisk)</u> - *a legendary **serpent** or **dragon** with lethal breath and glance*[1]

Would this first son of the Serpent become, in ways, the *successor* of his father?[2] Let's see.

The Sacrifice

The up-and-coming sacrifices of Cain and Abel, as already stated, would determine Adam's decision - whomever cared enough about their *own* sacrifice would, not only have the satisfaction of doing things right by God, but also get the beautiful, good-tempered woman as his wife.[3] This was Cain's proving ground.

Yet:

...Abel was a keeper of sheep, but Cain was a tiller of the ground.
- Gen. 4:2 (KJV)

As we already stated, there were signs around Cain, even at his birth, that indicated he may be a good "tiller of the ground," later on in life. We remember that, after being born, Cain picked up a piece of vegetation and gave it to his mother (as if he had some natural *inkling* towards working the earth). Abel, on the other hand, would end up leaning more towards having a sheep-herding career. Thus began a world of difference between the two, not only in lifestyles, but in *sacrifices*, as well.

*Hence Cain assisted in production of food for the primeval family, while Abel's duties were concerned with their **religious services** and clothing.*

(Pember, 1975, p. 118)[4]

It was now time for each to give their sacrifice - a blood sacrifice. Yes, *blood*, even back then, seemed necessary for the *remission* of one's sin. It was important, at least to God![5] Cain, however, began his sacrifice by thinking things should be done *his* way - using whatever elements of the world that *he* wanted! These thoughts, now, were about to betray him.

At the time of the sacrifice, Cain concluded it would probably be better to put some of his *vegetables* out, instead. And, why not? He grew them himself. That would be a *fair* way to show God his labor, and effort. Besides, it all looked good to *him*. Abel, on the other hand, did what he was instructed - he slaughtered a lamb, and (as messy as it all may sound) poured the lamb's blood on the altar. Let's look at what the Bible says happened next:

Gen. 4:
3 *And in the process of time it came to pass, that Cain brought of the fruit of the ground an offering unto the LORD.*
4 *And Abel, he also brought of the firstlings of his flock and of the fat thereof. And the LORD had respect unto Abel and to his offering.*
5 *But unto Cain and to his offering he had not respect.*

Topping it off, Cain went into his sacrifice with a *haughty* attitude. He strutted on the scene, assumed *his* ways were right, and presented whatever he felt was just. With this Serpent-like pride, he may have even concluded that he should be *entitled* to some sort of acceptance for his efforts. He deserved something - *just* for doing it! Was he correct, or was he acting just like his father, here?

*Abel, the younger, had respect for **justice** and, believing that God was with him in all his actions, paid heed of **virtue**... Cain, on the contrary, was thoroughly **depraved** and had an eye **only to gain**...*

- *Flavius Josephus* Jewish Antiquities 1:53-54[6]

*...one of them exercises a business, and takes care of living creatures, although they are devoid of reason... but the other devotes his attention to **earthly** and **inanimate objects**.* - *Works of Philo Judaeus* Questions and Answers on Genesis 1(59)[7]

The two seemed to have very different approaches to life, and two different outlooks, entirely. Cain's was one of pride, superiority and contempt for anything that stands in front of him he doesn't like, or approve of. Cain put out his vegetables and thought: "Good enough." God probably wouldn't be too keen on one *man's* interpretation of things, here.

According to one source, Cain even *ate* the best of the flax he put out (his vegetable sacrifice), and then left the *rest* to God.[8] How about that for reverence? How's that for obedience - to the God who created everything around you? There were major flaws in Cain's own perception of reality, and his approach to life. There were problems in what he thought was right or wrong. These self-serving philosophies, in the end, wouldn't hold up very well for him, however.

*As though his offense had not been great enough in offering to God fruit of the ground which **had been cursed by God**!*   (Ginzberg, 1909, p. 107-8)[9]

There are reasons why God wants things the way *He* wants them. Sometimes, He makes the reasons known to us; sometimes He doesn't. Here, part of the reason Cain's approach suffered was because it came from the very *ground* that God cursed in the first place! It's like taking water out of a polluted lake and giving it to a friend to drink. According to another source, Cain felt that it was proper to allocate grains even, once, trampled under his own two feet![10] No wonder his sacrifice was about to be abhorred, and rejected.

*Cain **became** tiller of the ground, and, therefore, had **reason** to feel the curse in all its bitterness.*   (Pember, 1975, p. 118)[11]

Cain's outlook on the world was so strange, at least compared to other people around him. *Man's* interpretation seemed to make more sense to him, rather than God's. Cain fancied and enjoyed the *material* elements of a cursed ground. He was too *proud* to follow anyone else's instruction. His free will told him what he should do, and what sacrifice to lay out. This was the first outward act of *man's* interpretation trumping God. Cain really thought there was nothing wrong with this way of thinking, though.

*"(Cain speaking to God)… according to **my** righteous labors have I offered it to you."*
- Armenian Apocryphal Adam Literature Abel and Cain 9[12]

These "ways" - obviously *not* God's ways - would soon be the essence of that which God universally hates: **idolatry** - the act of putting other people, places or things *above* God (including one's own self)!

Abel, on the other hand, did the opposite of Cain. He took the *best* of his lambs, turned it into a blood sacrifice, and made sure it was exactly how God wanted. And, most importantly, he did it all with another crucial element of the sacrifice: a sense of humility, reverence, and love for his Creator! Cain offered haughtily; Abel offered with humility.[13] As a result, Abel's sacrifice was about to be accepted.[14]

A "Black Heart" - And a Whole Lot More?

*And Cain was very wroth, **and** his **countenance** fell.*
- Gen. 4:5 (KJV)

What happened next to Cain comes without any definitive, Biblical evidence (although a number of different scriptural texts try to make sense of what going to happen). Theories abound on how God responded to Cain, for his actions, as we'll see.

It was now time for God to react to each sacrifice, individually. Abel's, obviously, went well:

Immediately a gentle breeze blew, and a light shone from heaven and illuminated the face of Abel. *- Armenian Apocryphal Adam Literature* Abel and Cain 12[15]

Something different was about to happen, in Cain's world. Something was about to fly in the face of a man who almost always thinks *his* ways were right:

> *A black cloud came over Cain's bundle (and) it thundered, and dust came forth from it, (and) it caused everything (to be) blown by the wind. It scattered the bundle, and destroyed everything.*
>   - *Armenian Apocryphal Adam Literature* Abel and Cain 10[16]

There was definitely a different response, by God, here. One common theory on what happened to Cain revolves around the following: if God was pleased with a sacrifice, a burning fire would be said to come down from the heavens, and consume it! And, the *rising* of burnt smoke, in Abel's case, was also considered symbolic of God's acceptance. God smelled the sweet savor (or smoke) of Abel's sacrifice, and was pleased, with the smoke rising up into the sky. With Cain's half-hazard attempt, the fire of God's approval did not come down and totally consume his sacrifice. It did just *the opposite*. The fire descended, yet the smoke did not go back up into heaven. Instead, it went all around Cain, almost suffocating him to death. The diversion of this "divine" smoke clearly signified God's utter rejection.[17]

As a consequence, everything around Cain "became dark." Many sources, here, state that Cain's face and body became *darkened*, in ways, by the smoke.[18] It could have been similar to those other angels who had fallen, around the time of Adam. As we recall, they were all "burnt." We're not sure exactly what happened to them: if they were burnt to a crisp, or, somehow, their appearance had changed.

With Cain, he was not burnt to a crisp, obviously. Could this *blackening* of Cain be a direct *contrast* to his once-heavenly, "angel-like" splendor? After he lost the bright countenance he once had, did he, somehow, turn very dark?[19] At the very least, we can assume Cain probably lost his heavenly *shine*, and looked like every other human being around him.

But, in certain other ways, things may have become a lot darker.

*...in fact, it has been noticed in our day that men **who have lost the spirit** of the Lord, and from whom his blessings have been withdrawn, have turned **dark** to such an extent as to excite the comments of all who have known them.*

("Juvenile Instructor, Vol. 26", n. d., p. 635)[20]

So many in the past assumed Cain became dark, or black, on the *outside*, but there's not a lot of ancient evidence for that (beyond some opinions). In fact, there seems more evidence to the contrary. Instead of outside, the *darkness* of Cain actually could have been some *internal* transformation - being "darkened" on the *inside*, if you will.

This makes sense, if we think about it. Let's explain: Cain, now, could have become blackened on the inside, in regards to his thoughts, with a good number of people around him now able to sense it, fairly easily. We recall that Cain already had some particularly negative thoughts brewing. Now, it was out of the bag, for so many to "sense." It's almost the same as when we come across a person who just doesn't seem "right," today. They try to act civil, but there's just something about them that screams "caution." Now, with Cain, his true colors began to be revealed. His inner negativities were beginning to be exposed, for all to see.

This theory leads us back to a verse in the Bible:

*And the LORD said unto Cain, Why art thou **wroth**? And why is thy **countenance fallen**?* 			- *Gen.* 4:6 (KJV)

After his sacrifice was rejected, God himself asked Cain why his countenance had "fallen." Assuredly, his shine or heavenly, angelic glow was now lost, forever. His countenance was now like the other Nephilim - fallen. And, the Bible doesn't allude to his being *darkened* any further on the outside. But, more or less, he now looked like any other human being. On top of it, we do notice there also seemed to be changes for Cain on the *inside*. He became "wroth" - humiliated, depressed, or even enraged. Could this have been what was meant by his being *darkened,* or *blackened*?

There are those out there - in the ancient and no-so-ancient past - who thought this incident was the point where Cain was *physically* turned "black as coal," equating him, today, with someone having a darker skin color:

He beat Cain's face with hail and blackened it like coal, and thus his face remained black.   - *Armenian Apocryphal Adam Literature* Abel and Cain 10[21]

It's understandable to ponder the meaning of all this, by reading texts such as the above. But, one thing we may need to understand is: the ancients probably wanted to find ways describe human *emotion*, as well as physical appearance, and probably had a hard time in doing so. How does one draw a picture of the symbolic "glow" an unusually-happy person might have? How do we picture someone with a *dark* heart? Could the physical descriptions of Cain's "blackness," such as in the above, actually be symbolic of these negative changes *inside* of Cain? Could it relate to how Cain now may have thought, for the most part? In the above situation, maybe his new, *negative* demeanor was "written all over his face."

There are actually a number of ancient texts that state Cain wasn't *darkened* at all (on the outside), but actually had blonde hair, ivory skin, and a yellow beard. So, if this could be true, then all of the blackness Cain had was, indeed, just internal.

*(God)… sent down smoke so that his face became **dirty with soot**. But Cain was **not ashamed** at God's displeasure.*   (Frankel, 1989, p. 37)[22]

As we see, in the above, any *external* darkening could have been a temporary discomfort for Cain. He only had to wipe the dark soot off of his face. The important thing to understand, here, is: any negative change of the *inside* would surely make things worse for Cain, overall. He, now, may begin to find it easier to "double down" on anything negative brewing in him already. It could, naturally, get even worse, until Cain's entire insides became black as **coal**.

Human nature might step in, now, and allow some to feel a little empathy for Cain, here… but his punishments *were* absolutely deserved. Cain's fall from grace came on to him because he wanted to do things his own way. And, God often dishes out His punishments to individuals "measure for measure." Cain wants to be stubborn and hard-headed against God; now, God will allow him to permanently experience what *true* negativity of the mind is. Funny, this was a lot like how He already dealt with the Serpent, and punished him. "Like father, like son."

Cain's Anger

Now that Cain was starting to capitalize on these additional thoughts brewing inside of him, God decided to confront him further:

Gen. 4:
6 *And the LORD said unto Cain, Why art thou **wroth**? And why is thy countenance fallen?*
7 *If thou doest well, shalt thou not be accepted? and if thou doest not well, **sin lieth at the door**. And unto thee [shall be] his desire, and thou shalt rule over him.*

Obviously, He pointed out that there would be darker things now working in Cain's mind, such as the "evil inclination." These thoughts, and other worldly temptations, were right there, crouching at the door to his heart. Would he let them in, and "seal" the *darkened* deal?

*"(God speaking)… I have placed in your hand control over the evil **inclination**, and you shall rule over it, whether for better or for worse (whether to be guilty, or innocent)."*   *- Genizah Manuscripts Gen. 4:7[23]*

*And into thy hand have I delivered the power **over evil passion**, and unto **thee** shall be the inclination thereof, that thou mayest have authority over it to **become righteous**, or to sin.*   *- Targum Pseudo-Jonathan IV[24]*

Although Cain still knew what was right (according to God), he turned the other way, and began to "cross the line," allowing those negativities within him to, for the most part, "take over."[25] Unlike Abel, he began to follow these, and any other inherited attributes of his blood-born ancestor, as well. Cain's thoughts soon mirrored the Serpent's anger, envy, wrath and pride.

The Wrath of Cain

Now, we discover another meaning for the name *Cain*: "as nought" and "the wrathful one."[26]

*Do not reveal to Cain the secret plan which you know, for he is a **son of wrath**.*
                                                    - Book of Adam [23]3.2[27]

Now, no matter what circumstances were in front of him, no matter if he was the majority of the problem, the denial of his sacrifice angered him to the utmost. He lost out on everything, and, of course, didn't want to blame himself. Cain went to Abel about his situation, and griped about it:

*...**I** perceive that the world was created in goodness, but it is not governed according to the fruit of good works, for there is respect to persons in judgment; therefore it is that thy offering was accepted, and mine not accepted **with good will**.*
                                                    - Targum Pseudo-Jonathan IV[28]

Cain further stated things, according to his own point of view:

*...I perceive that the world was not created in **mercy** and that it is not being conducted according to the fruits **of good words**, and that there is **favoritism** in judgment.*
                                                    - Targum Neofiti Gen. 4:8[29]

*...nor will good reward be given to the **righteous**, nor vengeance be taken of the wicked.*
                                                    - Targum Pseudo-Jonathan IV[30]

Assuming that he knew it all, Cain continued with comments such as: "This entire process is not **fair**. We're both the same. Our sacrifices were the same, *overall*. We both put forth an effort. Mine was just not accepted for some *unfair* reason." Abel, however, was not buying what Cain was selling, and had some honest words for him: "Mine was accepted because I love God; yours was rejected because you hate Him."[31] Abel told him the *real* truth, and why his sacrifice was not accepted. Cain, however, didn't appreciate this honesty. He really didn't want to hear this side of anything. It only prompted Cain to more and more *anger*, and resentment, which, eventually, allow him the "go ahead" to act on his inner, *blackened* emotions.[32]

The time was ripe for Cain to take action. According to one source, he was so upset with Abel he arrogantly blurted: "If I were to slay you today, who would demand your blood from me?" Abel, confident in his answer, replied: "Surely God will know your hiding place and will judge you for the evil you have proposed to do today!"[33] Another source stated that Abel already knew Cain was having negative feelings against him, and felt he needed to hide. Once Cain learned of it, he sent word to people around him, and asked them to help him find Abel... to tell him everything was "all right." Cain obviously lied to all of them, telling them he abandoned all negative thoughts when it was indeed the opposite. This deception allowed Cain a way to catch up with his brother again, and confront him one final time.[34]

He began a discussion with Abel, down in a near-by valley, using some of the same *subtleness* his father used.[35] But, for Cain, he emotions slowly began to overtake his conversation. And, in the middle of a verbal confrontation, Cain began to show more of his *violent* side, wrestling Abel to the ground. Abel, however, quickly overpowered Cain, and jumped on top of him. Cain cried out, helplessly, underneath.

Some sources suggested that Abel was, naturally, stronger than Cain. Another source stated that God was watching out for Abel - the same He did for Adam (when confronted by the fallen angels), and notified Abel that something bad was about to happen. God may have also encouraged Abel to severely *beat* Cain at this time, so he could get out of this situation. The interesting parallel here - Adam to Abel - is that: Adam fell in the Garden because he listened to God, but listened to Eve *more*. As we'll soon see, here, Abel probably did much of the *same*. Both Adam and Abel didn't trust God enough to go all the way with is. And, they both ended up paying the price - for adding in *their own interpretation*!

Upon hearing Cain's plea for mercy, Abel didn't follow God's advice, totally. He probably did what he thought was a *just* or *human* thing to do, and *compassionately* released the hold over Cain. While on top of him, Abel could have easily halted Cain's attempts, and stop Cain in his tracks, but he didn't choose that. It was possibly this decision which cost Abel his life.[36]

This was Cain's opportunity to act on his inner motives.

Lord Byron makes Lucifer say to Cain:
"First born of the first man
*Thy present state of sin - and **thou art evil**"...*
(Bristowe, 1927, p. 4)[37]

The Murder Occurs

*This **evil** in Cain (which destroys alike soul and body) **caused** him to kill Abel.*
- Yalkut Hadash[38]

*First, adultery came into being, afterward murder. And **he** was begotten in adultery, for he was **the child of the Serpent**. So he became a murderer, **just like his father**, and he killed his brother. Indeed, every act of sexual intercourse which has occurred between those unlike one another is adultery.* *- Gospel of Philip[39]*

The murder of Abel would be no accident, that's for sure. Cain took advantage of his brother's mercy and took a wooden stick (or, a reed), a rock, or some other tool, and hit Abel. He hit, and hit, and *hit* Abel. He did whatever he could to stop Abel from moving again. Another source stated Cain could have even *bit* his brother, like an *adder* (again, "like father, like son").[40]

*And Cain talked with Abel his brother: and it came to pass, when they were in the field, that Cain rose up against Abel his brother, and **slew** him.*
- Gen. 4:8 (KJV)

One source stated that Cain even tied Abel up with a grapevine, because he had difficulty finding a way to kill him outright. After all, no one ever really killed anyone before this time, so he wasn't sure how to do it. He was still intent on accomplishing the deed, however, and this bought him some time. He spent over an hour hitting him with his crude weapon, anything to finally end his life![41] Another source stated that he eventually used a sharpened rock, and stabbed Abel directly in the forehead.[42]

Whatever way it was finalized, Abel was down, paralyzed with pain. As he was lying there, close to death, he uttered a last request:

*...while he was slaughtering him Abel said "I am gone out of the world, but you **gain** the heart of our parents."*
                    - Armenian Apocryphal Adam Literature Abel and Cain 33[43]

Cain didn't care. Good riddance, as far as he was concerned. He, indeed, took *possession* of a lot more than his sister that day.

After Cain killed his brother, Abel's blood had spilled all over the ground. Cain tried to hide his body, burying it somewhere in the earth, and then fled the scene. He didn't do a very good job at hiding it, however. People around him found out what happened, and became very upset. God knew about it (obviously), and went over to confront Cain.

A small amount of Cain's thoughts, here, were of remorse. The majority, however, were bent on helping him *escape* what he had done. In fact, he even felt somewhat *glad* he did it, as well:

When he killed his brother, he went away cheerfully.
                    - Armenian Apocryphal Adam Literature Abel and Cain 34[44]

His Twisted Outlook

God would have none of this, and spoke to Cain. Another conversation arose:

And the LORD said unto Cain, Where [is] Abel thy brother? And he said, I know not: [Am] I my brother's keeper?   *- Gen.* 4:9 (KJV)

God knew he did it - and *Cain* knew he did it. In front of God, though, he *subtly* tried to get out of his shame using the "I didn't know" approach.[45] He also took the "victim-mentality" position. He began to act as a little child, and claim practically none of it was *actually* his fault. In one of his excuses, he claimed that he never saw a man murdered before, so how was *he* supposed to know what he did to Abel would end his life? "That's not fair." How despicable. But, yet, Again, he said and did whatever he could to weasel his way out of his own **responsibility**. These were becoming new characteristics of Cain's *blackened* mind. Do some of these sound familiar, today?

Yes, some people are truly sorry for their crimes. Some people are only sorry because they *were caught*. Thoughts like this occur, and prosper, within a twisted person's rationale. And, this was all, now, Cain… to a tee.

God wasn't buying any of it. Cain's punishment, now, was to be upon him:

Gen. 4:
10 *And he said, What hast thou done? the voice of thy brother's blood crieth unto me from the ground.*
11 *And now [art] thou cursed from the earth, which hath opened her mouth to receive thy brother's blood from thy hand;*
12 *When thou tillest the ground, it shall not henceforth yield unto thee her strength; a fugitive and a vagabond shalt thou be in the earth.*
13 *And Cain said unto the LORD, My punishment [is] greater than I can bear.*

Although God already tried to reason with Cain, Cain was at the point where he was not going accept any responsibility.[46] According to Cain, *God* was actually the one who was mean and unfair! He created the world. He did so much, here, to make the world what it was, yet, He couldn't do something as simple as to overlook this one act? God banished Adam and Eve from the Garden. And, now, He wants to banish Cain from his livelihood, as well, all over something Cain didn't even "realize" might happen! What a twisted reality! If one really thinks about it, we see so many of the *same*, twisted excuses echoing out of the mouths of people today, trying not to face reality, or themselves.

Cain may have tried to confront God, with this angle:

"Thou bearest the whole world," he said, *"and **my** sin **Thou canst not** bear? Verily, mine iniquity is too great to be borne! Yet, yesterday Thou didst banish my father from Thy presence, today, Thou dost banish me. In sooth, it will be said, it is **Thy way to banish**."*   (Ginzberg, 1909, p. 111)[47]

God didn't care. He had no compassion. He was mean and heartless. Within this entire twist, Cain now blurted out the famous statement: "My punishment is greater than I can bear" (Gen. 4:13). Now, what might this mean, for real? Maybe, it was not actually an admission of guilt, or one of sadness. Maybe, it was something proclaimed by Cain, out to the world, from one with a selfish, sarcastic mindset! Let's explain: as we begin to understand Cain's new, *darkened* mindset, it only makes sense to assume most of his words would be uttered to his *own* advantage. Here, he probably meant something like: "My punishment is greater than I can bear - it's too much for *me* to handle. God, how could you do this? How could you do this all to *me*? Why are you **so overbearing**? I can't handle all of this. Why don't you show the world what kind of merciful God you are and give me some help, here!"

Cain continued on, with this same rationality: "Is my iniquity *too great* to be forgiven by you, God?"[48]

*My sins are too great to bear; but there is much [ability] before **You** to pardon and to remit.*   *- Genizah Manuscripts Gen. 4:13*[49]

*Nevertheless there is power before Thee to absolve and **forgive** me.*
                                                        - Targum Pseudo-Jonathan IV[50]

"If you're such a great and compassionate God, show me, here!"

We see that Cain did practically everything "in the book" to divert the original cause of the problem: *himself*. He did whatever he could to skew the original crime *he* committed, and to blunt the necessity for *any* punishment to be administered… all of it done with skill and stealth, just like a serpent.

Cain, also, obviously never learned the value of humility (unlike *Adam*), or *introspection*.[51]

The Ultimate Complainer

*When Cain saw that God had accepted his brother's sacrifice and not his, he began to **mock** God before Abel. "What an unjust God this is who rules strictly by **whim**! See, your sacrifice has been chosen over mine for no good reason! And to think that I used to believe that God ruled the world fairly!"* (Frankel, 1989, p. 37)[52]

*"This world was not created in **mercy**; neither is it **ruled by compassion**. Why else has your (Abel's) offering been accepted and mine rejected?"*
(Graves and Patai, 1964, p. 91)[53]

Cain continued to go further off the ideological "deep end," in regards twisting his reality. When he began to feel that things were not going his way, Cain uttered out a statement of blasphemy: "There is no **law** and no judge!"[54] In other words, he was, now, even starting to deny God, and His authority over everything. His, in his own mind, was beginning to elevate *himself* into a "god-like" state. Cain's thoughts matter more, now, since God's doesn't. Man vs. God. This age-old conflict officially begins.

Cain went further: "It *shouldn't* matter what we do. What we choose to do is our *own* business. Nobody should judge me for just being *me*!"

He thought:

*...(Cain speaking) There is neither Justice nor Judge; there is **no retribution** for the wicked **nor reward** for the just, nor is there another world.*
- *Genizah Manuscripts* Gen. 4:8[55]

Wow, doesn't this also sound similar to a lot of our *modern-day* thought? People, today, often use these same rationales. They often seem so concerned with how *fair* something is. They promote one being emotional, and acting on their emotions, over rationality. They want others to live and breathe with *compassion*. Nobody should really be punished. It's inhuman. And, even, they may look only to science, and deny that God exists, or, at least, negate the possibility of God having any sway over our lives, or the world around us. More on this, a little later.

Continually escalating, Cain's excuses became even more *vain*.

*"(Cain to God) What will people say of **You** when they see me... You will become known as a God who delights in exile!"*   (Frankel, 1989, p. 38-9)[56]

Cain blamed his situation. He blamed God. He blamed almost everyone (and every situation) around him... that is, but himself.[57] Again, doesn't this sound like a lot of people, today? Isn't this how so many work today, to get around guilt and personal responsibility? Could the "victim-mentality" approach be the antidote that Cain was counting on, in order to save himself? We have an interesting commentary, regarding people who end up thinking with a lot of these same ways, and what their rationales *actually* end up pointing them towards:

*(You have) no reason to feel guilty. Your heart continues to tell you that you are the center of the universe. Your problems are somebody else's fault. This world owes you happiness. You are basically good and unselfish. You'll be happy if you get what you want. You will be happy when you follow your own heart... **You are under a curse.***
("Have We Gone the Way of Cain?", n. d., p. 6-7)[58]

Could these actually work to **curse** the individual, *over time*, or seem like it? Could these ways have originated from this "**seed of the Serpent**?" We recall, God may have punished Cain more *on the inside*, than out. So, now, maybe these all stem from Cain's new, *darkened* heart.

Although he was guilty - and, deep down inside, he probably *knew* it - he refused to confess his guilt. He refused liability, no matter what. And, as one who may know enough about psychology probably understands: a person with a good amount of self-esteem would be *man* enough (or *strong* enough) to admit their own faults, and accept responsibility. Those with *low* self-esteem find it the opposite a reality. It's so hard for them to "man up," if not impossible. Cain, obviously, must not have had a lot of self-esteem (or worth) to be able to do this, or else he would have stepped up. Who else had their self-esteem lowered (to the extreme), as a punishment in the Garden?

Cain's "Serpent-like" pride caused him to leave out any honor, or integrity, regarding his actions, here. The parallels, between father and son, just keep on coming.

The Cynical One

Interestingly, the following style of thought was said to have even *originated* in Cain, himself: *cynicism*. The name *Cain* is also considered root of the word "cynic," as well as "canine."[59] Well, what might this all mean, to our story?

cynical - 1. *distrustful of human nature: doubting or contemptuous of human nature or the motives, goodness, or sincerity of others.*
2. *sarcastic: mocking, scornful, or sneering.*[60]

The *Cynics* actually began as a Greek, philosophical sect in the 4th century B.C. A disciple of Socrates was considered founder of the movement. These learned scholars were also known as the *Canine* (or "dog-like") by people in ancient times, because the *dog* was once thought of as an animal with a lack of *shame*. These Cynics, then, "paraded their poverty, their antagonism to pleasure, and their indifference to others…" and also "…rejected the social values of their time, often flouting conventions in shocking ways to prove their point."[61] See all of this, as a connection to Cain, here, and how he acted? They delighted in mocking other people (and the "system"), and enjoyed being thought of as scornful or contemptuous. And, by also thinking in these ways, they somehow felt morally *superior* to others.[62] What a twisted way of looking at the world.

We'll also soon see how:

*…historically speaking a connection between the words **Cain**, Cynic and dog seems probable for, while the Epistle of Jude indicates that the evil character of Cain's later life was known to the Apostles, St. Paul and St. John head their lists of **evildoers** with the word "dogs," which one modern translator of the Bible has changed into "Cynics," a more convincing rendering than "dogs," for obviously **men** and not animals **are referred to**. Cain's wickedness… was thus vividly remembered in Palestine in the Apostles' time…* (Bristowe, 1927, p. 111)[63]

*Philologists agree that the word "Cynics"… given to certain Greek philosophers in the first century A.D. came from the Greek word for dog and that those philosophers were so-called because they were "prone to fall back into **animalism** pure and simple"…* (Bristowe, 1927, p. 111)[64]

Obviously, these Cynics, through these thoughts and actions, "outraged the dictates of common decency."[65]

> *"In the Old and New Testaments the dog is spoken of almost with abhorrence; it ranked amongst the unclean beasts; traffic in it was considered as an abomination."* The Cynics of Greece were evidently **proud** of their opprobrious title for they adopted a dog as their emblem or badge... *"They believed that Cain derived his existence from the **superior** power and Abel from the inferior power."*
> (Bristowe, 1927, p. 112)[66]

And, just *who or what* would have been that "superior power" ***Cain* drew from**? Would this, again, be the *Serpent* himself?

Now, from what we know about Cain already, it's easy to see where thoughts such as these probably originated from. It's so important to understand where people inherited ideals such as this, and what it all means to the construct of the world we live in. We need to know how to spot thoughts such as this, and why people say things like this. This *Cynic* movement - originating in **Cain** - is just one example of what we'll discover, when we begin to peel back the layers of techniques used by those under the spell of *Mystery Babylon*.

Cain: The First Alternate, "Free-Thinker?"

> *...Cain as "the first free-thinker"...*
> (Bristowe, 1927, p. 79)[67]

Some people, in the ancients, thought Adam was the first "thinker." Other people actually believed it was Cain. Why? Was it the different ways people looked at their world, maybe? Maybe, now, we could begin to see the *division* emanating between different groups of people, and, soon, we'll also see that there's *enmity* between then. And, we now see it begins with specific patriarchs, forbearers or "movers and shakers."

Moving on, we know that God confronted Cain about what was going on inside of him. He may have even told him the direct reasons *why* he killed his brother. Yet, Cain walked away from it all, believing something *different*. Wow. If even God tells Cain something, and he *still* doesn't believe it, that goes to show us that: there are some people out there who will *still* not believe anything, no matter *who* tell them! Sad, but reality.

God told it to Cain *as it was*, and made sure he knew that he committed a crime.

> *You are not his keeper; why did you become his murderer?*
> - *Armenian Apocryphal Adam Literature* Repentance 49[68]

But, Cain, still holding onto his own perceptions of reality, used his mind to become a *barrier* to understanding what was right in front of him. Throughout all of Cain's twisted thoughts, throughout all of his strange rationales, Cain ultimately acted on Abel because of something he truly hated, something he didn't want to face: *the truth*.[69]

Through conversation, God and Abel both gave Cain some insights that he couldn't quite shake. He couldn't rationalize *everything* out of his mind. That was one problem he still had - he *still* had somewhat of a conscience. All of what happened today wouldn't *totally* go away. Now, some internal *battles* would begin within him.

> *[God] offers him [Cain] an **amnesty**, imposing a benevolent and kindly law concerning the first on all judges - not that they may not destroy evil men, but that by hesitating a little and showing patience, they may cleave to mercy... **forgiveness is wont to produce repentance**.*
> - *Works of Philo Judaeus* Questions and Answers on Genesis 1(76, 82)[70]

Even with all of the excuses he gave, Cain, ultimately, couldn't totally get away from the truth bellowing inside of him:

> *Thus we (Adam and his brethren) walked in Light, but Cain and his brethren walked in darkness and anguish of soul. And Cain wrestled within himself, for the voice of Jehovah continued to call unto him, Where is thy brother whose blood crieth unto me from the ground for vengeance? To which Cain replied, Am I my brother's keeper? Nevertheless, he **knew** that he was lost in darkness and his mind was blighted and he became a fugitive and a vagabond in the earth, forever fleeing his memories and the **darkness** which pursued him and **grew within him**.*
> - *Book of the Generations of Adam* 5:11[71]

The above gives us an example of how Cain was *further* darkened, as a result of all this. Any guilt coming to Cain's mind, however, would begin to entrench itself in his own psyche. So, to counter-act this, he probably needed to *further* twist his thoughts, and continually go to deeper extremes, to rationalize anything like this which creeps in. Assuredly, this process may become *overwhelming*, at times.

Half a Dose of Regret

> *...the penitence of Cain... was not sincere. He was filled with remorse, but it was mingled with **envy** and hatred...* (Baring-Gould, 1881, p. 76)[72]

As already stated, some may feel sorry for their disobedience. Others feel sorry because they were *caught*. One may bitterly bemoan the severity of his punishment, because he's lives in the mode where it's "all about *him*." God was hoping Cain would cry out, repent, or feel *a little* guilty about what he did. God so wanted to dish out *a little* compassion here, at least.[73] But, with Cain, the *opposite* seemed true.

The Curses Upon Cain

God, as we know, didn't buy these attempts at manipulation. The time had now come. Cain had to show *some* responsibility, and accept some of it, whether he liked it or not. Now, there would be more punishments on the horizon, to make Cain understand his place in the murder - at least to a degree.

> *(Cain) shares in the responsibility for every soul that is wrongfully killed. That is because he was the first to institute killing.*
> *- al-Tabari: The History of al-Tabari - Vol. I: General Introduction and From the Creation to the Flood* Cain and Abel 144[74]

We recall that, up to the murder, Cain was considered to be exceptional at farming. After this dirty deed, however, he (and probably his descendants) may have been *cursed* from the ground, even more than Adam and others around him.[75] Farming, now, wouldn't seem as profitable for Cain, anymore.

> *The first curse was the judgment of God on the sin of Adam. Although the ground would bring forth thorns and thistles, its strength to produce abundant crops was not removed (Gen. 3:18). The second curse was the penalty of Cain's sin for shedding the righteous blood of Abel... And Cain was placed under a curse in which the ground was **no longer** able to yield its crops as it used to be. The harvest which were once plentiful had become barely sufficient.*
> ("The Mark of the Wicked Ones", n. d., p. 7)[76]

Cain (and probably his progeny) would not be alone, here. It seems that God wanted the rest of the human race to be, at least *somewhat*, cursed from the bountifulness of the earth, as compared to before. Possibly, this would serve as some kind of "universal remembrance" of **Cain's** murderous deed, here, for all to remember.

> *...May you be cursed... (upon) ground where you shed your brother's blood... (and) till the ground in toil and fatigue... And the earth will not give you its fruit, for with the blood of the righteous have you colored it.*
> - *Armenian Apocryphal Adam Literature* Repentance 51-54[77]

Now, Cain and his seed probably would be the least able to derive benefit from the earth, overall.[78] Even if they wanted to make the world a better place (and took the effort), Cain and his progeny would probably find it a little more difficult to get their tried and true results. This could have been called the ***Curse* of Cain** to some. And, it also seems to have been established in another ironic way: because Cain was the first to make the ground drink *blood* (i.e. the blood of Abel), the soiled ground would no longer provide as good a yield (or sustenance) to he and his own kind, as it did before.[79] All of this will actually become important, later on.

But, for now, Cain was about to experience more of God's wrath.

Half of a Fugitive and Vagabond

> *You see the foolishness of Cain… he answered God rudely and did not confess, so that he might* **make expiation** *and be* **justified** *(for killing Abel)… O, the* **beast,** *how foolishly did he respond!*
> *- Armenian Apocrypha Relating to Adam and Eve* Adam and his Grandsons 17[80]

As bad as Cain's attitude was, as diluted as Cain's repentance seemed to be, God still bent over backwards, and tried His best to find anything qualifying as an apology. But, Cain really didn't bite. He may have uttered a half-hearted apology at best, and God quickly concluded that wasn't really sincere.[81] So, in the end, the Lord could only go so far, here, and was no longer interested - punishments were soon due.

What a merciful God, though, to do His best - *even* to a son of the Serpent, himself! Cain, still, did not care:

> *Behold, thou hast driven me out this day from the face of the earth; and from thy face shall I be hid; and I shall be a fugitive and a vagabond in the earth; and it shall come to pass, [that] every one that findeth me shall slay me.* - Gen. 4:14 (KJV)

And, even though Cain perceived God as "brutal," the Lord still tried to give Cain credit for his *semi*-apology. Now, God originally destined Cain to become a fugitive **and** a vagabond (or wanderer) on the earth.[82] Yet, merciful God ended up removing half of Cain's punishment, here. After the murder, Cain surely was going to be wanted for murder by a number of those around him, just as any fugitive. Ancient sources tell us that other people around Cain, even the *animals*, wanted vengeance for what he did![83]

> *…wherever Cain went, swords sounded and flashed as though thirsting to smite him.*
> (Baring-Gould, 1881, p. 73)[84]

> *Adam said to Cain "Go away! You will always be afraid and not safe from anyone you see." Everyone… who passed by him shot (insults) at him.*
> *- al-Tabari: The History of al-Tabari - Vol. I: General Introduction and From the Creation to the Flood* Cain and Abel 144[85]

But, now, he was only to be a *vagabond* upon the earth. Now, he only was to roam about aimlessly, not really being happy, or satisfied, at any call, no matter where he ended up, or what he did![86] Sounds like more of the same, regarding all of the negativity already going on inside Cain's head.

God wasn't going to allow Cain to be hunted down and killed for Abel's murder. That would be too easy (for him to escape judgment). No, He wanted Cain to continue roaming about the earth, unabated, contemplating what he had done. God wanted it all to slowly eat away at Cain's soul![87] This way Cain, most likely, would not be able to find peace, nor rest, almost anywhere. He wouldn't be able to achieve full contentment in life until he actually took time and faced himself, and his actions.[88] God knew what was best for Cain's unruly heart, and that Cain was fighting Him every step of the way. So, as they say, "Let the punishment fit the crime." God's wisdom wins, again; because that punishment, according to many, was probably the worst punishment a person of Cain's mental stature would want.

> *No peace for him, no rest for him, treading the blood-drenched ground.*
> (Baring-Gould, 1881, p. 70)[89]

God set it all up, so that Cain's fate was now in his *own* hands, and his negative thoughts and attitudes were, often, going to come back to bite him. God knew that Cain probably wasn't going to consciously relent, even though he *could*, if he so wanted. C'est La Vie.

Cain's Nervous Trembling

> *He shuddered continually, and he walked upon the earth shaking incessantly, night and day.* - *Armenian Apocryphal Adam Literature* Repentance 60[90]

God would have a few other punishments, beyond those of the mind (or, at least it would seem that way). Next, God caused Cain to tremble and shake upon the earth, whenever he roamed about.[91] The ground reportedly seemed to "shake" under him (at least, that's the way he portrayed it).[92] His body was condemned to such a "shuddering" - non-stop, back and forth, and side to side - that he could barely even sit down peacefully, or bring his hand to his mouth accurately.[93] Another source stated that Cain "shook like a tree in the wind." He couldn't stand still, or stay in one place, for an extended period of time. We, today, may notice a pattern similar to this: in the shudder in a person who acts extremely *guilty* or *nervous*, or wanders about, to and fro, as if mentally unsettled, or unstable.

It's interesting, from what we already know about Cain, and his mindset, how this punishment also seems to "fit!"

*And He (God) said to him, "Where is thy brother?" To which he answered and said, "I know not." Then the Creator said to him, "Be trembling and quaking." Then Cain trembled and **became terrified**; and through this sign did God make him an example before all the creation, as the murder of his brother. And also did God bring trembling and terror upon him, that he might see the **peace** in which he was at first, and see also the trembling and terror he endured **at the last**; so that he might **humble** himself before God, and repent of his sin, and seek the peace he enjoyed at first... God was not seeking to kill Cain with the sword, but He sought to make him die of **fasting** and **praying** and **weeping by hard rule**, until the time that he was delivered from his sin... as to Cain, ever since he had killed his brother, he could not find rest in any place...*
      - First Book of Adam and Eve (The Conflict of Adam and Eve with Satan) 79:24-28[94]

*"Quaking and quivering shalt thou (Cain) be in the earth." That is, thy **soul shall shake**, and thy body shall quiver.*   *- Barhebraeus Gen. 4:12*[95]

So, again, in another case of irony, Cain may have been condemned in this way because he showed God **no** nervousness or trembling when engaged in conversation. Adam shuddered and feared God when He was talking to him. And, he wasn't condemned to any further punishment, such as this... because he gave God a show of respect. Cain, on the other hand, was different. God now had to *make* Cain shake and shudder - to, probably, act like he *should* have acted, all along! Now, this shudder would become a constant reminder of his former outbursts of pride and disrespect![96]

...with his feet and hands and every single limb he shuddered like a yew-tree.
*   - Armenian Apocryphal Adam Literature* Abel and Cain 41[97]

...May you shake like a tree in the winds... May you be tossed like the sea which is
agitated by the waves.
*   - Armenian Apocryphal Adam Literature* Repentance 55-56[98]

Cain, throughout this all, also began to be extremely *paranoid*, with constant suspicion and mistrust of those around him.[99] Because of it all, his life had truly become miserable, with constant insecurities, and without inner peace.

*...and God said to him, "Thou tremblest and art in fear; this shall **be thy sign**."*
(Baring-Gould, 1881, p. 74)[100]

More Signs Upon Cain

According to other ancient sources, Cain, from now on:

- *toiled*
- *groaned*
- *was removed from God*
- *did not **profit***[101]

He also developed:

- *a voracious hunger, never to be satisfied*
- *disappointment in every desire*
- *a perpetual lack of sleep*
- *a life where no man should either befriend or kill him*[102]

Also, from all of this, Cain seemed to have a hard time dealing even with the simplest elements of everyday life. Whenever he tried to do things, he often ended up with issues regarding his own satisfaction. Other ancient sources stated that, no matter how much food he ate (for example), he wasn't ever totally satisfied.[103] Assuredly, this didn't happen just with food. It probably occurred with most things he *touched*, or *dealt with* - material things around him, even interpersonal relationships. A lot just "didn't work out." Some might call it "Murphy's Law." In this case, it could be called "divine providence."

Cain's life, then, began to resonate with misery and anguish, because of it all. He couldn't sleep very well. Some ancient sources even stated he felt his situation was incurable, and wished to die.[104]

> *But when Cain killed Abel, Cain was stricken... (and) cried "Woe!" and "Alas"*
> *bitterly.   - Armenian Apocryphal Adam Literature* Abel and Cain 57[105]

Yet, all of these factors, regarding Cain and his punishments, are very important to the theme of this volume, as we'll see. It'll give us some insight into the soul of Cain, himself, the ancient side of the "Days of Noah" parallel, and also to what makes *Mystery Babylon* tick.

Nod - The Land of (Mental) Wandering?

> *And Cain went out from the presence of the LORD, and dwelt in the land of **Nod**, on*
> *the east of Eden.   - Gen. 4:16 (KJV)*

It was now time for Cain to make his way out into the world, a whole he helped to fashion. God forced him to dwell in the land (or forest) of *Nod*, which means "restlessness," "wandering" or even "exile."[106] Could this mean that Cain was also engaging in a lot of wandering "upstairs?"

And, to seal His promise, God provided *one* more thing to Cain, to help him along his way: his ***mark***.

The Prophecy for Cain

To keep His plans for Cain consistent, here, God not only delivered the prophecy of Genesis 3:15 to Adam and Eve, He also delivered a *warning* to anyone who interfered with one important punishment of Cain:

*And the LORD said unto him, Therefore whosoever slayeth Cain, vengeance shall be taken on him **sevenfold**...*   *- Gen.* 4:15 (KJV)

Simply, this meant that: if somebody interrupted Cain's "wandering," the offender and his future generations would be *punished* for a very long time - seventy-seven subsequent generations, in fact! Actually, this was an order of **protection**, by God, to stop the angry people around him from killing him! God wanted to make *sure* that nobody killed Cain before his time - to assure he was to remain alive, and *contemplate* what he had done.

The Mark of Cain

And the LORD set a mark upon Cain, lest any finding him should kill him.
                                                                  - Gen. 4:15 (KJV)

On top of his mental anguish, on top of his shuddering and wandering, God gave him his famous *mark* - the **mark of Cain**. No one, actually, knows for sure what this mark is. We *do* know it seemed to have an effect on other people around him: to make them recognize, avoid and, most importantly, to **keep him alive**.[107] This mark of Cain was actually for his own protection - to allow him to walk around freely, throughout the lands, without becoming *overwhelmingly* afraid of death.

Theories abound about what the mark actually was, but nothing is definitive. In one opinion, it was a physical mark, or *brand*, somewhere on the body, much like how a slave of ancient times had. Cain, according to some, could have been branded in this way to designate him as a special *protégé* of God, and God alone. It was to make sure everyone around Cain understood that he was a *ward* of God, and was "off limits."[108]

If we begin to follow this rationale, another thought that may come to mind is: just *who* would God need to protect Cain from, if he, Adam, and Eve were the only people on the earth at the time? Again, it supports the postulation that there were, probably, a good deal of *other* people around at this time.

Also, the name of the land he was destined to roam - *Nod* - could have even been associated with the word *nomad*.[109] So, if Cain was to wander some land, away from other settlements, then logic dictates there must have already been *other* settlements of people around at this time. There must have been, if people were already living in areas that Cain was forbidden to go. Also, could there have even been other *nomads* roaming areas, such as Nod... hence giving it the name?

> *Interestingly, we have further scriptural "proof" of pre-Adamites in the Bible a mark was put upon him as a protection against those people. This shows that, although we may assume that Adam was the first man into whom God breathed a "living soul," he was **not the first human being** upon the earth.* (Bristowe, 1927, p. 15)[110]

A couple of other interesting thoughts about this *mark* now may come to light, here.

The Cross

One way that God could have marked Cain, according to some, was to brand him with the letter "**T**" (or *Tau*). Possibly, this letter was placed on Cain left arm, or even on his forehead.[111] As the last letter of the Phoenician and Hebrew alphabet, this *Tav* was also considered a **cross**.

From the word *Tav* comes the Greek word *tau*. And, this *tau* was also said to have inspired another concept: crucifixion.[112]

> *The killing of Abel... could not but suggest to early Christians a parallel to the crucifixion - indeed, the specific mention of Abel's "blood(s)" implied a typological connection to "the sprinkled blood" of Jesus...* (Kugel, 1998, p. 168)[113]

We're already aware of the prophecy of Genesis 3:15. Could this *mark* - a mark placed upon this seed of the Serpent - have been a symbol of what would eventually be the way Jesus would use to conquer death? Could the *symbol* of what would be used to crucify Jesus actually be placed on Cain's forehead, way back then? Could this have been to show that the Serpent seed line was already destined to lose - by what happened on a cross? And, if so, it seems the *future* may have already been laid out, physically, upon Cain's head, since the beginning of this "enmity." We're not sure if this all has some meaning, but it's food for thought.

Another interesting thought abounds:

> One ancient rabbi thinks Cain killed Abel with **wood** - this was what Christ was crucified on.   (Baring-Gould, 1881, p. 72)[114]

Interestingly enough, we see that a symbol of the ancient pagan god *Tammuz* was *the cross*.[115] And, as we'll see in the next chapter, the origin of this pagan god was, most probably, *Abel* himself. Again, it seems totally fitting. Could this *cross*, then, also serve as a symbol of *Abel* - the righteous man that Cain destroyed - as some outward "justification" for this original murder?

And, also, if Cain killed Abel with a *wooden* stick, or reed, then maybe the reason Jesus was to die on a *wooden* cross was also to justify what happened, early on here. A lot of interesting parallels we could possibly have, here.

There's another famous interpretation of this mark.

The "Horn of Power"

Beyond this *Tav*, another interesting (and popular) interpretation of Cain's mark involves a *horn*. According to some, God caused Cain to be hairy on the outside, and also gave him an animal's **horn**, to be placed right on the middle of his forehead![116] Its purpose was, actually, to blow as a bugle.[117] Some even suggested this horn could continually announce to those around him, "Cain the fratricide is coming!"[118] So, by this up-and-coming procession, it continually alerted all of those around him, to get *away* and stay away! Interesting, as we'll see later.

Also, according to some, Cain became spiteful of this horn, and tried to "compliment" it by wearing animal skins, as clothing.[119] Maybe, in some weak attempt to raise his own self-esteem, Cain dressed this way to further *intimidate* anyone around him, and make *sure* they got away from him. In whatever way Cain used his hair and horn (if he even had them), there's something else to ponder: what a humbling experience this would be for Cain, at least in the beginning. Imagine a person seeing everyone around him run from him, wanting to get away. It probably would feel a little unnerving, at times, and upsetting.

Some sources even identify his mark as a "wild, ghastly look."[120] All of these things would have given Cain an unmistakable, and most unfavorable, fanfare, to say the least.

There was more:

*The mark or token, placed on his forehead, is said by the Rabbinical critics to have been a **horn** which grew on his head when the curse was pronounced, or, according to others, the sign consists only in the sun becoming brighter. Both sayings have the same meaning, for the horns of the sun are his rays, and it is clear that after the slaughter of the dawn brother, the sun (or **son**) driven forth to wander over the **earth** becomes brighter... as his "horn is exalted".* (Rogers, 1884, p. 12)[121]

If we think about it, this "horn" could even have symbolized something else: Cain, according to some ancient sources, actually became famous for wearing a *horned* helmet. Through *further* attempting to intimidate those running away from him, or trying to avoid him, Cain continually tried to find ways to make himself look stronger, or even appear as some *war-like* individual. Soon, this horn became a symbol of *power*, then - Cain's power! Interestingly enough, as we'll soon see, Cain *would* eventually want to have *power* over the people around him, and conquer them. And, as we'll also see, there seem to be a good number of interesting elements to Cain's story, here, whether they be actual, or only symbolic.

Still, there was another interpretation of this horn. We've just discovered how a *horn* could be the symbol of one's physical power. But, now, we'll see it also could represent the power inside of a person - inside *the human mind*! Also thought of as the *psychic function*, it could represent that "angel-like" power (or "divine," "third-eye" power) one might have, beyond human understanding. They may know something the average human wasn't capable of knowing, communicating something the average person wasn't capable of communicating. After all, as they say: "knowledge is power!"

So, Cain, according to some sources, may have had access to this knowledge, possibly because he was a son of the Serpent. And, possibly, a number of those who had terrestrial, Nephilim blood could have had access to some of this power, as well. Interestingly enough, horns such as these were often pictured on a person *exactly* where one might think a person with psychic abilities would have it - right in the middle of their forehead! That's where your average psychic will tell you their power resides, where their "third eye" sets.

The "Horn" of the Mind

Could God have allowed Cain to have some of these *psychic* powers, as well, to assist him in his own protection efforts?[122] At least, a knowledge of how this earth works would be nice!

> *Intellectually, Cain was as smart and cunning as his father, the Serpent. He had not only inherited the evil traits from the wicked one, the devil, but was also full of* **worldly wisdom**... *with his intellectual shrewdness he would be able to escape unscathed... With the mark set on him, Cain must have been more* **subtle** *than his Serpent father. His intellectual and sagacious mind must have helped him to outwit his pursuers in many situations when he was being hunted.*
> ("The Mark of the Wicked Ones", n. d., p. 10-11)[123]

Could this Mark of Cain also relate to his ability to understand insights and introspections beyond this world? This would assuredly help him avoid any possible sabotage, or plots against him. As Cain became an expert in the "ways of the world," he may have also become a master of the *occult*.

Some sources stated God may have even allowed Cain to grow bigger and taller, physically, to aid in his attempt to intimidate others away from him:[124]

*Cain, a white man endowed with **superhuman knowledge** and **physique** and rendered **invulnerable** by some divine talisman.*
(Bristowe, 1927, p. 15-16)[125]

All of it would assuredly have helped Cain survive, and escape any thoughts of persecution, or any rush to judgment by those around him. It would continually keep him "one step ahead" of any and all who may plot revenge, and want to, somehow, hurt him.

Cain, with whatever *mark* he inherited, wouldn't really want to use it to improve himself morally, or use it to help him become a better person in any way. Not Cain. He would want to take advantage of anything he now had, and, actually, take it in the *opposite* direction, as we'll soon see:

*...the sign was that when he was going forward, he was **thrust backward**.*
- *Barhebraeus* Gen. 4:16[126]

The "Abused" One - Not a Murderer

He (God) made him an example for murderers... He made him an example to penitents... the Lord made Cain a sign (to others)... of the fear that haunts a murderer (and) of the saving power of repentance, which Cain displayed, so that God did not put him to death immediately.   - *Genesis Rabbah* 22:12 (and notes)[127]

Whatever happened to Cain, and whatever reason God may have had to do things to him, he continually took it the wrong way. The mark was actually meant to protect Cain; but, he took it as something horrible, wrong, and disrespectful to *his* ego. This, as we'll see, would become a usual thought pattern of so many who begin to adopt Cain's way of thinking:

*...the paradox is that you can't bear the **mark** of God's grace without it reflecting the **marks of sin**. God's (protective) seal upon us should make us appreciative. But I am almost sure that Cain **only saw** the negative aspect of his mark. He only saw that he was **marked** as a murderer.*
("Sermon: Have We Gone in the Way of Cain?", n. d., p. 8)[128]

*His punishment, however, **far from being** taken as a warning, only served to **increase his vice**.* - *Flavius Josephus* Jewish Antiquities 1:59-64[129]

Instead of remorse, Cain, again, became even more rebellious:

He (Cain) would never let anybody walk over him, or take an insult, or allow anyone to besmirch his imagined "honor". ("The Mark of Cain", n. d., p. 6)[130]

All of these thoughts would lay the cornerstone of whom Cain would, eventually, begin to idolize - lock, stock and barrel.

The "Son of Perdition"

perdition - *a state of final spiritual ruin*[131]
> *complete and irreparable **loss**, ruin*
> *loss of the soul*[132]

Interestingly enough, though, there is a *Perdition*, and a *son of Perdition*, in the Bible. Now, just who were they? The definition of *perdition*, besides "eternal damnation" or "Hell," could also have meanings such as the *above*.

If we example the word *loss* a little further, we see that it could also mean, "the act of *losing* possession."[133] Wow. Isn't one of the meanings of *Cain* - "possession?" How fitting. Could this represent the Serpent, and his son?

Cain and the Serpent - The Same "Perdition"

*...Cain, who had been led by the adversary to break the law, and the murdered Abel (and) the **perdition** brought on him and given through **the lawless one**.*
- *Apocalypse of Abraham 24:5-6*[134]

*...and Cain, that Son of Darkness who had become **Perdition**... ministered in them mysteries of darkness, showing himself to be god through satanic powers.*
- *Book of the Generations of Adam 9:6*[135]

As we see, the Serpent was also known as:

*...**perdition** personified, like Sheol (hell) and Abaddon.*
(Jung, 1974, p. 155)[136]

We also see, now, how *perdition* becomes another important link between Cain and his real father, the Serpent.[137]

So, now, as a result of Cain's excessive desire to acquire **things**, he, eventually, would be destined towards the opposite extremes of this all, in so many ways. Instead of acquiring, he was destined to *lose* a lot of what he once had, over time and over circumstance. Even if he ended up with a lot, he would still, continually, be *in want*, and never really feel satisfied. So much of his problem was up in his head. He would eventually lose a lot of the *self-esteem* he continually tried to gather for himself. That was all part of his punishment, as we recall.

Ultimately, Cain was cursed to feel *perdition*, in one way or another.

Generations Ripe for Destruction

On top of this, there are some other definitions of *perdition*: "eternal misery," "destruction" and "ruin" - all trademarks of how Cain, and his eventual followers, may eventually feel, and may affect those around them, if they so allow.[138]

*Why doth they brother's blood cry from under the altar against thee? Behold, is not his blood upon they flesh, a mark which shall not be eradicated until the end of time? Thou wicked Cain, thou art Perdition and thy deeds shall follow thee for from thee shall flow murder and bloodshed, wars and contentions, until the earth shall hide her face from the wickedness and pollution of mankind. Depart from before my face, for **thine existence is a pollution** to the sanctity of this spot. Nevertheless, no man shall slay thee, for thou shalt live to see the full measure flowing from thine iniquity, until the final destruction of the darkness of this world.*
- Book of the Generations of Adam 5:8[139]

We see, in the above, that wars and contention may quite easily flow from Cain, his progeny, and his conformists. The word *contention* can also be defined as, "verbal strife, dispute, argument, controversy, a statement or point that one argues for as true or valid." Vines Expository Dictionary of New Testament Words says this about - what the Bible calls - the "Son of Perdition":

*...(the) "son of perdition" signifies the proper destiny of the person mentioned; metaphorically of men **persistent in evil**... vessels of wrath **fitted themselves for "destruction"**... of professing Christians, really enemies of the Cross of Christ... of professing... adherents who shrink back into unbelief...*
("Vines Expository Dictionary, *Perdition*", n. d., p. 1)[140]

Often, there is not a lot of good that comes from people who connect themselves with Cain, and their chosen ways of life.

God's Prophecy Set Into Motion

Ultimately, we understand that Cain spilled blood. We know that Cain killed someone for an immoral reason. And, we also know that God set up a prophecy for Cain, to stop anyone set on revenge, because of it:

*And the LORD said unto him, Therefore whosoever slayeth Cain, vengeance shall be taken on him **sevenfold**...*   *- Gen. 4:15 (KJV)*

Next, we'll look more into how Cain's descendants, through these tendencies to head towards *perdition*, could, often, be more prone to diminish other people, places and things around them… as well as destroy *themselves*. We know that Cain opposed whatever punishment he had, for every reason, and ending up heading in the *opposite direction* of where God wanted him to head (in so many ways). As a true rebel, he used almost every tool he now had against God - not to remain *humble* (as Adam was). He, rather, tried to magnify himself and his own ways of thinking and living, above all the rest. His arrogance, of course, would not last forever.

So, let's now take a look at what Cain *did* to influence the world around him, after all of this, and continue to bring others down to his *own* level - by adopting the ways of his true father, the Serpent. We'll also discover how some descendent of Cain would actually interfere with the plans God had for him, and mess things up even more! This, in turn, would bring *more* problems to Cain, to his descendants, and to the world as a whole.

Chapter 10

"Raising Cain" - Founder of an Ancient Religion and Empire

*Was not Cain the **foremost** of all the "wandering stars for which the **blackness** of darkness hath been reserved for ever?"*   (Bristowe, 1927, p. 153)[1]

Cain, his soon-to-be descendants, and other conformists after him, would seem to fall under the domain of these negative (or *darkened*) ways of thinking and living. And, over time, many would probably go on to *suffer* under them, one way or another. And, one way or another, many would go on to, at least partly, fulfill one side of that Genesis 3:15 Prophecy (i.e. the *Protoevangelium*). Those of the Serpent would be at *enmity* with those of Adam. We'll soon look at some of the pathways Cain traveled, where he ended up, and how he was able to influence so many people after him… to help formulate a massive group against Adam, and those who would follow him.

Let's concentrate on one side of this "great division" - the side of Cain (and his father, the Serpent). Let's also explore the political and religious *empires* they were about to set up, and push, throughout the old world.

The World - According to Cain

As we know, there are usually two sides to every story. The same in this case (of the two seeds of Genesis 3:15). The Bible has one story - or opinion - of Cain, and a number of other ancient texts out there seem to have another. So much of the world's ancient pagan myth and legend seems to point towards Cain, not in a negative way, but in a very *positive* one. Not only that, we'll see that most of these other accounts preferred to adopt what *he* believed, and looked to the ways he followed, hands down.

The book, *The Parthenon Code*, gives us some interesting thoughts on how most ancient pagan views compare to the Bible:

*Ancient Greek religion, what we call mythology, tells the same story as the Book of Genesis, except from the **point of view** that the **serpent** is the enlightener of mankind rather than our deceiver.*   (Johnson, 2004, p. 9)[2]

*The Judeo-Christian tradition says God is the measure of all things; the **Greek religious system says man** is the measure of all things. Both stem from **the same source**.*   (Johnson, 2004, p. 26)[3]

This last quote is oh, so *important*. We now begin to see an ancient *rift* developing - two different *ideologies* being formed (each forming, seemingly, in parallel along with a particular seed line)! And, on top of this, a good amount of ancient pagan lore seems to have similarities with the story of Genesis (believe it or not), but, it seems to come from an entirely different point of view.[4] In so many cases, it seems to represent an *opposite* point. Why? Of course, it only makes sense to figure this as part of the parallel, as well.

In the case with Cain, by looking at these alternate sources, we find Cain was not really the bloodthirsty murderer the Bible portrayed, but, more or less, a *hero*. Obviously, it depends on *who's* telling the story, here, and what *their stake* is in what they're trying to push to the populous:

*Two of the most recent writers upon the Babylonian inscriptions unintentionally support... that the Genesis stories came down in 'two streams,' and also my theory that one stream came down through the descendants of Seth (a true son of Adam) and the other through **Cain** in Babylonia.*   (Bristowe, 1927, p. 13)[5]

The *valley* between these opposing differences was beginning to widen, further and further. Cain and the Serpent's ways would begin to challenge the true ways of God, in every capacity. In these other points of view, Cain was not going to be turned into the lowest common human denominator, but one of the greatest, "god-like" heroes of antiquity! We'll see.

This was evident, even thousands of years later, in *Gnostic* thought:

*The Cainites (descendents of Cain) are sometimes called libertine Gnostics for believing that true perfection, and hence salvation, comes only by **breaking** all the laws of the Old Testament. The violation of biblical prescriptions was, therefore, **a religious duty**... the Cainites did not look for salvation in the created world but rather **escape from it**. Their subversion of biblical stories allowed them to use Sacred Scripture to support their dualist view of existence.*

("Britannica Online Encyclopedia, *Cainite*", n. d., p. 5)[6]

*(A Cainite also was considered a) member of a **Gnostic** sect mentioned by Irenaeus and other early Christian writers as flourishing in the 2nd century AD... (The ancient theologian) Origen declared that the Cainites had "entirely abandoned Jesus." (The Gnostic) reinterpretation of Old Testament texts reflected the view that Yahweh (God)... was positively evil because His creation of the world was perversely designed to **prevent** the **reunion** of the **divine element in man** with the unknown perfect God (i.e. the Serpent). The Cainites also **reversed biblical values** by **revering** such rejected figures as Cain, Esau, and the Sodomites, all of whom were considered to be **bearers** of an esoteric, saving knowledge (gnosis).*

("Britannica Online Encyclopedia, *Cainite*", n. d., p. 5)[7]

Some ancient texts referred to certain people as "giants;" not because they were physically large, but because of how influential their deeds were! Their popularity made them "giants." The Bible doesn't really refer to their patriarchs as "giants," per se', but a number of non-Biblical sources have stated how Adam and Noah were "giants" - "giants" of character and moral fortitude. However, along this same line, there are also some non-Biblical sources that state the descendants of Adam were "giants," but in a very *negative* tone.[8] Instead of being *protagonists*, as the Bible might portray them, instead of being looked upon as wonderful, God-fearing beings, they were thought of as, more or less, giant *troublemakers* or antagonists. We'll get into more of this, later on.

As we already stated, these two points of view, now beginning to flow down into two separate "streams" of information, were beginning to make things difficult for the average individual to weed through this rhetoric. It became harder for each to decipher *true* right from wrong, here. These opposing viewpoints will also make it difficult for anyone "off the street" to understand what was true history back then - and that, assuredly to Cain and his kind, was probably meant to be that way.

With enough study, however, we will, hopefully, be able to conglomerate it into one *real* story, and start to find the truth. They say there are two sides to every story, and somewhere in the middle you find truth. So, let's look at the combination of these two streams of information, and put it all of the pieces together. Let's begin to decipher the *untold* story of Cain, assembled from the four corners of our ancient, written world, to see what ancient history, here, may *really* be trying to tell us!

Cain Didn't Wander for Long

Moving further, we know that, after God caused him to become a vagabond on earth, Cain quickly did want to accept this type of punishment.[9] He didn't want to go along with God's commandments to roam about, to contemplate what he did. Instead, soon after his banishment, he began to strive for the *opposite* - to settle in one place (at least for a little while), not to be very concerned about the murder![10] We already know how Cain, through his sacrifice, always seemed to want things to be done *his* way. And, we also know that, in his mind, he believed he was actually *innocent* of the murder charge, depending how one "looks at it." He thought, for the most part, he was a *victim* of extraneous circumstances, such as Abel and God "not understanding" his way of looking at the world, or merely just "picking on him."

He also believed that, by his style of "negations," he may have even "pulled one over" on almighty God, in a number of ways.

> *...he threw the words behind him and went out, like one who would **deceive** the Almighty.*   *- Genesis Rabbah 22:13*[11]

All of what he did to Abel was, now, beginning to look *justified* in his mind, even though evidence to the contrary was so overwhelming:

> *...Cain was the only one of the first few Adamites to **rebel against** the sentence of death pronounced upon all mankind.*   (Bristowe, 1927, p. 79)[12]

He had convinced himself everything was all about him. By this stubborn mindset and desire for (wrongful) change, Cain would go on to have more of an effect on our world than most of us could ever have dreamed. Not only would he *physically* begin to go his own way, he also was the first to go his own way as far as *religious* ideology. This was the kicker that launched him into eternal stardom, if you will. He was the first to show inklings of a *new* belief system, contrary to God, and more in his favor. This was an ideology based, in part, on the way Cain looked at the world. But, most probably, it was coached into existence with **influences** of the Serpent, his father, and other fallen angels around him.[13] God, now, was beginning to be "in the way," in regards to their overall attempts at advancing themselves in this fallen world, and all the world may have to offer.

On top of establishing some sort of *counter-religion*, Cain also began to establish an **empire**, sub-doing others around him, while indoctrinating as many as possible into his same mode of thought. Wandering Cain, soon, was about to become a very cunning man, just like his father. He would soon be a great leader into "wicked courses."[14]

The Most Famous Men of Ancient Times - "Sargon" and "Khan"

If we are to connect Cain with the origin of this counter-belief, this empire, and new ways of thinking and living resulting from it all, we need to look at some ancient mythological or pagan accounts. And, interestingly enough, we *do* seem to be able to identify him with a couple of the most famous people of their day! Let's look at a few connections *Cain* may have had, with some famous individuals of old:

> *Another indication of the identity of Cain with the Babylonian **Sargon** is that the name variously rendered Sargon, Sargoni, Sarrukinu, Shargani, etc., may reasonably be taken as synonymous with "**King Cain**," the first syllable Sar or Shar meaning ruler or King in Babylonia and obviously the origin of Shah, Czar, Sahib, Sire, Sir, etc., while the second syllable gon, gani, gina or kinu, is very like Cain. George Smith writes: "Several of the other names of antediluvian patriarchs correspond with Babylonian words and roots such as Cain with gina and kinu." (Chaldean Genesis, p. 295. Early edition.)...* (Bristowe, 1927, p. 31)[15]

We now see that **Sargon** was considered one of the most famous people in the ancient land of Babylonia (i.e. modern Iraq), and was noted as one of the earliest *conquerors* of recorded history. This ancient land could also have easily been the area where the Garden of Eden was once located, so it all makes sense.

Many of us have, as well, heard of the famous "Genghis-Khan" - conqueror of western Asia. Interestingly enough, the word "Khan," here, could also stand for *ruler*. And, there seemed to be a number of "Khans" out there, in our ancient world. The first probable conqueror - the original "Khan" - might, actuality, have been none other than **Cain**, himself.[16] Let's see.

> ...the "**Kan**" or "**Gan**" of the Babylonian texts was 'obviously the historical origin of the "Cain" of the Hebrew Genesis, and that his father, King Adar or Adda or Addamu was the historical origin of "Adam" of the "Garden of Eden"'...
> (Bristowe, 1950, p. 19)[17]

Some ancient sources stated that Cain probably lived about 700 years or so - more than enough time to expand influences to those around him.[18] A lot of ancient people in Cain's day, according to the Bible, lived up to 900 years, or even more. Methuselah was a perfect example (a total of 969 years). Could *Cain* have found ways to conquer a number of people around him, during this time-frame, allowing himself more and more feelings of *self-importance* and *relevance*, as a result of all this control? Could his extended years have allowed him enough time to solidify the first **empire** of the post-Fall world? Could *Khan* or *Sargon* - both famous conquerors of old - be the earliest, pagan avatars of *Cain*?

> ...Sargon's date was about 3800 B.C., at which time Cain, according to the Bible dates, may have been alive. (Bristowe, 1927, p. 150)[19]

Both *Cain* and *Sargon*, interestingly enough, were also thought to have shared a similar profession, as well as the same language:

> (Sargon)... was a **gardener** when young... (and his) language (Ancient Babylonian) resembled Hebrew, which was presumably that of Cain.
> (Bristowe, 1927, p. 22)[20]

God Maker… Developer of the First "Religion"

*…Sargon is called in inscriptions "the first **high priest**."*
(Bristowe, 1927, p. 84)[21]

After he killed Abel, the Bible tells us that Cain *did* go out from the presence of the Lord. But, Divine Providence tells us that God is everywhere, so what could this have meant? Most probably, Cain went out from the presence of the Lord in regards to his *thought* or *ideology*. He could never step anywhere to get away from God, but he did step away in a religious sense. The birth of this first counterfeit, anti-God, pagan religion was now underway. And, interestingly enough, some sources stated that Cain's rebellious belief-system originated in the *very* outdoor field where he committed the murder!

The online source *Wikipedia* states that the word *pagan* derives from a Latin word, meaning, "of or relating to the *countryside*" or "*country* dweller." How ironic! How fitting, here!

Even though Cain could have officially abandoned God in a field, now being *far* from God in thought or deed, he still was be able to advance himself, taking on a great deal of knowledge and worldly understanding that was now out there. Some of the (legitimate) information came from Adam and Eve. Most came from the Serpent and other fallen angels around. And, as one could guess, most of this he received was twisted in favor of the Serpent, and the ways *he* favored:[22]

*Cain, type of the religious natural man, who believes in a God, and in "**religion**," but after his own **will**, and who rejects redemption by blood… the apostate teacher explains it away.* - *Schofield Reference Bible* Jude 1:11 (notes)[23]

*These had so **perverted** the truth as to offer sacrifices unto Jehovah in the name of Satan, taking the fruit of the ground and offering it up in an unholy parody of the holy ordinance.* - *Book of the Generations of Adam* 5:5[24]

We know Sammael/Satan influenced the Serpent, way back in the Garden. Now, the same thing happened with Cain, from *his* father. He began to whisper in Cain's ear where to go, and what to do. Thus became the foundation of **idolatry**: looking to one's own prideful self, or looking to other pagan "gods" around, as a modem of advancing one's own salvation, one's enlightenment, or their ego-gratification:

*...Cain introduced that knowledge, and used it as the basis of idolatry by ascribing Divine attributes to the gods of his **own** invention.*
(Bristowe, 1927, p. 117)[25]

So, *where* did this multitude of "gods" - that gods that pagan belief was originally noted for - really come from?

Parents Turned Into Gods - The Origins of Ancestor Worship

The examination of names is the beginning of learning.
- *Socrates*[26]

A number of ancient sources stated the earliest "gods" of pagan lore and religion were, at one time, very *human*:

*Did not the pagans by attributing God-like qualities to **men**, change "the un-corruptible God into an image made like to corruptible man?"*
(Bristowe, 1927, p. 63)[27]

*...as early as the 4th century A.D. the Christian Bishop Augustine of Africa, wrote in his book, De Civita Dei: "Alexander the Great told his mother in a letter that even the higher gods were **men**"...*
(Bristowe, 1950, p. 46)[28]

*...the view propounded by Euemerus (316 B.C.), according to whom the **myths** were **history in disguise** and: "all gods **were once men** whose real feats have been decorated and distorted by later fancy" (Ency. Brit., Ed. II. Mythology)".*
(Bristowe, 1927, p. 62-63)[29]

Cain probably began to set up a belief system based on whatever he saw around him, and knew of. Simple enough. So, he could have, of course, desired to deify whomever he saw important in his life (beyond God, of course). Now, not only did Cain turn one's veneration *away* from God, and towards *material things* of this world, but he also helped turn people into worshipping anyone he considered *close* to him:

> *...Cain, armed with superhuman knowledge and power, came into Babylonia bringing with him the marvelous story of the Creation of the world and the Garden of Eden... No wonder the old times were perpetually harped upon in inscriptions in which are **veiled allusions** to Adam and Eve - the Fall of Adam - Eve's sorrow for Abel and her anger against Cain - the coming of Cain to Babylonia and his alliance with the Devil.*
> (Bristowe, 1927, p. 57)[30]

As we can decipher, from looking at ancient works of the past, Cain still probably maintained a great deal of respect for Adam and Eve, *especially* for his mother. His first move towards "deification" began with the conversation of *them* both into gods and goddesses. This, most probably, was the true origin of **ancestor worship** - a widely held belief in ancient pagan cultures of old.

Adam, Eve, the Serpent and Abel

> *These illusions are cloaked in the form of mythology which originated (as I hope to show) in Cain's travesty of the truth in transferring the Divine attributes of the Creator to **three false gods**, whom he called **Anu** and **Ea**, after his parents, and **Bel**, after the Devil.*
> (Bristowe, 1927, p. 57)[31]

> *The Professor tells us that the first Babylonian gods were a trio - "the supreme gods Anu, Mul-lil and Ea," and there was a **fourth god** called **Tammuz**. These four gods seem to be regarded by Assyriologists as the models from which **Adam, Eve, the Devil** and **Abel** were drawn, but my contention is that, on the contrary, they were the deified representatives of those Bible characters, and that it was Cain who deified their memories by transferring to them some of the attributes of God.*
> (Bristowe, 1927, p. 70)[32]

Sargon, as we know, was probably another name for Cain. Now, as we see, this ancient king established four main gods - originating in Adam, Eve, Abel *and* the Serpent.[33] Hence, we have the first major *gods* of paganism, with even *more* ancient avatars reading and willing to spring out from them, as well. For example:

Eve - descended deities such as *Ea, Enki, Ishtar, Ashtoreth*[34]
Adam - descended deities such as *Anu, Atum, Shamash, Zeus*[35]
The Serpent - descended deities such as *Enlil, Mul-lil, Bel, Sin the moon god, Akki* [36]
Abel - descended deities such as *Tammuz*[37]

Throughout the ages, these original gods would develop even further:

According to the Babylonian priests, several gods took part in the creation of the world, and the gods Anu, Ea and Bel at first, and in later times Shamas, Ishtar and Sin ruled the heavens, earth, sea and "the affairs of men".
(Bristowe, 1927, p. 115)[38]

Beginning in the ancient lands of Mesopotamia (a.k.a. Sumeria, Akkad, Babylonia, etc.), the launch of Cain's new religion began to spread in all directions. It was spread, for the most part, by this new *empire* Cain had also established. Beyond these primary names, they would become transformed, over time, into many *other* gods and goddesses since, leeching out into most every culture, religion and empire since.

The Obscured Accounts of Old?

*...the knowledge of God and of His laws was taken into Babylonia in the very earliest times and... that knowledge came to be **suppressed** or **travestied almost beyond recognition**.*   (Bristowe, 1927, p. 151)[39]

*...(the Sumerian story of the Creation) is only one of the **corrupt** versions of the Creation story handed down from the time of Cain by the Babylonian priests.*
(Bristowe, 1927, p. 49)[40]

According to ancient accounts, these gods, sometimes, were brother and sister. Sometimes they were looked upon as mother and son, sometimes married, sometimes single. Sometimes, they were thought of as male, sometimes female. There were a variety of reasons why the details surrounding these ancient gods were changed: sometimes, it was over time; sometimes, it was because of inaccurate oral retelling; sometimes, it was inaccurate copying onto parchment. And, of course, there's also the real possibility that a number of these ancient gods and goddesses were *intentionally* blurred, or covered up, over time![41] *Why*? It's because there were certain individuals out there who needed to obscure things, so they would continue to profit off of them, pure and simple. Some people don't want everyone to understand their primary "gods" were originally based on Cain, the Serpent, and other Biblical patriarchs of the day - of course, because it exposes them for who they *really* were, and, of course, they wouldn't want to give the Bible any validation for anything. See how it all works? It's time for them to erase any incendiary references coming out of the true Word of God.

So, whatever "gods" they would developed into next, it is important to realize, here, that they all probably had the same origin - the time right after the Fall.

Eve - The Goddess Mother

We have some interesting quotes on the probability of *Eve* being the origin of many early goddesses (and even some gods, also):

> *...Sargon is called the son of **Ea** (Eve)...*
> (Bristowe, 1927, p. 151)[42]

> ***Ishtar's*** *countless titles include those of "Lady of Eden," "Goddess of the Tree of Life," "Mother of Mankind," and "Beloved of Anu (i.e. Adam)."*
> (Bristowe, 1950, p. 10)[43]

Under Mother's Care?

As we recall, Cain had great respect for his mother. This is reflected in ancient pagan lore, as well:[44]

> *...the Babylonians themselves attributed Sargon's superhuman knowledge to **his mother's teaching**.* (Bristowe, 1950, p. 5)[45]

*...the following inscription refers to Cain's indebtness to his mother for his knowledge: "Moreover he... possessed all... Ea's wisdom;" "My child" Ea had said to him, "What is there that thou knowest not and what could I teach thee? What **I know thou knowest** also" (Mesopotamia, Delaporte, p. 141).*

(Bristowe, 1927, p. 84)[46]

After the murder of Abel, things began to change a little, between Eve and her son. Instead of great affection, Eve developed a distain for Cain, at least for a while. We see this in ancient mythology:

*That Sargon is represented in inscriptions as the gardener of Anu (Adam), as Beloved of Ishtar (Eve) and **only loved by her for a certain period**, since he says: "When I was a gardener Ishtar loved me," which may refer to the fact that after the murder of Abel, Eve renounced Cain.*　　　　　　　　(Bristowe, 1927, p. 151)[47]

...another "Penitential Hymn"... was used as part of a temple ritual... and its great importance... is that it records Cain's first step in idolatry... in the very same words as he addresses to the Creator... We read:... "I knew not that I sinned. May Ishtar, my mother be appeased again, for I knew not that I sinned, God knoweth that I knew not... God, in the strength of his heart, has taken me, Ishtar, my mother, has seized me, and put me to grief."　　　　(Bristowe, 1950, p. 40)[48]

Assuredly, it's understandable why. But, it didn't last for very long. Eve, being the loving mother that she was, couldn't turn her back on her son for all time, no matter what dark places he was heading.

Adam - The Father God

Now, we have some reveling quotes on the possibility of *Adam* also being the origin of some early gods:

*Abu (is the)... "Lord of the **Plants**"... It seems so obvious that "Abu," who's name means "father," represented Adam...*　　　　　　(Bristowe, 1950, p. 62)[49]

*That Sargon (Cain) is represented in inscriptions as the **gardener** of Anu (Adam)...*
(Bristowe, 1927, p. 151)[50]

...(an) inscription in which Anu and Ishtar are called lord and lady of the holy mound is probably an allusion to the Garden of Eden. (Bristowe, 1927, p. 73)[51]

We'll, also, see that Adam was known by other names, beyond *Abu* or *Anu*. In ancient Egypt, for example, Adam could have been made into the god *Atum*. Atum apparently arose "out of these chaotic waters," and even had a son named Seth (by which Adam did, as well).[52] As we see, some of this is similar to the Adam of the Bible.

The Greek god *Zeus* could also be another title for the Biblical Adam.

Zeus and Hera, a husband/wife and brother/sister pair, are pictures of Adam and Eve. (Johnson, 2004, p. 9)[53]

The meaning of Zeus' name has led us directly back to the Garden of Eden, and to the time when Eve and Adam accepted the serpent's wisdom as their own... He (Adam) may very well have desired to possess the knowledge of good and evil for himself... Homer says that Zeus is "the father of men and gods"... (and) Athena is born out of Zeus just as Eve came out of Adam... (Johnson, 2004, p. 173)[54]

The Serpent - Also Now a "God"

And, on top of these two, we also have revealing quotes on the possibility of **the Serpent** being the origin of a number of pagan gods:

*King Sargina (Sargon)... listening obediently to the god **Enlil** (the Serpent)...* (Bristowe, 1950, p. 44)[55]

*...the chief god was Enlil, whose name is translated... "lord of **demons**" by various authorities.* (Mackenzie, 1915, p. 35)[56]

We, also, see the pagan god *Dati-Enlil* could have been the original of our word *devil*:

***Sargon** says in... (one) legend that he "knew not his father," while he elsewhere claims **Dati-Enlil** as his father.* (Bristowe, 1927, p. 95)[57]

That while St. John says that Cain was "of the wicked one," Sargon is called the "king-priest of Enlil" (the Devil); and is made to call his father **"Dati-Enlil"** *(the* **Devil***).*   (Bristowe, 1927, p. 150)[58]

On top of this, in ancient pagan mythology, we have a number of references to a "dragon." And, we already know that the *dragon* was probably another symbol of the *Serpent*. So, could the god *Bel*, *Mul-lil* and *the dragon* all be one in the same?

Professor Sayce seems to identify the second god of the great trio with Satan by writing: "The supreme **Bel** *was* **Mul-lil** *who was called the god of the lower world, his messengers were nightmares and demons of the night, and from whom came the plagues that oppressed mankind (Hibbert Lectures, p. 147)."*
                                                         (Bristowe, 1927, p. 71)[59]

Neither in Hebrew nor Babylonian literature are Bel and the Dragon represented as antagonists. They are obviously, on the contrary, different forms of **the same god** *and there is no authority, therefore, for concluding that this drawing represents a fight between the two. It is even possible that the word* **Dragon** *came from Dagon which, according to Professor Jastrow, was only another name for* **Bel***... And Professor Sayce says... "Dagon is identified as Mul-lil" (Hibbert Lectures, 1887, p. 1888).*
                                                         (Bristowe, 1927, p. 100)[60]

There's another ancient pagan god, known as *Sin the Moon God*. This deity was very popular in the ancient Middle East. Interestingly enough, this god *also* seems to fulfill one's visual perception of the devil:

As Robert Browning wrote: "Note that the climax and the crown of things. Invariably is - the Devil appears himself - Armed, accoutered, horns and hoofs and tail." And sure enough those baneful signs are inseparable from the Babylonian religion; for in their drawings all their gods and heroes are represented with **horns** *or* **hoofs** *or* **tail***.*
                                                         (Bristowe, 1927, p. 55)[61]

Another popular god of the land of ancient Mesopotamia was *Akki*. The following quote, not only links *Akki* with the Serpent, but also gives us insight into Sargon's (i.e. Cain's) early life:[62]

*In the "Legend of **Sargon**" he (Sargon) calls his adopted father "**Akki**," which is evidently another name for the Devil, for it is closely connected with the name of **Nakash** the Hebrew serpent - with Ahi, the water-god and serpent - with Ahri-man, who in the Persian religion is the "source of all evil, the devil" - with Agni, the Indian god of fire - with the Egyptian Naka, the serpent - with Naga, the Indian serpent-god... and with Agu or Acu, another name for the Babylonian moon-god, otherwise called **Sin**. The moon-god Sin is evidently **Bel** or **En-lil** under another name, for in later times the original trio Anu, Ea and Bel became Shamash, Sin and Ishtar (Shamash supplanting Anu, Ishtar supplanting Ea, and Sin, Bel).*

(Bristowe, 1927, p. 93)[63]

The more we research, the more it all seems to come from *one* source.

Cain - Also Turned Into a "God" Himself

Cain seems to have been transformed into a "god," as well:

*It can hardly be considered a coincidence that while St. John says that Cain was "of that wicked one," referring to the Devil, Sargon is described by the Babylonian priests as being the son or protégé of the Devil. This is one of the strongest indications of the identity of **Cain** with Sargon, who in different inscriptions is called "**son of Bel** the just," "the son of Itti-Bel," and the "son of Dati-Enlil," while Sargon's country is called the "realm of Enlil" (or Bel)...* (Bristowe, 1927, p. 93)[64]

*...in a Babylonian text **Sargon** proclaims himself "The **Divine** Sargani, the illustrious king, a son of Bel the Just, the King of Agade, and of **the children of Bel**" (The First Bible, Conder).* (Bristowe, 1950, p. 8)[65]

As another major "god," Cain could have, in the Bible (in Jer. 50:2), been known as *Merodach* (or *Marduk*).[66]

*Nebuchadnezzar calls Merodach in inscriptions "the **first**-born, the glorious, the first-born of the gods, Merodach the prince," suitable titles, one would think, for the first-born of Adam's race... To crown their (the Babylonian scribes') inconsistencies, in the story of the Creation, Merodach's father is called, not Ea as elsewhere, but Anu. Since Anu represents Adam, and Ea and Ishtar represent Eve, **who could** Merodach their eldest born have represented but **Cain**?* (Bristowe, 1927, p. 80-81)[67]

As with Cain, Merodach was once considered a farmer:

> ..."Merodach" is described in another text as "Donor of **fruitfulness**, founder of agriculture and creator of grain and plants, who causes the green herb to spring forth" (Origin of Bible Traditions, p. 211, Clay).   (Bristowe, 1950, p. 66)[68]

Children of the "Sun" God

In the ancient past, the words *son* and *sun* could have been similar in meaning, practically synonymous. A rounded disk, as in the shape of the *sun*, could have also been symbolic of one's *own* son, or even someone's reincarnated soul.[69] So, the next time we hear of a *sun god*, we may need to ask ourselves: could it be, in some way, connected to Cain, the *son* of someone considered a deity? Or, what about the Serpent? Could he, also, have some sort of connection with the sun, as a deity?[70]

> ...the founder of the Babylonian empire was Cain and that he was flimsily disguised in mythology as Merodach, or Marduk the **Sun-god** who, **together with Bel (the Serpent)**, was worshipped in Babylon up to the end of that city.
>   (Bristowe, 1950, p. 45)[71]

> Merodach... is the solar hero who belongs **to the darkness** and not to the light.
>   (Sayce, 1898, p. 154)[72]

It's interesting that many ancient people have also thought of themselves as **Children of the Sun**. Could they have considered themselves *actual* descendants of Cain, possibly, or even the Serpent? Or, could they have been among those who had ancestors, so long ago, who chose to subscribe to their ways?

> ...if Cain... was the human original of the Babylonian Sun-god whose followers spread a high grade of civilization all over the ancient world, the nature of the **religion** which accompanies that civilization **witnesses against him**. Wherever the "Children of the Sun" raised their pyramids and dolmens, their stately palaces and temples... all... as we have seen, can be traced back to **Sargon**.
>   (Bristowe, 1927, p. 127)[73]

The Greek "Lord of Light"

Ancient mythologies, from Egypt to Persia, from Greece to Rome, contain "gods" that probably originated from a civilization before them. Ultimately, most of them originated in ancient Mesopotamia or Babylonia, which, according to many, could have also been the original location of the *Garden of Eden*. So, it only makes sense that their ancient "gods" were probably based on these same, famous individuals of the land, as well.

> *...the Greeks themselves not only adopted the ancient mythology of **Babylonia**, but added to it some even worse features...* (Bristowe, 1927, p. 64)[74]

We know that Cain, and even the Serpent, were probably connected with the "sun god" - those with a "brilliant" countenance. And, since the gods of *Greek* Mythology were often thought of as borrowed from ancient Babylonian gods, then we can start to see connections, here. The philosopher Socrates described the Greek god *Hephaistos* as, "the princely lord of **light**."[75] Obviously, these gods were not only thought to consist of light, they "enlightened" others to follow them, and their ways, as well.

Interestingly enough, Zeus, of whom we now know was probably the Greek version of *Adam*, was considered father of Hephaistos. Interesting, the correlation, here. The god Hephaistos will also become a little more important to our story, as we move further.

Abel - Their Arch Enemy

> *Abel resolves into **Ab** (Snake) and **El** (God/shining)... and therefore he is a "snake god" or "shining snake."* (Gardiner, 2006, p. 18)[76]

We know Abel was probably another son of the Serpent (and we see more evidence in the above, as well). And, as we remember, ancient pagan accounts often seem to consider the heroes of the Bible as antagonists - the *real* problems in the world. Abel was no exception. In some cases, Abel was even thought of as the god of "enmity," which seems to bring us back to the Genesis 3:15 Prophecy. How fitting, knowing what we already know about the prophecy.

As expected, Abel seemed to have found a place in ancient mythological lore, as well:

*Professor Sayce says about the fourth god Tammuz, whom he calls the prototype of Abel: "The primitive home of Tammuz had been in that Garden of Eden or Edin... hence his mother... is called 'the lady of Edin.'" (Hibbert Lectures, p. 23.) He also says that like Abel, Tammuz was a **shepherd** and was killed when young.*
(Bristowe, 1927, p. 70-71)[77]

*In some inscriptions Tammuz also is called the son of Ea... and so is shown to be the brother of Merodach as **Abel** was of Cain...*   (Bristowe, 1927, p. 81)[78]

We also see that Cain (i.e. Sargon) was given credit for accomplishing one more thing:

*...Sargon... is shown to be the brother of Tammuz (Abel) and (as the god Adar) to have **killed** Tammuz.*   (Bristowe, 1927, p. 151)[79]

The Essence of Cain's Religion

Now that we know who helped establish the ancient pagan "gods" of old, let's take a look at how Cain and the Serpent would twist the true ways of God, as well. In our first example, we see that, according to Cain, God was *not* really the creator, protagonist and benefactor of the world - *the Serpent*, in the Garden, was!

*...Greek poets and artists are telling us the same story from an **opposite** viewpoint - one that says that the serpent did not delude Adam and Eve in the ancient garden, but rather, **enlightened them**.*   (Johnson, 2004, p. 7)[80]

The "True" Enlightener

Famous throughout ancient mythology, the "wisdom of the serpent" may also have origins in the Garden of Eden. According to Cain, what *the Serpent* brought to mankind was important, more important than what God had already laid out:

*In Genesis, the fruit of the tree was "good for food," brought a "yearning to the eyes," and was "to be coveted as the tree to **make one intelligent**." It is for embodying this last quality for which Athena (**Eve**), as goddess of the serpent's **wisdom**, was specifically and especially revered.*   (Johnson, 2004, p. 189)[81]

The Serpent seduced Eve, and, through it all, she acquired the "**Knowledge** of Good and Evil." This was the first incidence of how the Serpent's knowledge was given to mankind, all for his "enlightenment."[82] As we see, the whole incident of the Garden was now twisted - in their favor. The moment Eve ate of the fruit was the point she made a step in a *positive* direction, not disobedience to God. There was knowledge out there that, at least in God's eyes, was probably not meant for human beings to acquire. Cain claimed just the opposite.

Just as Eve was given credit for receiving this "enlightenment," other ancient pagan "gods," such as *Adam*, were thought to have taken, or even "stole," this same enlightenment. It was, of course, all due to the blessings of the Serpent.[83]

*To the Greeks, the **serpent** freed mankind from bondage to an oppressive God, and was therefore a savior and illuminator of our race.*   (Johnson, 2004, p. 12)[84]

The "Enlightened" Eve

Eve, then, would go on to form a huge element of this pagan, "illumination" concept:

*Under the name of Nina or Nintu Ishtar is said to have divined all the mysteries of the gods - surely a reference to Eve's **acquisition of God-like knowledge** described in the Bible.*   (Bristowe, 1927, p. 74)[85]

*Athena's (Eve's) familiar and endearing intimacy with the serpent is undeniable, and it points **straight to Eden**. Her being is indissolubly coupled with the serpent: she is the goddess of **the serpent's wisdom**... (Athena) is the serpent's Eve, reborn and exalted... she is the new representative of Eve in the Greek age.*

(Johnson, 2004, p. 6, 22)[86]

Also, the "Enlightened" Adam

Adam (a.k.a. *Zeus*) also had a part in achieving this "illumination," even though he wasn't as prominent:[87]

*The presence of snakes around the other gods indicated that they were part of the serpent's system of enlightenment and sacrifice. But **Zeus** is not a subordinate part of the serpent's system - he is the serpent... The Judeo-Christian viewpoint has Adam ashamed of himself after eating of the tree. But on... (one ancient) vase we have a picture of an **unashamed** Adam who has eaten its fruit. From the viewpoint of Zeus-religion, taking the fruit from the tree of the knowledge of good and evil did not bring shame, but **Victory**.* (Johnson, 2004, p. 171, 244)[88]

Cain still loved Adam, and had respect him as a "pseudo-father," even though he wasn't totally on board to what Cain was beginning to develop. Cain made him a "god" to the people, regardless.

In conclusion, we are beginning to see *two* spiritual "pathways to wisdom" being laid out, each contrary to the other. This Genesis 3:15 *division* was coming to fruition, just as God predicted. People were beginning to follow, either these *new* ways of the Serpent, or the old ways of God (through *Adam's* teaching and example).

Cain - King of the Ancient World

According to this *new* way, Adam, Eve, the Serpent and Cain were the real "gods." Ancestor worship and worship of the "sun god" were now to be the norm. The Serpent's "enlightenment" now represented the proper pathway to divine reconciliation. Not only would Cain begin to control people through this Serpent-based religion, he also began to control them, *politically*, through the first "world empire."

*...**Cain** (was)... the ancestor of all the impious generations that were **rebellious** toward God, and rose up against Him.* (Ginzberg, 1909, p. 105)[89]

A "Fiery" Beginning

Cain also took it upon himself to conquer people in military-like fashion. He established an empire that would go on to influence future civilizations, and the way they did business, from then on. Cain, through this, was also able to keep people at a safe *distance* from him (at least in his mind). As we recall, he was paranoid that people around him would want revenge for the murder of Abel, and he figured, by conquering them, it would also help to keep them away from acting on these thoughts.

Also, anyone questioning Adam and the ways of God may, now, begin to find solace in all of what Cain was starting to offer. Cain introduced the knowledge of the Serpent and other fallen Nephilim, all in exchange for elevating these beings into some kind of "**godhood**." In one example, Cain assuredly learned about how to use fire. But, he learned a lot more about *fire* from these angelic beings - not only how to use it for upright purposes, but sinister reasons, as well. Cain adopted it as part of *his* ways of worship. He may have even directed people use it to provide sacrifices to *his* newfound "gods," the same.[90]

*Iblis (the Serpent?) came (to Cain) and said to him: "Abel's offering was accepted and consumed by fire because he used to serve and worship **fire**. So, you, too, set up a fire for yourself and your descendents!" Cain thus built a fire temple. He was the first to set up and **worship fire**.*
        - al-Tabari: The History of al-Tabari - Vol. I: General Introduction and From the Creation to the Flood Adam's Descendants to Jared 167[91]

*These had so perverted the truth as to offer sacrifices unto Jehovah in **the name of Satan**, taking the fruit of the ground and offering it up in an unholy parody of the holy ordinance.* *- Book of the Generations of Adam 5:5*[92]

The Blacksmith

Interestingly enough, another meaning of the word *Cain* is "smith."[93] In some areas of our ancient world, the occupation of "smith" had certain stigmas attached to it. A smith was often considered an alien, an intruder or "tinker in the old world." He could have also been considered a *magician*, or performer in some sort of "forbidden art."[94] The word "blacksmith" could even have become popular because many "smiths" were probably into the *black* arts.[95] We're not sure. But, either way, this, most probably, was a skill the Serpent, or some other fallen angel, helped Cain to refine. Whatever the situation, the stigmas around this occupation often seemed to point to its human originator.[96]

Interestingly enough, we've already mentioned the Greek god *Hephaistos* (of whom we know was equated with Cain). He was also known as the god of *techne* - a discipline by which we get the word *technology*.[97] Interesting. Was Cain truly the human originator of the art of metallurgy, and, ultimately, a force behind the **technical** and **industrial advancements** of people in our earliest ages?

The Opposite of Farmer

*Cain, says Josephus, sought to gain livelihood by farming methods which depleted the soil... God put a stop to Cain's way - the way of **getting**. If Cain and his heirs had been allowed to continue their agricultural pursuits, soils all over the world would long ago have been rendered unfit for cultivation... The geological record tells us what God did to save the soil from utter depletion... Wherever Cain wandered his agricultural pursuits came to **naught**. When it should have rained, the weather turned dry. Just as he was about to reap the ripening crop, a storm blew in. Nothing turned out right... He and the generations who followed him eked out a wretched living.*
(Hoeh, 1962, p. 9-10)[98]

Cain, as we know, was once a farmer. And, he was good at it. After the murder (and the "curse of Cain"), all of that had changed. The farming methods used by most people at the time would no longer would work as well with Cain and his progeny. Because it "just seemed" to become a little more difficult for his crops to grow, or for whatever other reason, Cain decided to get out of the farming business, began to devise ways to exploit the land in *other ways*. Instead of roaming about, even instead of attempting to farm, Cain thought it would be more advantageous to him to create more permanent structures - solid *buildings* and the like. He used the technological advancements the angels taught him to diverge people from their traditional, tent-dwelling ways they had - a life, of course, originally designated by God. Again, he strived for the "opposite."

And, obviously, since Cain's thoughts were not on the ways of God *above*, he began to concentrate his efforts on exploiting the world the *below*, and shaping it around him (to his advantage, of course). He began to mold the material world into something *he* considered better, and more suiting, for humanity![99]

Cain was also considered the first to initiate boundary stones around fields. Beyond the Garden, there were, now, *new* walls springing up in many areas, helping to secure each person their own property border.[100] As far as Cain was concerned, he wanted to make sure that everyone truly knew what was theirs, and also that everyone truly knew *what was his*. He wanted to keep out any undesirables, in order to lessen his paranoia a little.

The Builder of Large Structures

Beyond solid-structured living areas, beyond walls, Cain, also worked on perfecting his irrigation techniques, providing a solid system of aqueducts for the people. This helped to deliver **water** on a massive scale.[101] The knowledge of weights and measures were also attributed to *Cain's* initial promotion, here. They, assuredly, would have helped him a great deal in seeing these projects to fruition.[102] Of course, Cain received a lot of his initial knowledge from the Serpent and other terrestrial angels, and used all of it to further defy the one now he considered his real enemy: God.

We'll now see there was *one* more undertaking by Cain, something that even the Bible says was attributed to him… something huge:

Gen. 4:
16 *And Cain went out from the presence of the LORD, and dwelt in the land of Nod, on the east of Eden.*

17 *And Cain knew his wife; and she conceived, and bare Enoch: and he builded a* **city**...

Again, if we think about it, Cain further went down the *opposite* pathways that God originally decreed:

*As A.E. Knock has written, "**Cities** display the highest achievements of mortals and glorify mankind." The word city (**naked** in Hebrew) indicates that the ground has been **denuded of vegetation**. But living, growing plant life is God's achievement, and reminds us of his vital power, wisdom, and glory.* (Johnson, 2003, p. 54)[103]

Cain just wanted to continue on, building things and gaining control over the people, by reason, among other things, so that nobody could get to him. Of course, the rush he began to have, due to originating it all, was probably a good reprieve from all of the mental anguish he usually had inside. Quite possibly, the building of a city was Cain's vain attempt to, somehow, immortalize *himself* and this way of living.[104]

And, interestingly enough, it does seem to further prove that there were a lot *more* people on the earth at this time. A city is a lot for one person to build. Where did all of his help come from? We are not talking about a house here, or even a couple of neighborhoods - but a *city*.[105] He must have been able to recruit help from many people around him, whether they be of his immediate family, or on the outside.

Poets and painters have depicted Cain as going into exile accompanied by an Adamite wife and family, but the Bible leads us to infer that before the birth of Seth only Cain and Abel had been born to Adam and Eve. We are prepared, therefore, to find that Cain had settled among a non-Adamite race when he built a city and founded a family... (Bristowe, 1927, p. 14)[106]

If there were a good number of people on the earth at this time, all of them, once, must have been located close to the Garden of Eden. And, as more and more began to look to Cain for their "salvation," they began to flock to the cities Cain had underway. They also felt that they, if needed, could exploit whatever resources around them, for their own needs, as well.[107] Ancient sources tell us that Cain not only built one city, but *seven*.[108]

As in today, the cities of Cain's day eventually became filled with violence and debauchery. Cain, and others who came to power under him, assuredly amassed wealth by the rapine of the land, as well as over other groups of individuals.

> *A Jewish history says: "Cain dwelt in the earth trembling according as God had appointed him after he slew Abel his brother." But it adds "and he began to build cities" and "he founded seven cities," which indicates that new **courage** came to him; and the Babylonian inscriptions show whence it came. According to them it was the **Devil** who adopted Sargon and in exchange for his worship and obedience gave him **power** and **wealth**.*
> (Bristowe, 1927, p. 152)[109]

> *This building of (Cain's) cities was a godless deed, for he surrounded them with a wall, forcing his family to remain within. All his other doings were equally impious. The punishment God had ordained for him did not effect any improvement... He also introduced a change in the **simplicity** wherein men had lived before, and he was the author of measures and weights. And whereas men lived **innocently** while they knew nothing of such arts, he changed the world into cunning craftiness.*
> (Ginzberg, 1909, p. 117)[110]

The innocent, tent-dwelling lives of so many before, as in those who followed the ways of God, were coming to an end.[111] The world of those who lived under Cain were about to become a lot more complicated. His desire to build things, as well as *possess* things, became forefront in his mind. Eventually, he began to move beyond this immediate area, and expand his ways of living to all the people he came across.[112]

Cain's Power - Beginning at Eden?

One of the earliest cities of Sargon (i.e. Cain) was called *Eridu*, in southern Babylonia. Could this have, actually, been located in the same place *Eden* was once located?

> *The primitive home of Tammuz had been in that Garden of Eden or Edin which Babylonian tradition placed in the immediate vicinity of **Eridu**. (Hibbert Lectures, p. 23.)... It was at **Eridu** that the Garden of the Babylonian Eden was placed.*
> (Bristowe, 1927, p. 70-71 (and notes))[113]

*Sir Leonard Woolley... says "the Sumerians believed (Eridu) to be the **oldest city** upon the earth" (Ur of the Chaldees, p.13).*   (Bristowe, 1950, p. 65)[114]

Beyond Eridu, other cities built by Cain were called *Ur*, *Enoch*, and, of course, one of the most famous city of ancient times: ***Babylon***.[115]

*...in the Encyclopedia Britannica we read: "The history of the city of **Babylon** can now be traced back to the days of **Sargon** of Agade (before 3000 B.C.), who appears to have given that city its name".*   (Bristowe, 1927, p. 80)[116]

*If we rule out the possibility of its having been built by the pre-Adamites, **Babylon** may have been one of the **seven cities** attributed to Cain in Jewish traditions.*
                                    (Bristowe, 1927, p. 80)[117]

Cain Ruled Over Groups of People

What about the *pre-Adamites* and *Adamites* who lived in these areas around the Garden, the ones Cain was beginning to unite in these cities?

*At **Babylon** there was a great resort of people... who... lived in a lawless manner like the beasts of the field.*   - Berossus Of the Cosmology and Deluge [118]

One way or another, *Cain* probably made use of this angelic knowledge to become a very crafty and powerful leader. We recall that one interpretation of Cain's "mark" was the *horn*. Could this *horn* have been part of his warrior attire? Or, could this have signified that Cain had divine *knowledge* on his side?

*Perhaps the story of the horn arose from the fact that **Sargon** wore a horned helmet... Professor King says: "He wears a **helmet** adorned with the **horns** of a bull, and he carries a battle-axe and a bow and arrow."*   (Bristowe, 1927, p. 142 (notes))[119]

Beyond his knowledge, he probably used physical *suggestion* to get his point across. He looked intimidating, one way or another. According to ancient sources, Cain could have then conquered a number of different kinds, or races, of people. Many of them, as well, may have once made Cain fearful, so he showed no discretion on who he ruled. As previously stated, he was probably afraid that any and all would take vengeance upon him, for Abel's murder:

> *...the black race... (were the)... race of whom Cain was afraid.*
> (Bristowe, 1950, p. 7)[120]

> *If, as Professor Sayce thinks probable, Babylonia was the country to which Cain journeyed and if, as the same authority suggests, the first inhabitants of that country were blacks, it is easy to imagine Cain, a white man endowed with **superhuman knowledge** and physique and rendered invulnerable by some **divine talisman**, taking command...*
> (Bristowe, 1927, p. 15-16)[121]

Imagine someone everyone knows of, running around, adored with horns and animal skins, sporting a lot of divine knowledge and power? That would be quite shocking to most! And, yet again, we learn another meaning of the word *Cain*: a *spear*. Yes, he became, probably, very war-like indeed! Of course, he probably was able to create weapons of war because of his knowledge of being a *smith*. See how it all ties together?

Also, the original Hebrew for the English word *spear*, as in the above, is *Qayin*. It not only means *Cain*, but also something else:

<u>Qayin (7014)</u> - *Kajin, the name of first child (Cain)... (and) an **Oriental** tribe*[122]

Could Cain have had some type of connection to Oriental tribes, back then? Could he have once been a *leader* of them? Were they under his *spear* of domination? We're not sure. But, assuredly, people of all colors, along with descendents of Adam, were probably being subdued by Cain, and made to move into his new cities.[123]

We also see that:

*Again, for straws show which way the wind blows, the **Chinese** Imperial title, Ruler of the Yellow, the coveted order of the Yellow Jacket, the Yellow titles of the Imperial palaces and the temples, the Yellow Imperial color and the Yellow River are all curiously suggestive considering that, for some unknown reason, **yellow is Cain's traditional color**. Shakespeare wrote: "a little beard, a **Cain**-colored beard;" and in ancient tapestries Cain's **beard** is always **yellow**.*

(Bristowe, 1927, p. 148-149)[124]

Maybe those who eventually crossed into *China* took Cain's influences with them. This also seems to give us a little information on what Cain may have really looked like. Obviously, he wasn't *blackened* by God on the outside, or made to have *black* skin. He wasn't any father of black people - he *conquered* a lot of them. He conquered Orientals/Asians, as well. He conquered Whites. He even conquered a number of Adam's descendants in the area, as well. People from every creed and location were beginning to take his lead.

And, the above tells us that Sargon (a.k.a. Cain) was, actuality, described as being light-skinned, with thick, prominent-looking blonde hair (and a most-prominent beard of the same color). With his intimidating dress, his divine knowledge, and his angelic power-backing, Cain probably found a great role for himself as world-conqueror:

*It must be remembered too, that the theory of **Cain's** presence in Babylonia offers the best explanation for the sudden arrival in that country of a marvelous civilization and culture, and relieves us of the necessity of believing that it was gradually evolved... that it seems to be the key to... the problem of the origin of idolatry - to the problem of the ancient civilizations attributed to the **Children of the Sun-god**...*

(Bristowe, 1927, p. 151)[125]

The "Sun-God"... How His Ideas Spread About

After solidifying his empire, a number of people began to spread, throughout the ancient world, and probably brought these influences of Cain along with them, and onto their descendants.[126]

*...Cain was the **human original** of the Sun-god whose followers wandered into every climate, carrying with them the culture of the ancient Babylonians and the leaven of malice and wickedness as well.* (Bristowe, 1927, p. 129)[127]

*In some **far-off lands** the Sun-god's name was "**Kane**" (The Children of the Sun. W. J. Perry, p. 167).* (Bristowe, 1927, p. 88 (notes))[128]

So, now, we are beginning to see just how much *Cain* and *the Serpent* influenced the human race, as we know it. How much more could these other, terrestrial angels of the time strive to expand *themselves*, and *their influences*, to the world, as well (with more of the same)? Where would all these pagan influences begin to take our world, in consequence? More coming up, in part 2.

- End of Part 1 -

Endnotes

Preface

[1] Thinkexist.com, *Dr. Carl Sagan quotes*, http://en.thinkexist.com/quotes/Dr._Carl_Sagan/ (accessed Dec. 22, 2009).

[2] *Luke* 17:26 (KJV).

[3] J. Preston Eby, *The World System*, 2, http://www.theshop.net/giess/world.html (accessed Aug. 17, 2000) 4.

[4] Andrew Collins, *From the Ashes of Angels* (Rochester, Vermont: Bear & Company, 1996), 20.

Chapter 1

[1] Robert Graves and Raphael Patai, *Hebrew Myths: The Book of Genesis* (Garden City, New York: Doubleday & Company, 1964), 45.

[2] *Targum Neofiti 1: Genesis / Translated, With Apparatus and Notes*, 3:24, trans. Martin McNamara (Collegeville, Minnesota: Liturgical Press, 1992), 63; James L. Kugel, *Traditions of the Bible* (Cambridge, Massachusetts: Harvard University Press, 1998), 57.

[3] *The First Earth Age*, 1-2, http://www.adamqadmon.com/nephilim/firstearthage.html (accessed Dec. 7, 2000); Stephen Quayle, *Genesis 6 Giants: The Master Builders of Prehistoric and Ancient Civilizations* (Bozeman, Montana: End Time Thunder Publishers, 2005), 10-16, 23.

[4] *The Book of the Mysteries of the Heavens and the Earth and Other Works of Bakhayla Mikael (Zosimas)*, trans. E.A. Wallis Budge (London: Oxford University Press, 1935), 8.

[5] J. Preston Eby, *The World System*, 1, http://www.theshop.net/giess/world.html (accessed Aug. 17, 2000); Strong's G2889 - *kosmos*, http://www.blueletterbible.org/lang/lexicon/lexicon.cfm?Strongs=G2889&t=KJV.html (accessed Dec. 23, 2009).

[6] Stephen Quayle, *Genesis 6 Giants: The Master Builders of Prehistoric and Ancient Civilizations* (Bozeman, Montana: End Time Thunder Publishers, 2005), 12, 14, 20-22.

[7] Strong's H7725 - *re'shiyth*, http://www.blueletterbible.org/lang/lexicon/lexicon.cfm?Strongs=H7225&t=KJV.html (accessed Dec. 23, 2009).

[8] The Bible, Genesis & Geology, *Understanding the Biblical Difference Between the Words "World" and "Earth"*, http://www.kjvbible.org/theworlds.html (accessed Dec. 23, 2009).

[9] Strong's G104 - *aei*, http://www.blueletterbible.org/lang/lexicon/lexicon.cfm?Strongs=G104&t=KJV.html (accessed Dec. 23, 2009).

[10] Strong's H8414 - *tohuw*, http://www.blueletterbible.org/lang/lexicon/lexicon.cfm?Strongs=H8414&t=KJV.html (accessed Dec. 23, 2009).

[11] Strongs's H922 - *bohuw*, http://www.blueletterbible.org/lang/lexicon/lexicon.cfm?Strongs=H922&t=KJV.html (accessed Dec. 23, 2009).

[12] Strong's H1961 - *hayah*, http://www.blueletterbible.org/lang/lexicon/lexicon.cfm?Strongs=H1961&t=KJV.html (accessed Dec. 23, 2009).

[13] Robert Bowie Johnson, Jr., *The Parthenon Code: Mankind's History in Marble* (Annapolis, Maryland: Solving Light Books, 2004), 205.

[14] J. Preston Eby, *The World System*, 5, http://www.theshop.net/giess/world.html (accessed Aug. 17, 2000 **4**); *The Companion Bible*, Appendix 146 (Grand Rapids, Michigan: Kregel Publications, 1990), 171; Robert Bowie Johnson, Jr., *The Parthenon Code: Mankind's History in Marble* (Annapolis, Maryland: Solving Light Books, 2004), 206.

[15] Strong's G2602 - *katabole*, http://www.blueletterbible.org/lang/lexicon/lexicon.cfm?Strongs=G2602&t=KJV.html (accessed Dec. 23, 2009).

[16] The Bible, Genesis & Geology, *Understanding the Biblical Difference Between the Words "World" and "Earth"*, http://www.kjvbible.org/theworlds.html (accessed Dec. 23, 2009).

[17] Greg Killian, *The Days of Noah*, 29-30, www.adamqadmon.com/nephilim/gkillian000 (accessed Dec. 6, 2000).

[18] Robert Bowie Johnson, Jr., *The Parthenon Code: Mankind's History in Marble* (Annapolis, Maryland: Solving Light Books, 2004), 45.

[19] The Bible, Genesis & Geology, *Understanding the Biblical Difference Between the Words "World" and "Earth"*, 5, http://www.kjvbible.org/theworlds.html (accessed Dec. 23, 2009).

[20] *The First Earth Age*, 4, http://www.adamqadmon.com/nephilim/firstearthage.html (accessed Dec. 7, 2000).

[21] *Pseudo - Philo (The Biblical Antiquities of Philo)*, 3:9, trans. M. R. James (1917), 81, http://www.sacred-texts.com/bib/bap/bap19.htm (accessed July 13, 2006).

[22] *The Works of Philo Judaeus*, Questions and Answers on Genesis II, 54, trans. C. D. Yonge (London: H. G. Bohn, 1854-1855).

[23] *Saltair na Rann*, 2437-2340, trans. David Greene.

[24] Stephen Quayle, *Genesis 6 Giants: The Master Builders of Prehistoric and Ancient Civilizations* (Bozeman, Montana: End Time Thunder Publishers, 2005), 52.

[25] The Bible, Genesis & Geology, *Subject: 12,000-Year-Old Human Hair DNA Has No Match With Modern Humans*,

3, http://www.kjvbible.org/earthfilesstory.html (accessed Dec. 11, 2007).

26 Stephen Quayle, *Genesis 6 Giants: The Master Builders of Prehistoric and Ancient Civilizations* (Bozeman, Montana: End Time Thunder Publishers, 2005), 57-58.

Chapter 2

1 *The Sibylline Oracles, Translated from the Greek into English blank Verse*, First Fragment (Notes), trans. Milton S. Terry (New York: Hunt & Eaton, 1890).

2 *The First Book of Adam and Eve (The Conflict of Adam and Eve with Satan)*, 27:10, trans. S. C. Malan (London: Williams and Norgate, 1882).

3 Augustine, *The City of God*, Book 11, Chapter 9 - What the Scriptures Teach Us To Believe Concerning the Creation of the Angels, http://www.newadvent.org/fathers/120111.htm (accessed Dec. 15, 2009).

4 Answers.com, *light*, 1, http://www.answers.com/topic/light (accessed Oct. 3, 2005).

5 Rabbi Leo Jung, Ph. D., *Fallen Angels in Jewish, Christian and Mohammedan Literature* (New York: KTAV Publishing House, 1974), 99.

6 Robert Graves and Raphael Patai, *Hebrew Myths: The Book of Genesis* (Garden City, New York: Doubleday & Company, 1964), 102; James L. Kugel, *The Bible As It Was*, (Cambridge, Massachusetts: Harvard University Press, 1997), 58, 60; *The Book of the Rolls (Kitab Al-Magall)*, 6, trans. Margaret Dunlop Gibson, Apocrypha Arabica (London: C.J Clay and Sons, 1901), 3; Christian Geology: Science and Scripture, *Introduction: Beyond Gap Theory Interpretation of Genesis*, 8, http://kjvbible.org/gap_theory.html (accessed Aug. 29, 2005); *The Lebor Gabala Erren*, 2, http://www.ancienttexts.org/library/celtic/irish/lebor.html (accessed May 26, 2005); James L. Kugel, *Traditions of the Bible* (Cambridge, Massachusetts: Harvard University Press, 1998), 76; *The Book of Jubilees*, 2:2, trans. R. H. Charles, The Apocrypha and Pseudepigrapha of the Old Testament (Oxford, Clarendon Press, 1913).

7 *The Shepherd of Hermas*, First Book: Visions, Third Vision, Ch. IV, 6, Roberts-Donaldson English Translation, http://www.earlychristianwritings.com/text/shepherd.html (accessed Dec. 16, 2009).

8 *The Book of the Cave of Treasures*, The First Thousand Years: Adam to Yared (Jared), The Creation, First Day, trans. Sir E. A. Wallis Budge (London: The Religious Tract Society, 1927), 43-46.

9 *The Book of Jubilees*, 2:2 (also 2:8), trans. R. H. Charles, The Apocrypha and Pseudepigrapha of the Old Testament (Oxford: Clarendon Press, 1913).

10 Louis Ginzberg, *The Legends of the Jews Volume I: From the Creation to Jacob* (Baltimore, Maryland: The Johns Hopkins University Press, 1909), 135.

11 *2 Enoch (The Book of the Secrets of Enoch)*, 25:1, trans. W. R. Morfill, M. A. (Oxford: Clarendon Press, 1896).

12 Louis Ginzberg, *The Legends of the Jews Volume I: From the Creation to Jacob*, trans. Henrietta Szold (Baltimore, Maryland: The Johns Hopkins University Press, 1909), 135.

13 *The Book of the Bee*, Chapter 2: Of the Creation of the Seven Natures (Substances) in Silence, trans. Earnest A. Wallis Budge, M.A., http://www.sacred-texts.com/chr/bb/bb02.htm (accessed Dec. 23, 2009).

14 *The Penitence of our Forefather Adam*, Adam and Abel's Funerary Rites [47]39.3, trans. Gary A. Anderson and Michael E. Stone, http://www2.iath.virginia.edu/anderson/viat/english/vita.arm.html (accessed Dec 26, 2009).

15 Augustine, *The City of God*, Book XI, Chapter 9 - What the Scriptures Teach Us To Believe Concerning the Creation of the Angels, http://www.newadvent.org/fathers/120111.htm (accessed Dec. 15, 2009).

16 *The Book of Jubilees*, 2:2, trans. R. H. Charles, The Apocrypha and Pseudepigrapha of the Old Testament (Oxford: Clarendon Press, 1913).

17 *The Book of the Mysteries of the Heavens and the Earth and Other Works of Bakhayla Mikael (Zosimas)*, trans. E.A. Wallis Budge (London: Oxford University Press, 1935), 12.

18 Answers.com, *dark*, 1, http://www.answers.com/topic/dark (accessed Oct. 3, 2005).

19 Watchmen Bible Study Group, *When Was the Beginning?*, 6, http://biblestudysite.com/begin.html (accessed Dec. 6, 2006).

20 Answers.com, *night*, 1, http://www.answers.com/topic/night (accessed Oct. 3, 2005).

21 Stephen Quayle, *Genesis 6 Giants: The Master Builders of Prehistoric and Ancient Civilizations* (Bozeman, Montana: End Time Thunder Publishers, 2005), 16; G. H. Pember, M. A., *Earth's Earliest Ages and their Connection With Modern Spiritualism, Theosophy, and Buddhism* (Grand Rapids, Michigan: Kregel Publications, 1975), 69.

22 Answers.com, *black and white dualism*, 1, http://www.answers.com/topic/black-and-white-dualism (accessed Feb. 9, 2010).

23 Answers.com, *chthonic*, 1-2, http://www.answers.com/topic/chthonic (accessed Feb. 9, 2010).

24 *The Book of the Mysteries of the Heavens and the Earth and Other Works of Bakhayla Mikael (Zosimas)*, trans. E.A. Wallis Budge (London: Oxford University Press, 1935), 13.

25 Stephen Quayle, *Genesis 6 Giants: The Master Builders of Prehistoric and Ancient Civilizations* (Bozeman, Montana: End Time Thunder Publishers, 2005), 16; *On the Origin of the World*, 1-2, http://www.earth-history.com/Judaism/origin-world.htm (accessed May 10, 2007).

26 Stephen Quayle, *Genesis 6 Giants: The Master Builders of Prehistoric and Ancient Civilizations* (Bozeman, Montana: End Time Thunder Publishers, 2005), 16-17.

27 Wikipedia, the Free Encyclopedia, *Pre-existence*, 1-4, http://en.wikipedia.org/wiki/Pre-existence (accessed May 14, 2007).

28 Watchmen Bible Study Group, *When Was the Beginning?*, 8-12, http://biblestudysite.com/begin.html (accessed Dec. 6, 2006).

29 *Welcome to 3 World Ages*, 1, http://www.geocities.com/Vienna/6787/word4.html (accessed Oct. 21, 2005).

30 *The Book of Jubilees*, 2:7, trans. R. H. Charles, The Apocrypha and Pseudepigrapha of the Old Testament (Oxford: Clarendon Press, 1913).

31 The Bible, Genesis & Geology, *Understanding the Biblical Difference Between the Words "World" and "Earth"*, 4, http://www.kjvbible.org/theworlds.html (accessed Sept. 29, 2005).

Chapter 3

1 *Genizah Manuscripts of Palestinian Targum to the Pentateuch Volume One*, Genesis 2:20, trans. Michael L. Klein (Cincinnati: Hebrew Union College Press, 1986), 2.

2 *The Companion Bible*, Appendix 13 (Grand Rapids, Michigan: Kregel Publications, 1990), 19.

3 *The Zohar*, Volume 11, Safra Det'zniuta, Section 3. Third Chapter, 38, https://www2.kabbalah.com/k/index.php/p=zohar/zohar&vol=22&sec=816 (accessed March 16, 2010).

4 *The Babylonian Talmud*, Jews' College / Soncino English Translation, Yebamoth 98a, http://www.halakhah.com/yebamoth/yebamoth_98.html (accessed Dec. 28, 2010).

5 *The Writings of Abraham*, 29:8, http://www.earth-history.com/Pseudepigrapha/Mormonism/writings-abraham-1.htm (accessed May 10, 2007); *Armenian Apocrypha Relating to the Patriarchs and Prophets*, The Words of Adam To Seth 1, 16, 18, trans. Michael E. Stone (Jerusalem: The Israel Academy of Sciences and Humanities, 1982), 12-13.

6 Dictionary.com, *behemoth*, 3, http://dictionary.reference.com/search?r=2&q=behemoth (accessed May 16, 2007).

7 Bible Hub, *Genesis 7:14*, 2, http://biblehub.com/text/genesis/7-14.htm (accessed June 5, 2017); Bible Hub, *5775. oph*, 1, http://biblehub.com/hebrew/5775.htm (accessed June 5, 2017).

8 *The Midrash Rabbah*, Bereshith (Genesis) 1:3 (& notes), trans. Rabbi Dr. H. Freedman and Maurice Simon (London: The Soncino Press, 1961).

9 *The Book of Adam*, 19:2, trans. J. P. Mahe, http://www.pseudepigrapha.com/pseudepigrapha/TheBookOfAdam.htm (accessed June 27, 2005).

10 Johann Andreas Eisenmenger, *The Traditions of the Jews, Contained in the Talmud and other Mystical Writings* (London: J. Robinson, 1748), 130-131; Mrs. Sydney Bristowe, *Sargon the Magnificent* (London: The Covenant Publishing Co., 1927), 102; Andrew Collins, *From the Ashes of Angels* (Rochester, Vermont: Bear & Company, 1996), 57-59; *The Penitence of our Forefather Adam*, Separation of Adam and Eve 20.2, trans. Gary A. Anderson and Michael E. Stone, http://www2.iath.virginia.edu/anderson/viat/english/vita.arm.html (accessed Dec 26, 2009).

11 *The Book of Adam*, 20:2, trans. J. P. Mahe, http://www.pseudepigrapha.com/pseudepigrapha/TheBookOfAdam.htm (accessed June 27, 2005).

12 Bob Curran, *Dark Fairies* (Pompton Plaines, New Jersey: The Career Press, Inc., 2010), 65.

13 *Acts 17:26*, 1, http://biblehub.com/text/acts/17-26.htm (accessed Dec. 23, 2016).

14 Blue Letter Bible, *Acts 17:26*, 1, https://www.blueletterbible.org/kjv/act/17/1/t_conc_1035026 (accessed Dec. 23, 2016); Blue Letter Bible, Strong's G129 - *haima*, 1, https://www.blueletterbible.org/lang/lexicon/lexicon.cfm?Strongs=G129&t=KJV (accessed Dec. 23, 2016).

15 (From Dr. William Boyd, *Races and People* (1955), 145) *Was Adam the First Man?*, 5, http://www.seek-info.com/adam.htm (accessed Sept. 10, 2000).

16 Wikipedia, the free encyclopedia, *Polygenism*, 1, http://en.wikipedia.org/wiki/Polygenism (accessed Nov. 21, 2006).

Chapter 4

1 *The Sibylline Oracles, Translated from the Greek into English blank Verse*, Second Fragment, Lines 13-18, trans. Milton S. Terry (New York: Hunt & Eaton, 1890).

2 Mrs. Sydney Bristowe, *Sargon the Magnificent* (London: The Covenant Publishing Co., 1927), 17.

3 *The Zohar*, Volume 15, Tazria, Section 22, Man, person, 107, https://www2.kabbalah.com/k/index.php?p=zohar/zohar&vol=30&sec=1090 (accessed Feb. 26, 2010).

4 S. Baring-Gould, *Legends of the Patriarchs and Prophets and Other Old Testament Characters* (New York: American Book Exchange, 1881), 28.

5 *The Companion Bible*, Appendix 14 (Grand Rapids, Michigan: Kregel Publications, 1990), 21; *Gen.* 1:26, 2:5, 5:1 (KJV).

6 *The Companion Bible*, Appendix 14 (Grand Rapids, Michigan: Kregel Publications, 1990), 21; *Gen.* 2:7, 2:8, 2:15 (KJV).

7 *The Companion Bible*, Genesis 2:7, Appendix 14 (Grand Rapids, Michigan: Kregel Publications, 1990), 5, 21.

8 *The Companion Bible*, Appendix 14, Appendix 24 (Grand Rapids, Michigan: Kregel Publications, 1990), 21, 27; Mrs. Sydney Bristowe, *Sargon the Magnificent* (London: The Covenant Publishing Co., 1927), 17.

9 *Targum Pseudo-Jonathan (Targum of Palestine / Targum of Jonathan Ben Uzziel)*, On the Book of Genesis, Section 3, Berashith, http://targum.info/pj/pjgen1-6.htm (accessed Oct. 2, 2009).

[10] *The History of al-Tabari - Volume I: General Introduction and From the Creation to the Flood*, The Story of Adam, 87, trans. Franz Rosenthal (Albany: New York Press, 1989), 258.

[11] *The History of al-Tabari - Volume I: General Introduction and From the Creation to the Flood*, The Story of Adam, 91, trans. Franz Rosenthal (Albany: New York Press, 1989), 263.

[12] *The Bible, The Koran, and the Talmud (Biblical Legends of the Mussulmans)*, Adam (A Mohammedan Legend), trans. Dr. G. Weil (New York, 1863), 22.

[13] Strongs's H6754 - *tselem*, http://www.blueletterbible.org/lang/lexicon/lexicon.cfm?Strongs=H6754&t=KJV.html (accessed Dec. 17, 2009).

[14] Stephen Quayle, *Genesis 6 Giants: The Master Builders of Prehistoric and Ancient Civilizations* (Bozeman, Montana: End Time Thunder Publishers, 2005), 23-4.

[15] Strong's G444 – *anthropos*, http://www.blueletterbible.org/lang/lexicon/lexicon.cfm?Strongs=G444&t=KJV.html (accessed Dec. 17, 2009).

[16] *The Book of the Bee*, 14, trans. Earnest A Wallis Budge, M.A., http://www.sacred-texts.com/chr/bb/bb14.htm (accessed Oct. 10, 2004); *Armenian Apocrypha Relating to Adam and Eve*, 9, 13, 25, trans. Michael E. Stone (Leiden: E. J. Brill, 1996), 33, 35, 45; James L. Kugel, *Traditions of the Bible* (Cambridge, Massachusetts: Harvard University Press, 1998), 114-5; *Barhebraeus' Scholia on the Old Testament Part I: Genesis - II Samuel*, Genesis 2:25, trans. Martin Sprengling and William Creighton Graham (Chicago, Illinois: University of Chicago Press, 1931), 25.

[17] *Saltair na Rann*, 1789-1796, trans. David Greene.

[18] E. S. G. Bristowe, *Cain - An Argument* (Leicester: Edgar Backus, 1950), 91-92.

[19] *Targum Pseudo-Jonathan (Targum of Palestine / Targum of Jonathan Ben Uzziel)*, On the Book of Genesis, Section 2, Berashith, http://targum.info/pj/pjgen1-6.htm (accessed Oct. 2, 2009).

[20] *The Book of the Mysteries of the Heavens and the Earth and Other Works of Bakhayla Mikael (Zosimas)*, trans. E.A. Wallis Budge (London: Oxford University Press, 1935), 8.

[21] *The History of al-Tabari - Volume I: General Introduction and From the Creation to the Flood*, The Story of Adam, 91, trans. Franz Rosenthal (Albany: New York Press, 1989), 263.

[22] E. S. G. Bristowe, *Cain - An Argument* (Leicester: Edgar Backus, 1950), 7; *The First Book of Adam and Eve (The Conflict of Adam and Eve with Satan)*, 34:14, trans. S. C. Malan (London: Williams and Norgate, 1882).

[23] Mrs. Sydney Bristowe, *Sargon the Magnificent* (London: The Covenant Publishing Co., 1927), 16-17.

[24] *2 Enoch (The Book of the Secrets of Enoch)*, 65:2, trans. W. R. Morfill, M. A. (Oxford: Clarendon Press, 1896).

[25] *The First Book of Adam and Eve (The Conflict of Adam and Eve with Satan)*, 34:8, trans. S. C. Malan (London: Williams and Norgate, 1882).

[26] *The Words of the Heavenly Lights* (The Dead Sea Scrolls), (4Q504), Fr. 8 recto, trans. Geza Vermes, *The Complete Dead Sea Scrolls in English* (New York: Penguin Books, 1997), 367.

[27] *Targum Pseudo-Jonathan (Targum of Palestine / Targum of Jonathan Ben Uzziel)*, On the Book of Genesis, Section 2, Berashith, http://targum.info/pj/pjgen1-6.htm (accessed Oct. 2, 2009).

[28] *The Book of Jubilees*, 4:15, trans. R. H. Charles, The Apocrypha and Pseudepigrapha of the Old Testament (Oxford: Clarendon Press, 1913).

[29] *The Companion Bible*, Gen. 2:7, Appendix 14 (Grand Rapids, Michigan: Kregel Publications, 1990) 5, 21.

[30] *The Book of the Cave of Treasures*, The First Thousand Years: Adam to Yared (Jared), The Revolt of Satan, and the Battle in Heaven, trans. Sir E. A. Wallis Budge (London: The Religious Tract Society, 1927) 55-59; *The Armenian Apocryphal Adam Literature*, History of the Repentance of Adam and Eve, the First Created Ones, and How They Did It 21, trans. William Lowndes Lipscomb (Ann Arbor, Michigan: University Microfilms International, 1983), 224; *Saltair na Rann*, 2245-2248, trans. David Greene; *The History of al-Tabari - Volume I: General Introduction and From the Creation to the Flood,* The Story of Adam, 87, trans. Franz Rosenthal (Albany: New York Press, 1989), 258-259.

[31] *The Book of the Cave of Treasures*, The First Thousand Years: Adam to Yared (Jared), The Creation of Adam, trans. Sir E. A. Wallis Budge (London: The Religious Tract Society, 1927), 51-55.

[32] *The Book of Adam*, [37]10.3, trans. J. P. Mahe, http://www.pseudepigrapha.com/pseudepigrapha/TheBookOfAdam.htm (accessed June 27, 2005).

[33] Strong's H119 - *adam*, http://www.blueletterbible.org/lang/lexicon/lexicon.cfm?Strongs=H119&t=KJV (accessed Dec. 17, 2009).

[34] Wikipedia, the Free Encyclopedia, *Adam*, 5, http://en.wikipedia.org/wiki/Adam (accessed Aug 28, 2007).

[35] E. S. G. Bristowe, *Cain - An Argument* (Leicester: Edgar Backus, 1950), 60.

[36] *Saltair na Rann*, 1401-1412, trans. David Greene; Wikipedia, the Free Encyclopedia, *Adam*, 5, http://en.wikipedia.org/wiki/Adam (accessed Aug 28, 2007).

[37] *The Book of Enoch*, 106:2, trans. R. H. Charles (Montana: Kessinger Publishing, 1912).

[38] *Barhebraeus' Scholia on the Old Testament Part I: Genesis - II Samuel*, Genesis 2:7, trans. Martin Sprengling and William Creighton Graham (Chicago, Illinois: University of Chicago Press 1931), 19.

[39] Gesenius' Lexicon - *aphar*, http://www.blueletterbible.org/lang/lexicon/lexicon.cfm?Strongs=H6083&t=KJV (accessed Dec. 17, 2009).

[40] *The Apocalypse of Moses / Apocalypsis Mosis*, 6:2, 9:3, trans. R. H. Charles, http://www.pseudepigrapha.com/pseudepigrapha/aprmose.htm (accessed June 27, 2005); *The Book of Adam*, [36]9.3,

trans. J. P. Mahe, http://www.pseudepigrapha.com/pseudepigrapha/TheBookOfAdam.htm (accessed June 27, 2005).

[41] Star Wars, *Lesson Seven - The Serpent*, 1, http://usa-the-republic.com/religion/star%20wars/Star%20Wars%20-%20Lesson%20Seven.htm (accessed April 23, 2005).

[42] *Targum Pseudo-Jonathan (Targum of Palestine / Targum of Jonathan Ben Uzziel)*, On the Book of Genesis, Section 3, Berashith, http://targum.info/pj/pjgen1-6.htm (accessed Oct. 2, 2009).

[43] Strong's H6635 - *tsaba*, http://www.blueletterbible.org/lang/lexicon/lexicon.cfm?Strongs=H6635&t=KJV# (accessed Jan. 4, 2010); Lambert Dolphin, *The Ruin of Creation*, 1, http://www.adamqadmon.com/nephilim/dolphin-ruin.html (accessed Dec 5, 2000).

[44] *The Sibylline Oracles, Translated from the Greek into English blank Verse*, Second Fragment, Lines 13-18, trans. Milton S. Terry (New York: Hunt & Eaton, 1890). ·

[45] *The Book of the Generations of Adam*, 1:3, 3:1, http://www.earth-history.com/Pseudepigrapha/generations-adam.htm (accessed May 5, 2007).

[46] Mrs. Sydney Bristowe, *Sargon the Magnificent* (London: The Covenant Publishing Co., 1927), 29.

[47] *The Chronicles of Jerahmeel* (*The Hebrew Bible Historiale*), 6:14, trans. M. Gaster, Ph. D. (London: The Royal Asiatic Society, 1899) 17.

[48] *The Chronicles of Jerahmeel* (*The Hebrew Bible Historiale*), 6:14, trans. M. Gaster, Ph. D. (London: The Royal Asiatic Society, 1899), 17.

Chapter 5

[1] Andrew Collins, *From the Ashes of Angels* (Rochester, Vermont: Bear & Company, 1996), 151; *The Theme of Paradise*, 1, http://www.adamqadmon.com/watchers/paradise.html (accessed Feb. 10, 2001); Wikipedia, the Free Encyclopedia, *Garden of Eden*, 2, http://en.wikipedia.org/wiki/Garden_of_Eden (accessed April 23, 2007); James L. Kugel, *Traditions of the Bible* (Cambridge, Massachusetts: Harvard University Press, 1998), 110.

[2] Ezekiel 28:14 (KJV); James L. Kugel, *Traditions of the Bible* (Cambridge, Massachusetts: Harvard University Press, 1998), 162; Robert Graves and Raphael Patai, *Hebrew Myths: The Book of Genesis* (Garden City, New York: Doubleday & Company, 1964), 73, 105.

[3] Wikipedia, the Free Encyclopedia, *Garden of Eden*, 2, http://en.wikipedia.org/wiki/Garden_of_Eden (accessed April 23, 2007); Andrew Collins, *From the Ashes of Angels* (Rochester, Vermont: Bear & Company, 1996), 151.

[4] Andrew Collins, *From the Ashes of Angels* (Rochester, Vermont: Bear & Company, 1996), 151; *The Theme of Paradise*, 1, http://www.adamqadmon.com/watchers/paradise.html (accessed Feb. 10, 2001).

[5] *The Penitence of our Forefather Adam*, Serpent's Approach to Paradise [44]17.3, trans. Gary A. Anderson and Michael E. Stone, http://www2.iath.virginia.edu/anderson/viat/english/vita.arm.html (accessed Dec 26, 2009).

[6] *The Book of Adam*, [32]7.3b-[33].1, trans. J. P. Mahe, http://www.pseudepigrapha.com/pseudepigrapha/TheBookOfAdam.htm (accessed June 27, 2005).

[7] Andrew Collins, *From the Ashes of Angels* (Rochester, Vermont: Bear & Company, 1996), 69.

[8] *The Armenian Apocryphal Adam Literature*, History of the Creation and Transgression of Adam 1, trans. William Lowndes Lipscomb (Ann Arbor, Michigan: University Microfilms International, 1983), 118.

[9] *The First Book of Adam and Eve (The Conflict of Adam and Eve with Satan)*, 13:4, trans. S. C. Malan (London: Williams and Norgate, 1882).

[10] *The History of al-Tabari – Volume I: General Introduction and From the Creation to the Flood*, The Story of Iblis, 81, trans. Franz Rosenthal (Albany: New York Press, 1989), 252.

[11] *2 Enoch (The Book of the Secrets of Enoch)*, 31:1-5, trans. W. R. Morfill, M. A. (Oxford: Clarendon Press, 1896).

[12] Robert Graves and Raphael Patai, *Hebrew Myths: The Book of Genesis* (Garden City, New York: Doubleday & Company, 1964), 85; *The Penitence of our Forefather Adam*, Fall of Satan 12.1, trans. Gary A. Anderson and Michael E. Stone, http://www2.iath.virginia.edu/anderson/viat/english/vita.arm.html (accessed Dec 26, 2009).

[13] *The History of al-Tabari - Volume I: General Introduction and From the Creation to the Flood*, The Story of Iblis, 84, 81, trans. Franz Rosenthal (Albany: New York Press, 1989), 252-253, 255

[14] *The Midrash Rabbah*, Bereshith (Genesis) 26:7, trans. Rabbi Dr. H. Freedman and Maurice Simon (London: The Soncino Press, 1961).

[15] *The Armenian Apocryphal Adam Literature*, History of the Creation and Transgression of Adam 1-4, trans. William Lowndes Lipscomb (Ann Arbor, Michigan: University Microfilms International, 1983), 118-119.

[16] *Saltair na Rann*, 1729-1752, 1777-1784, 1821-1844, 1865-1880, trans. David Greene; *The Armenian Apocryphal Adam Literature*, History and Sermon: Concerning the Creation of Adam and the Incarnation of Christ Our God 1-5, trans. William Lowndes Lipscomb (Ann Arbor, Michigan: University Microfilms International, 1983), 261.

[17] G. H. Pember, M. A., *Earth's Earliest Ages and their Connection With Modern Spiritualism, Theosophy, and Buddhism* (Grand Rapids, Michigan: Kregel Publications, 1975), 37.

[18] *The History of al-Tabari - Volume I: General Introduction and From the Creation to the Flood*, The Story of Adam, 85-86, trans. Franz Rosenthal (Albany: New York Press, 1989), 256-257.

[19] S. Baring-Gould, *Legends of the Patriarchs and Prophets and Other Old Testament Characters* (New York: American Book Exchange, 1881), 21.

[20] E. S. G. Bristowe, *Cain - An Argument* (Leicester: Edgar Backus, 1950), 39.

[21] Mrs. Sydney Bristowe, *Sargon the Magnificent* (London: The Covenant Publishing Co., 1927), 120; *The Armenian Apocryphal Adam Literature*, The History of the Creation and Transgression of Adam 5, 9, trans. William Lowndes Lipscomb (Ann Arbor, Michigan: University Microfilms International, 1983), 119.

[22] *The Armenian Apocryphal Adam Literature*, History of the Creation and Transgression of Adam 1, trans. William Lowndes Lipscomb (Ann Arbor, Michigan: University Microfilms International, 1983), 119.

[23] *The History of al-Tabari - Volume I: General Introduction and From the Creation to the Flood*, The Story of Adam, 86, trans. Franz Rosenthal (Albany: New York Press, 1989), 257.

[24] *The Zohar*, Volume 1, Beresheet A, Section 20. The five types of the mixed multitude, 226, https://www2.kabbalah.com/k/index.php/p=zohar/zohar&vol=2&sec=41 (accessed Feb. 24, 2010).

[25] *The History of al-Tabari - Volume I: General Introduction and From the Creation to the Flood*,   The First House on Earth, 130, trans. Franz Rosenthal (Albany: New York Press, 1989), 300.

[26] *Pirke De Rabbi Eliezer*, Chapter 13: The Serpent in Paradise (15A.ii.), trans. Gerald Friedlander (New York: Sepher-Hermon Press, 1981), 91.

[27] *The History of al-Tabari - Volume I: General Introduction and From the Creation to the Flood*, The First House on Earth, 130, trans. Franz Rosenthal (Albany: New York Press, 1989), 300.

[28] *The Book of the Cave of Treasures*, The First Thousand Years: Adam to Yared (Jared), The Creation of Adam, trans. Sir E. A. Wallis Budge (London: The Religious Tract Society, 1927), 51-55.

[29] *The Chronicles of Jerahmeel* (*The Hebrew Bible Historiale*), 6:13, trans. M. Gaster, Ph. D. (London: The Royal Asiatic Society, 1899), 17.

[30] Johann Andreas Eisenmenger, *The Traditions of the Jews, Contained in the Talmud and other Mystical Writings* (London: J. Robinson, 1748), 25.

[31] *The Chronicles of Jerahmeel* (*The Hebrew Bible Historiale*), 6:12, trans. M. Gaster, Ph. D. (London: The Royal Asiatic Society, 1899), 14.

[32] S. Baring-Gould, *Legends of the Patriarchs and Prophets and Other Old Testament Characters* (New York: American Book Exchange, 1881), 26.

[33] *The Book of the Cave of Treasures*, The First Thousand Years: Adam to Yared (Jared), The Creation of Adam (notes), The Revolt of Satan, and the Battle in Heaven, trans. Sir E. A. Wallis Budge (London: The Religious Tract Society, 1927), 55-59; *The History of al-Tabari - Volume I: General Introduction and From the Creation to the Flood*, The Story of Iblis, 80, trans. Franz Rosenthal (Albany: New York Press, 1989), 251.

[34] S. Baring-Gould, *Legends of the Patriarchs and Prophets and Other Old Testament Characters* (New York: American Book Exchange, 1881), 26.

[35] S. Baring-Gould, *Legends of the Patriarchs and Prophets and Other Old Testament Characters* (New York: American Book Exchange, 1881), 15.

[36] *The Chronicles of Jerahmeel* (*The Hebrew Bible Historiale*), 7:1, trans. M. Gaster, Ph. D. (London: The Royal Asiatic Society, 1899), 18; Rabbi Leo Jung, Ph. D., *Fallen Angels in Jewish, Christian and Mohammedan Literature* (New York: KTAV Publishing House, 1974), 75.

[37] Johann Andreas Eisenmenger, *The Traditions of the Jews, Contained in the Talmud and Other Mystical Writings* (London: J. Robinson, 1748), 195.

[38] James L. Kugel, *Traditions of the Bible* (Cambridge, Massachusetts: Harvard University Press, 1998), 121.

[39] *The Book of Jubilees*, 2:17-21 (notes), trans. R. H. Charles, The Apocrypha and Pseudepigrapha of the Old Testament (Oxford: Clarendon Press, 1913); James L. Kugel, *Traditions of the Bible* (Cambridge, Massachusetts: Harvard University Press, 1998), 121; *The History of al-Tabari - Volume I: General Introduction and From the Creation to the Flood*, The Story of Iblis, 82, The Story of Adam, 90, trans. Franz Rosenthal (Albany: New York Press, 1989), 253, 62-63; *The Book of Adam*, [44]16.3b, trans. J. P. Mahe, http://www.pseudepigrapha.com/pseudepigrapha/TheBookOfAdam.htm (accessed June 27, 2005); *The Qur'an* (Yusufali), 7. Al-Araf (The Heights), 007.011, http://www.usc.edu/schools/college/crcc/engagement/resources/texts/muslim/quran/007.qmt.html (accessed Dec. 30, 2010).

[40] *The History of al-Tabari - Volume I: General Introduction and From the Creation to the Flood*, The Story of Iblis, 81, trans. Franz Rosenthal (Albany: New York Press, 1989), 252; Psalms 104:4 (KJV); James L. Kugel, *Traditions of the Bible* (Cambridge, Massachusetts: Harvard University Press, 1998), 75.

[41] *The Qur'an* (Yusufali), 15. Al-Hijr (Al-Hijr, Stoneland, Rock City), 015.027, http://www.usc.edu/schools/college/crcc/engagement/resources/texts/muslim/quran/015.qmt.html (accessed Dec. 30, 2010).

[42] Johann Andreas Eisenmenger, *The Traditions of the Jews, Contained in the Talmud and Other Mystical Writings* (London: J. Robinson, 1748), 192.

[43] *The History of al-Tabari - Volume I: General Introduction and From the Creation to the Flood*, The Story of Adam, 93, trans. Franz Rosenthal (Albany: New York Press, 1989), 264; *The Silence of the Hosts of Angels*, 4, http://adamqadmon.com/nephilim/acollins2.html (accessed Dec. 5, 2000); *The Qur'an* (Yusufali), 15. Al-Hijr (Al-Hijr, Stoneland, Rock City), 015.026 - 015.035, http://www.usc.edu/schools/college/crcc/engagement/resources/texts/muslim/quran/015.qmt.html (accessed Dec. 30,

2010).

[44] *The Book of the Cave of Treasures*, The First Thousand Years: Adam to Yared (Jared), The Revolt of Satan, and the Battle in Heaven, trans. Sir E. A. Wallis Budge (London: The Religious Tract Society, 1927), 55-59.

[45] *The Book of the Cave of Treasures*, The First Thousand Years, The Revolt of Satan, and the Battle in Heaven, trans. Sir E. A. Wallis Budge (London: The Religious Tract Society, 1927), 55-59.

[46] *The First Book of Adam and Eve (The Conflict of Adam and Eve with Satan)*, 13:14, trans. S. C. Malan (London: Williams and Norgate, 1882).

[47] *The Armenian Apocryphal Adam Literature*, Concerning the Creation of Adam and the Incarnation of Christ Our God 10, trans. William Lowndes Lipscomb (Ann Arbor, Michigan: University Microfilms International, 1983), 262; Johann Andreas Eisenmenger, *The Traditions of the Jews, Contained in the Talmud and other Mystical Writings* (London: J. Robinson, 1748), 195; Rabbi Leo Jung, Ph. D., *Fallen Angels in Jewish, Christian and Mohammedan Literature* (New York: KTAV Publishing House, 1974), 76; Stephen Quayle, *Genesis 6 Giants: The Master Builders of Prehistoric and Ancient Civilizations* (Bozeman, Montana: End Time Thunder Publishers, 2005), 30.

[48] *Vita Adae Et Evae (The Life of Adam and Eve)*, 13:2-15:3, trans. R. H. Charles, *The Apocrypha and Pseudepigrapha of the Old Testament* (Oxford: Clarendon Press, 1913).

[49] *The Book of the Cave of Treasures*, The First Thousand Years, The Revolt of Satan, and the Battle in Heaven, trans. Sir E. A. Wallis Budge (London: The Religious Tract Society, 1927), 55-59.

[50] *The First Book of Adam and Eve (The Conflict of Adam and Eve with Satan)*, 6:7, trans. S. C. Malan (London: Williams and Norgate, 1882).

[51] *The First Book of Adam and Eve (The Conflict of Adam and Eve with Satan)*, 13:2-5, trans. S. C. Malan (London: Williams and Norgate, 1882).

[52] *The Penitence of our Forefather Adam*, Fall of Satan 12.1-16.2, trans. Gary A. Anderson and Michael E. Stone, http://www2.iath.virginia.edu/anderson/viat/english/vita.arm.html (accessed Dec 26, 2009).

[53] S. Baring-Gould, *Legends of the Patriarchs and Prophets and Other Old Testament Characters* (New York: American Book Exchange, 1881), 18.

[54] James L. Kugel, *Traditions of the Bible* (Cambridge, Massachusetts: Harvard University Press, 1998), 124; *The Armenian Apocryphal Adam Literature*, The History of the Creation and Transgression of Adam 11, trans. William Lowndes Lipscomb (Ann Arbor, Michigan: University Microfilms International, 1983), 120; *The History of al-Tabari - Volume I: General Introduction and From the Creation to the Flood*, The Story of Iblis, 81, 82, The Story of Adam, 93 (and notes), trans. Franz Rosenthal (Albany: New York Press, 1989), 252, 253, 264-265; S. Baring-Gould, *Legends of the Patriarchs and Prophets and Other Old Testament Characters* (New York: American Book Exchange, 1881), 39.

[55] S. Baring-Gould, *Legends of the Patriarchs and Prophets and Other Old Testament Characters* (New York: American Book Exchange, 1881) 23, 39; *The Armenian Apocryphal Adam Literature*, History of the Creation and Transgression of Adam 11, trans. William Lowndes Lipscomb (Ann Arbor, Michigan: University Microfilms International, 1983), 120.

[56] S. Baring-Gould, *Legends of the Patriarchs and Prophets and Other Old Testament Characters* (New York: American Book Exchange, 1881), 16.

[57] Johann Andreas Eisenmenger, *The Traditions of the Jews, Contained in the Talmud and other Mystical Writings* (London: J. Robinson, 1748), 196; Alan Unterman, *Dictionary of Jewish Lore and Legend* (London: Thames and Hudson, 1991), 170; S. Baring-Gould, *Legends of the Patriarchs and Prophets and Other Old Testament Characters* (New York: American Book Exchange, 1881), 16.

[58] Johann Andreas Eisenmenger, *The Traditions of the Jews, Contained in the Talmud and other Mystical Writings* (London: J. Robinson, 1748), 190, 192-193.

[59] Alan Unterman, *Dictionary of Jewish Lore and Legend* (London: Thames and Hudson, 1991), 170; Johann Andreas Eisenmenger, *The Traditions of the Jews, Contained in the Talmud and other Mystical Writings*, By (London: J. Robinson, 1748), 188; Rabbi Leo Jung, Ph. D., *Fallen Angels in Jewish, Christian and Mohammedan Literature* (New York: KTAV Publishing House, 1974), 80.

[60] *3 Enoch (The Hebrew Book of Enoch)*, 26:12 (notes), trans. Hugo Odeberg (New York: KTAV Publishing House, Inc., 1973), 93; *Azazel and Atonement (No. 214)*, 6, http://www.adamqadmon.com/me[jo;o,/huie003.html (accessed Dec. 5, 2000); Johann Andreas Eisenmenger, *The Traditions of the Jews, Contained in the Talmud and other Mystical Writings* (London: J. Robinson, 1748), 186, 188.

[61] *Zech.* 3:1-7 (KJV); *3 Enoch (The Hebrew Book of Enoch)*, Chapter 26:12 (and notes), trans. Hugo Odeberg (New York: KTAV Publishing House, Inc., 1973), 93.

[62] G. H. Pember, M. A., *Earth's Earliest Ages and their Connection With Modern Spiritualism, Theosophy, and Buddhism* (Grand Rapids, Michigan: Kregel Publications, 1975), 52, 56; *Rev.* 12:10 (KJV).

[63] Johann Andreas Eisenmenger, *The Traditions of the Jews, Contained in the Talmud and Other Mystical Writings* (London: J. Robinson, 1748), 189.

[64] Philip Gardiner and Gary Osborn, *The Shining Ones: The World's Most Powerful Secret Society Revealed* (London: Watkins Publishing, 2006), 145.

[65] Philip Gardiner and Gary Osborn, *The Shining Ones: The World's Most Powerful Secret Society Revealed* (London: Watkins Publishing, 2006), 134.

[66] Philip Gardiner and Gary Osborn, *The Shining Ones: The World's Most Powerful Secret Society Revealed* (London: Watkins Publishing, 2006), 146.

[67] Strong's H1711 - *dagah*, http://www.blueletterbible.org/lang/lexicon/lexicon.cfm?Strongs=H1711&t=KJV# (accessed Jan. 5, 2010).

[68] Gesenius' Lexicon - *dagah*, http://www.blueletterbible.org/lang/lexicon/lexicon.cfm?Strongs=H1711&t=KJV# (accessed Jan. 5, 2010).

[69] Donald Mackenzie, *Myths of Babylonia and Assyriai*, Chapter 2 (1915), 28.

[70] S. Baring-Gould, *Legends of the Patriarchs and Prophets and Other Old Testament Characters* (New York: American Book Exchange, 1881), 47-48.

[71] *The Zohar*, Volume 10, Mishpatim, Section 18. Two Messiahs, 482, www2.kabbalah.com/k/index.php?p=zohar/zohar&vol=20&sec=702 (accessed Feb. 24, 2010),

[72] Johann Andreas Eisenmenger, *The Traditions of the Jews, Contained in the Talmud and Other Mystical Writings* (London: J. Robinson, 1748), 193.

[73] *The Zohar*, Volume 10, Mishpatim, Section 18. Two Messiahs, 482, www2.kabbalah.com/k/index.php?p=zohar/zohar&vol=20&sec=702 (accessed Feb. 24, 2010),

[74] Johann Andreas Eisenmenger, *The Traditions of the Jews, Contained in the Talmud and other Mystical Writings*, By (London: J. Robinson, 1748), 205-206.

[75] Johann Andreas Eisenmenger, *The Traditions of the Jews, Contained in the Talmud and other Mystical Writings*, By (London: J. Robinson, 1748), 187.

[76] Johann Andreas Eisenmenger, *The Traditions of the Jews, Contained in the Talmud and other Mystical Writings*, By (London: J. Robinson, 1748), 186-187.

[77] Robert Graves and Raphael Patai, *Hebrew Myths: The Book of Genesis* (Garden City, New York: Doubleday & Company, 1964), 65.

[78] *Genizah Manuscripts of Palestinian Targum to the Pentateuch Volume One*, Genesis 2:20, trans. Michael L. Klein (Cincinnati: Hebrew Union College Press, 1986), 2.

[79] Strong's H3335 - *yatsar*, http://www.blueletterbible.org/lang/lexicon/lexicon.cfm?Strongs=H3335&t=KJV (accessed Jan. 5, 2010).

[80] Johann Andreas Eisenmenger, *The Traditions of the Jews, Contained in the Talmud and Other Mystical Writings* (London: J. Robinson, 1748), 22.

[81] *The Chronicles of Jerahmeel* (*The Hebrew Bible Historiale*), 23:1, trans. M. Gaster, Ph. D. (London: The Royal Asiatic Society, 1899), 48.

[82] James L. Kugel, *Traditions of the Bible* (Cambridge, Massachusetts: Harvard University Press, 1998), 113.

[83] J. E. Hanauer, *Folklore of the Holy Land: Moslem, Christian and Jewish*, II: Our Father Adam (London: BiblioBazaar, 2007), 9; James L. Kugel, *Traditions of the Bible* (Cambridge, Massachusetts: Harvard University Press, 1998), 113-114.

[84] J. E. Hanauer, *Folklore of the Holy Land: Moslem, Christian and Jewish*, II: Our Father Adam (London: BiblioBazaar, 2007), 9.

[85] Robert Graves and Raphael Patai, *Hebrew Myths: The Book of Genesis* (Garden City, New York: Doubleday & Company, 1964), 65.

[86] J. E. Hanauer, *Folklore of the Holy Land: Moslem, Christian and Jewish*, II: Our Father Adam (London: BiblioBazaar, 2007), 9.

[87] J. E. Hanauer, *Folklore of the Holy Land: Moslem, Christian and Jewish*, II: Our Father Adam (London: BiblioBazaar, 2007), 9.

[88] S. Baring-Gould, *Legends of the Patriarchs and Prophets and Other Old Testament Characters* (New York: American Book Exchange, 1881), 34.

[89] S. Baring-Gould, *Legends of the Patriarchs and Prophets and Other Old Testament Characters* (New York: American Book Exchange, 1881), 34.

[90] Louis Ginzberg, *Legends of the Jews: Volume 1*, trans. Henrietta Szold (Baltimore, Maryland: The Johns Hopkins University Press, 1909), 62.

[91] *The Chronicles of Jerahmeel* (*The Hebrew Bible Historiale*), 22:1, trans. M. Gaster, Ph. D. (London: The Royal Asiatic Society, 1899), 46.

[92] Hyman E. Goldin, *The Book of Legends: Tales From the Talmud and Midrash* (New York: The Jordan Publishng Co., 1929), 16; *The History of al-Tabari - Volume I: General Introduction and From the Creation to the Flood*, Adam is Taught All the Names, 98-99, trans. Franz Rosenthal (Albany: New York Press, 1989), 270-271; *The Armenian Apocryphal Adam Literature*, History and Sermon: Concerning the Creation of Adam and the Incarnation of Christ Our God 9, trans. William Lowndes Lipscomb (Ann Arbor, Michigan: University Microfilms International, 1983), 262; *Pirke De Rabbi Eliezer*, Chapter 13: The Serpent in Paradise [15A. ii.], trans. Gerald Friedlander (New York: Sepher-Hermon Press, 1981), 91.

[93] S. Baring-Gould, *Legends of the Patriarchs and Prophets and Other Old Testament Characters* (New York: American Book Exchange, 1881), 23; *Pirke De Rabbi Eliezer*, Chapter 13: The Serpent in Paradise [15A. ii.], trans. Gerald Friedlander (New York: Sepher-Hermon Press, 1981), 91.

[94] *Pirke De Rabbi Eliezer*, Chapter 13: The Serpent in Paradise [15A.ii.], trans. Gerald Friedlander (New York: Sepher-Hermon Press, 1981), 91.

[95] Ellen Frankel, *The Classic Tales: 4000 years of Jewish Lore* (Northvale, New Jersey: Jason Aronson Inc., 1989), 27.

[96] *The Chronicles of Jerahmeel* (*The Hebrew Bible Historiale*), 22:1, trans. M. Gaster, Ph. D. (London: The Royal Asiatic Society, 1899), 46.

[97] Robert Graves and Raphael Patai, *Hebrew Myths: The Book of Genesis* (Garden City, New York: Doubleday & Company, 1964), 62.

[98] *The Zohar*, Volume 19. Balak, Section 43. Aza and Azael, "falling down, but having his eyes open", 416, 419, https://www2.kabbalah.com/k/index.php/p=zohar/zohar&vol=43&sec=1518 (accessed Feb. 24, 2010); *3 Enoch (The Hebrew Book of Enoch)*, 40:3, trans. Hugo Odeberg (New York: KTAV Publishing House, Inc., 1973), 126; *The Chronicles of Jerahmeel* (*The Hebrew Bible Historiale*), 6:3, trans. M. Gaster, Ph. D (London: The Royal Asiatic Society, 1899); S. Baring-Gould, *Legends of the Patriarchs and Prophets and Other Old Testament Characters* (New York: American Book Exchange, 1881), 17.

[99] *The History of al-Tabari - Volume I: General Introduction and From the Creation to the Flood*, The Story of Iblis, 84, trans. Franz Rosenthal (Albany: New York Press, 1989), 255.

[100] *The Babylonian Talmud*, Book VII, Tract Sandhedrin, Part II (Haggada), Chapter XI, 369, trans. by Michael L. Rodkinson, http://www.sacred-texts.com/jud/t08/t0814.htm (accessed Jan 31, 2011).

[101] Louis Ginzberg, *Legends of the Jews: Volume 1*, trans. Henrietta Szold (Baltimore, Maryland: The Johns Hopkins University Press, 1909), 53.

[102] *The Zohar*, Volume 2, Beresheet B, Section 69. "The Nefilim were on the earth", 423, https://www2.kabbalah.com/k/index.php/p=zohar/zohar&vol=3&sec=142 (accessed Feb. 24, 2010).

[103] Louis Ginzberg, *Legends of the Jews: Volume 1*, trans. Henrietta Szold (Baltimore, Maryland: The Johns Hopkins University Press, 1909), 151.

[104] *The Zohar*, Volume 1, Beresheet A, Section 20. The five types of the mixed multitude, 227, https://www2.kabbalah.com/k/index.php/p=zohar/zohar&vol=2&sec=41 (accessed Feb. 24, 2010).

[105] *The Zohar*, Volume 2. Beresheet B, Section 69. "The Nefilim were on the earth", 423-424, https://www2.kabbalah.com/k/index.php/p=zohar/zohar&vol=3&sec=142 (accessed Feb. 24, 2010); *The Zohar*, Volume 1. Beresheet A, Section 20. The five types of the mixed multitude, 226, https://www2.kabbalah.com/k/index.php/p=zohar/zohar&vol=2&sec=41 (accessed Feb. 24, 2010). *The Zohar*, Volume 1. Beresheet A, Section 50. Aza and Azael, 464, https://www2.kabbalah.com/k/index.php/p=zohar/zohar&vol=2&sec=71 (accessed Feb. 24, 2010).

[106] *Pirke De Rabbi Eliezer*, Chapter 22: The Fall of the Angels [26A. i.], trans. Gerald Friedlander, 160.

[107] *The Zohar*, Volume 2, Beresheet B, Section 69. "The Nefilim were on the earth", 423, https://www2.kabbalah.com/k/index.php/p=zohar/zohar&vol=3&sec=142 (accessed Feb. 24, 2010).

[108] Malcolm Godwin, *Angels: An Endangered Species* (New York: Simon & Schuester, 1990), 86.

[109] *The Zohar*, Volume 1. Beresheet A, Section 20. The five types of the mixed multitude, 226, https://www2.kabbalah.com/k/index.php/p=zohar/zohar&vol=2&sec=41 (accessed Feb. 24, 2010); *Sefer 'Uza Wa-'Aza(z)el: Exploring Early Jewish Mythologies of Evil*, 1, http://www.religiousstudies.uncc.edu/jcreeves/sefer_uzza_waazazel.htm (accessed July 1, 2005).

[110] *The Zohar*, Volume 2. Beresheet B, Section 69. "The Nefilim were on the earth", 423, https://www2.kabbalah.com/k/index.php/p=zohar/zohar&vol=3&sec=142 (accessed Feb. 24, 2010). *The Zohar*, Volume 1. Beresheet A, Section 50. Aza and Azael, 466, https://www2.kabbalah.com/k/index.php/p=zohar/zohar&vol=2&sec=71 (accessed Feb. 24, 2010).

[111] *Pirke De Rabbi Eliezer*, Chapter 13: The Serpent in Paradise [15A.ii.], trans. Gerald Friedlander, 91.

Chapter 6

[1] *Vita Adae Et Evae (The Life of Adam and Eve)*, 16:4, trans. R. H. Charles, *The Apocrypha and Pseudepigrapha of the Old Testament* (Oxford: Clarendon Press, 1913).

[2] *The Book of the Cave of Treasures*, The First Thousand Years: Adam to Yared (Jared), The Symbolism of Eden, trans. Sir E. A. Wallis Budge (London: The Religious Tract Society, 1927), 62-63.

[3] *The Apocalypse of Moses / Apocalypsis Mosis (The Life of Adam and Eve)*, 15:3, trans. R. H. Charles, http://www.pseudepigrapha.com/pseudepigrapha/aprmose.htm (accessed June 27, 2005); *The Book of Adam*, trans. J. P. Mahe, [32]7.3b, [44]15.3, [44]17.3, http://www.pseudepigrapha.com/pseudepigrapha/TheBookOfAdam.htm (accessed June 27, 2005); *The Bible, The Koran, and the Talmud (Biblical Legends of the Mussulmans)*, Adam (A Mohammedan Legend), trans. Dr. G. Weil (New York, 1863), 2.

[4] *The Book of the Cave of Treasures*, The First Thousand Years, The Making of Eve (notes), trans. Sir E. A. Wallis Budge (London: The Religious Tract Society, 1927), 61.

[5] David Goldstein, *Jewish Legends (Library of the World's Myths and Legends)* (New York: Peter Bedrick Books, 1933), 4.

[6] Mrs. Sydney Bristowe, *Sargon the Magnificent* (London: The Covenant Publishing Co., 1927), 120.

[7] *The Book of Adam*, trans. J. P. Mahe, [38]11.1,

http://www.pseudepigrapha.com/pseudepigrapha/TheBookOfAdam.htm (accessed June 27, 2005).

[8] *Saltair na Rann*, 1193-1196, trans. David Greene.

[9] Andrew Collins, *From the Ashes of Angels* (Rochester, Vermont: Bear & Company, 1996), 59.

[10] Malcolm Godwin, *Angels: An Endangered Species* (New York: Simon & Schuester, 1990), 71.

[11] Johann Andreas Eisenmenger, *The Traditions of the Jews, Contained in the Talmud and other Mystical Writings* (London: J. Robinson, 1748), 189.

[12] *The Life of Adam and Eve (The Apocalypse of Moses / Apocalypsis Mosis)*, 26:3, trans. R. H. Charles, http://www.pseudepigrapha.com/pseudepigrapha/aprmose.htm (accessed June 27, 2005); Alan Unterman, *Dictionary of Jewish Lore and Legend* (London: Thames and Hudson Ltd., 1991), 176.

[13] Andrew Collins, *From the Ashes of Angels* (Rochester, Vermont: Bear & Company, 1996), 103.

[14] Alan Unterman, *Dictionary of Jewish Lore and Legend* (London: Thames and Hudson Ltd., 1991), 176.

[15] Rabbi Leo Jung, Ph. D., *Fallen Angels in Jewish, Christian and Mohammedan Literature* (New York: KTAV Publishing House, 1974), 115.

[16] *Timeline of Nephilim Movement Through the World*, 1-2, http://www.ziarah.net.timeline.html (accessed March 19, 2007).

[17] *The Book of Enoch*. 87:2, trans. R. H. Charles (Montana: Kessinger Publishing, 1912).

[18] *2 Enoch (The Book of the Secrets of Enoch)*, 1:6, trans. W. R. Morfill, M.A. (Oxford: Clarendon Press, 1896).

[19] Louis Ginzberg, *The Legends of the Jews Volume V: Notes for Volume One and Two*, II. Adam, 124, trans. Henrietta Szold (Baltimore, Maryland: The Johns Hopkins University Press, 1909), 131; Andrew Collins, *From the Ashes of Angels* (Rochester, Vermont: Bear & Company, 1996), 156, 158.

[20] *Gates of Hell: The Descent of Ishtar to the Netherworld*, 3 (*Ancient Near Eastern Texts*, trans. E. A. Speiser and George A. Barton), http://www.piney.com/Ishtar.html (accessed Dec. 30, 2010).

[21] Andrew Collins, *From the Ashes of Angels* (Rochester, Vermont: Bear & Company, 1996), 48.

[22] *The Testament of Amram* (The Dead Sea Scrolls), (4Q544) Fr. 1, trans. Geza Vermes, *The Complete Dead Sea Scrolls in English* (New York: Penguin Books, 1997), 535.

[23] Andrew Collins, *From the Ashes of Angels* (Rochester, Vermont: Bear & Company, 1996), 255-256, 258-261, 268; *Timeline of Nephilim Movement Through the World*, 1-2, www.ziarah.net/timeline.html, (accessed March 19, 2007).

[24] *The Apocalypse of Abraham*, 23:7, translator unknown, http://www.pseudepigrapha.com/pseudepigrapha/Apocalypse_of_Abraham.html (accessed Oct 5, 2006); Louis Ginzberg, *The Legends of the Jews Volume V: Notes for Volume One and Two*, II. Adam, 117, trans. Henrietta Szold (Baltimore, Maryland: The Johns Hopkins University Press, 1909), 121; *The Writings of Abraham*, 23:7, 23:35, http://www.earth-history.com/Pseudepigrapha/Mormonism/writings-abraham-1.htm (accessed May 10, 2007); Strong's G1404 - *drakon*, http://www.blueletterbible.org/lang/lexicon/lexicon.cfm?Strongs=G1404&t=KJV (accessed Dec 29, 2010).

[25] Strong's H8314 - *seraph*, http://www.blueletterbible.org/lang/lexicon/lexicon.cfm?Strongs=H8314&t=KJV, (accessed Jan. 12, 2010); *dragon*, 1, https://www.blueletterbible.org/search/search.cfm?Criteria=dragon&t=KJV#s=s_primary_0_1 (accessed Dec. 29, 2016).

[26] Johann Andreas Eisenmenger, *The Traditions of the Jews, Contained in the Talmud and Other Mystical Writings* (London: J. Robinson, 1748), 187-189.

[27] Kingdom Bible Studies: Studies in End-Time Revelation, *The Heavens Declare Part 18: Scorpio - the Scorpion*, 1, http://www.sigler.org/eby/heavens18.html (accessed Sept. 11, 2000).

[28] Adam Clarke, *Nachash, The Serpent*, 3, http://wesley.nnu.edu/wesleyctr/books/0901-1000/HDM0999.PDF (accessed Jan. 5, 2010).

[29] *The Companion Bible*, Appendix 19 (Grand Rapids, Michigan: Kregel Publications, 1990), 24-25.

[30] *Satan's Seed*, 1, http://www.thetruword.com/satansseed.htm (accessed Sept. 11, 2000); *The Doctrine of Original Sin Part I: The Garden of Eden (No. 246)*, 8, 24, http://www.adamqadmon.com/nephilim/gardeneden/html (accessed Feb. 10, 2001).

[31] Gary Osborn, *Shining Ones*, http://garyosborn.moonfruit.com/#/shining-ones-notes/4519248692 (accessed Dec. 30, 2010).

[32] Andrew Collins, *From the Ashes of Angels* (Rochester, Vermont: Bear & Company, 1996), 50; *The Doctrine of Original Sin Part I: The Garden of Eden (No. 246)*, 8, http://www.adamqadmon.com/nephilim/gardeneden/html (accessed Feb. 10, 2001); Louis Ginzberg, *The Legends of the Jews Volume V: Notes for Volume One and Two*, II. Adam, 131, trans. Henrietta Szold (Baltimore, Maryland: The Johns Hopkins University Press, 1909), 124.

[33] *3 Enoch (The Hebrew Book of Enoch)*, 26:8 (notes), trans. Hugo Odeberg (New York: KTAV Publishing House, Inc., 1973), 92.

[34] Malcolm Godwin, *Angels: An Endangered Species* (New York: Simon & Schuester, 1990), 25.

[35] Encyclopedia Mithica, *Seraphim*, 1, http://www.pantheon.org/mythica/articles/seraphim.html (accessed July 1, 2000).

[36] *The Book of the Mysteries of the Heavens and the Earth and Other Works of Bakhayla Mikael (Zosimas)*, trans. E.A. Wallis Budge (London: Oxford University Press, 1935), 17.

[37] Andrew Collins, *From the Ashes of Angels* (Rochester, Vermont: Bear & Company, 1996), 41, 52-53; *The Doctrine of Original Sin Part I: The Garden of Eden (No. 246)*, 8, 24, http://www.adamqadmon.com/nephilim/gardeneden/html (accessed Feb. 10, 2001); G. H. Pember, M. A., *Earth's Earliest Ages and their Connection With Modern Spiritualism, Theosophy, and Buddhism* (Grand Rapids, Michigan: Kregel Publications, 1975), 112; Malcolm Godwin, *Angels: An Endangered Species* (New York: Simon & Schuester, 1990), 25-26; *The Silence of the Hosts of Angels*, 4, http://www.adamqadmon.com/nephilim/acollins2/html (accessed Dec. 5, 2000).

[38] *The Apocalypse of Abraham*, 23:11-2, translator unknown, http://www.pseudepigrapha.com/pseudepigrapha/Apocalypse_of_Abraham.html (accessed Oct 5, 2006).

[39] Malcolm Godwin, *Angels: An Endangered Species* (New York: Simon & Schuester, 1990), 112.

[40] Hitchcock's Bible Name Dictionary, *Azaz*, 7, http://www.adamqadmon.com/nephilim/definitions/biblenames.html (accessed March 8, 2001); *Azazel and Atonement (No. 214)*, 32, http://www.adamqadmon.com/nephilim/huie003.html (accessed Dec. 5, 2000).

[41] *Azazel and Atonement (No. 214)*, 32, http://www.adamqadmon.com/nephilim/huie003.html (accessed Dec. 5, 2000).

[42] Louis Ginzberg, *The Legends of the Jews Volume V: Notes for Volume One and Two*, II. Adam, 121, trans. Henrietta Szold (Baltimore, Maryland: The Johns Hopkins University Press, 1909), 117; Wikipedia, the Free Encyclopedia, *Azazel*, 2, http://en.wikipedia.org/wiki/Azazel (accessed Oct. 05, 2006).

[43] Louis Ginzberg, *The Legends of the Jews Volume V: Notes for Volume One and Two*, II. Adam, 121, trans. Henrietta Szold (Baltimore, Maryland: The Johns Hopkins University Press, 1909), 117; Malcolm Godwin, *Angels: An Endangered Species* (New York: Simon & Schuester, 1990), 113.

[44] *The Book of Enoch*, 69:4-12, trans. R. H. Charles (Montana: Kessinger Publishing, 1912); Louis Ginzberg, *The Legends of the Jews Volume V: Notes for Volume One and Two*, II. Adam, 131, IV. Noah, 10, trans. Henrietta Szold (Baltimore, Maryland: The Johns Hopkins University Press, 1909), 124, 170-1; Malcolm Godwin, *Angels: An Endangered Species* (New York: Simon & Schuester, 1990), 113.

[45] *The Book of Enoch*, 69:6, trans. R. H. Charles (Montana: Kessinger Publishing, 1912); Malcolm Godwin, *Angels: An Endangered Species* (New York: Simon & Schuester, 1990), 113; Louis Ginzberg, *The Legends of the Jews Volume V: Notes for Volume One and Two*, II. Adam, 121, trans. Henrietta Szold (Baltimore, Maryland: The Johns Hopkins University Press, 1909), 116.

[46] *The Book of Enoch*, 69:4-12, trans. R. H. Charles (Montana: Kessinger Publishing, 1912); Louis Ginzberg, *The Legends of the Jews Volume V: Notes for Volume One and Two*, II. Adam, 121, trans. Henrietta Szold (Baltimore, Maryland: The Johns Hopkins University Press, 1909), 116; Malcolm Godwin, *Angels: An Endangered Species* (New York: Simon & Schuester, 1990), 113; *The Apocalypse of Abraham*, 22:33, 23:34, 23:36, translator unknown, http://www.pseudepigrapha.com/pseudepigrapha/Apocalypse_of_Abraham.html (accessed Oct 5, 2006).

[47] Jayim Nahman Bialik and Yehoshua Hana Ravnitzky, *The Book of Legends (Sefer Ha-Aggadah): Legends from the Talmud and Midrash* (New York: Shocken Books, 1992), 22; *The Chronicles of Jerahmeel (The Hebrew Bible Historiale)*, 6:4, 6:13, 7:2, trans. M. Gaster, Ph. D. (London: The Royal Asiatic Society, 1899), 15, 17, 18.

[48] Hyman E. Goldin, *The Book of Legends: Tales From the Talmud and Midrash* (New York: The Jordan Publishing Co., 1929), 20.

[49] Johann Andreas Eisenmenger, *The Traditions of the Jews, Contained in the Talmud and Other Mystical Writings* (London: J. Robinson, 1748), 196.

[50] Ellen Frankel, *The Classic Tales: 4000 Years of Jewish Lore* (Northvale, New Jersey: Jason Aronson Inc., 1989), 28.

[51] Rabbi Leo Jung, Ph. D., *Fallen Angels in Jewish, Christian and Mohammedan Literature* (New York: KTAV Publishing House, 1974), 69.

[52] Johann Andreas Eisenmenger, *The Traditions of the Jews, Contained in the Talmud and Other Mystical Writings* (London: J. Robinson, 1748), 198.

[53] Merriam-Webster Dictionary, *Dainty*, http://www.merriam-webster.com/dictionary/dainty (accessed Feb. 3, 2010).

[54] Rabbi Leo Jung, Ph. D., *Fallen Angels in Jewish, Christian and Mohammedan Literature* (New York: KTAV Publishing House, 1974), 73-74.

[55] *Barhebraeus' Scholia on the Old Testament Part I: Genesis - II Samuel*, Genesis 3:1, trans. Martin Sprengling and William Creighton Graham (Chicago, Illinois: University of Chicago Press 1931), 25.

[56] *Star Wars, Lesson Seven*, 6, http://usa-the-republic.com/religion/star%20wars/Star%20Wars%20-%20Lesson%20Seven.htm (accessed April 23, 2005).

[57] *The History of al-Tabari - Volume I: General Introduction and From the Creation to the Flood*, The Story of Iblis, 83, trans. Franz Rosenthal (Albany: New York Press, 1989), 254.

[58] Shira Halevi, *The Life Story of Adam and Havah*, Genesis 3:1a (Northvale, New Jersey: Jason Aronson, Inc., 1997), 166.

[59] *Genizah Manuscripts of Palestinian Targum to the Pentateuch Volume One*, Genesis 3:1, trans. Michael L. Klein (Cincinnati: Hebrew Union College Press, 1986), 3.

[60] Merriam-Webster Dictionary, *Shrewd*, http://www.merriam-webster.com/dictionary/shrewd (accessed Feb. 3, 2010).

[61] *Star Wars, Lesson Seven*, 7, http://usa-the-republic.com/religion/star%20wars/Star%20Wars%20-%20Lesson%20Seven.htm (accessed April 23, 2005).

[62] Louis Ginzberg, *The Legends of the Jews Volume V: Notes for Volume One and Two*, II. Adam, 117, trans. Henrietta

Szold (Baltimore, Maryland: The Johns Hopkins University Press, 1909), 121.

[63] *The History of al-Tabari - Volume I: General Introduction and From the Creation to the Flood*, The Story of Adam, 91, trans. Franz Rosenthal (Albany: New York Press, 1989), 262.

[64] *The History of al-Tabari - Volume I: General Introduction and From the Creation to the Flood*, The Story of Iblis, 83, trans. Franz Rosenthal (Albany: New York Press, 1989), 254.

[65] *The History of al-Tabari - Volume I: General Introduction and From the Creation to the Flood*, The Story of Iblis, 83, trans. Franz Rosenthal (Albany: New York Press, 1989), 254; *The History of al-Tabari - Volume I: General Introduction and From the Creation to the Flood*, The Story of Iblis, 80, trans. Franz Rosenthal (Albany: New York Press, 1989), 250-251.

[66] *The History of al-Tabari - Volume I: General Introduction and From the Creation to the Flood*, The Story of Iblis, 80, trans. Franz Rosenthal (Albany: New York Press, 1989), 250-251.

[67] *The First Book of Adam and Eve (The Conflict of Adam and Eve with Satan)*, 46:4, trans. S. C. Malan (London: Williams and Norgate, 1882).

[68] *Pirke De Rabbi Eliezer*, Chapter 13: The Serpent in Paradise [15A.ii.], trans. Gerald Friedlander (New York: Sepher-Hermon Press, 1981), 91.

[69] *The Book of Adam*, [44]16.3a-16.4, trans. J. P. Mahe, http://www.pseudepigrapha.com/pseudepigrapha/TheBookOfAdam.htm (accessed June 27, 2005).

[70] *Pirke De Rabbi Eliezer*, Chapter 13: The Serpent in Paradise [15A. ii.], trans. Gerald Friedlander (New York: Sepher-Hermon Press, 1981), 92; *The Apocalypse of Moses / Apocalypsis Mosis*, 16:5, 17:4, trans. R. H. Charles, http://www.pseudepigrapha.com/pseudepigrapha/aprmose.htm (accessed June 27, 2005); James L. Kugel, *Traditions of the Bible* (Cambridge, Massachusetts: Harvard University Press, 1998), 124-125.

[71] *The Penitence of our Forefather Adam*, Temptation of Eve [44]18.3, trans. Gary A. Anderson and Michael E. Stone, http://www2.iath.virginia.edu/anderson/viat/english/vita.arm.html (accessed Dec. 26, 2009); *The History of al-Tabari - Volume I: General Introduction and From the Creation to the Flood*, God's Testing of Adam, 105, 109, trans. Franz Rosenthal (Albany: New York Press (1989), 276, 281; *The Book of Adam*, [44]16.1-4, trans. J. P. Mahe, http://www.pseudepigrapha.com/pseudepigrapha/TheBookOfAdam.htm (accessed June 27, 2005).

[72] *The History of al-Tabari - Volume I: General Introduction and From the Creation to the Flood*, The Story of Iblis, 83, trans. Franz Rosenthal (Albany: New York Press (1989), 254.

[73] Louis Ginzberg, *The Legends of the Jews Volume V: Notes for Volume One and Two*, II. Adam, 131, trans. Henrietta Szold (Baltimore, Maryland: The Johns Hopkins University Press, 1909), 124.

[74] *The Apocalypse of Moses / Apocalypsis Mosis*, 16:1-18:6, trans. R. H. Charles, http://www.pseudepigrapha.com/pseudepigrapha/aprmose.htm (accessed June 27, 2005).

[75] *Barhebraeus' Scholia on the Old Testament Part I: Genesis - II Samuel*, Genesis 3:1-4, trans. Martin Sprengling and William Creighton Graham (Chicago, Illinois: University of Chicago Press 1931), 25.

[76] *The Book of Enoch*, 10:9, trans. R. H. Charles (Montana: Kessinger Publishing, 1912).

Chapter 7

[1] *2 Enoch (The Book of the Secrets of Enoch)*, 31:5, trans. W.R. Morfill, M.A. (Oxford: Clarendon Press, 1896).

[2] Rabbi Leo Jung, Ph. D., *Fallen Angels in Jewish, Christian and Mohammedan Literature* (New York: KTAV Publishing House, 1974), 68-69.

[3] *The Apocalypse of Moses / Apocalypsis Mosis*, 15:3 (notes), trans. R. H. Charles, http://www.pseudepigrapha.com/pseudepigrapha/aprmose.htm (accessed June 27, 2005); Andrew Collins, *From the Ashes of Angels* (Rochester, Vermont: Bear & Company, 1996), 40.

[4] Andrew Collins, *From the Ashes of Angels* (Rochester, Vermont: Bear & Company, 1996), 40; J. E. Hanauer, *Folklore of the Holy Land: Moslem, Christian and Jewish*, 2: Our Father Adam (London: BiblioBazaar, 2007), 10; Alan Unterman, *Dictionary of Jewish Lore and Legend* (London: Thames and Hudson Ltd., 1991), 176.

[5] Dominick McClausland, *Adam and the Adamite; or, The Harmony of Scripture and Ethnology* (London, Richard Bentley and Son, 1872), 130.

[6] Robert Graves and Raphael Patai, *Hebrew Myths: The Book of Genesis* (Garden City, New York: Doubleday & Company, 1964), 85; James L. Kugel, *Traditions of the Bible* (Cambridge, Massachusetts: Harvard University Press, 1998), 122.

[7] Greg Killian, *The Days of Noah*, 19-20, http://www.adamqadmon.com/nephilim/gkillian000 (accessed Dec. 6, 2000); James L. Kugel, *Traditions of the Bible* (Cambridge, Massachusetts: Harvard University Press, 1998), 110.

[28] 4 Maccabees 18:7-8 (Revised Standard Version), http://quod.lib.umich.edu/cgi/r/rsv/rsv-idx?type=DIV1&byte=4496061 (accessed Jan. 31, 2011).

[9] *Pirke De Rabbi Eliezer*, Chapter 13: The Serpent in Paradise [15A. ii.], trans. Gerald Friedlander (New York: Sepher-Hermon Press, 1981), 94.

[10] *Pirke De Rabbi Eliezer*, Chapter 13: The Serpent in Paradise [15A. ii.], trans. Gerald Friedlander (New York: Sepher-Hermon Press, 1981), 94.

[11] Shira Halevi, *The Life Story of Adam and Havah*, Genesis 3:5 - 3:6a (Northvale, New Jersey: Jason Aronson, Inc., 1997), 167-168.

[12] *The Book of Adam*, [44]15:3-4, trans. J. P. Mahe, http://www.pseudepigrapha.com/pseudepigrapha/TheBookOfAdam.htm (accessed June 27, 2005).

[13] *The Book of Adam*, [44]18.1, 19.1-20.5, trans. J. P. Mahe, http://www.pseudepigrapha.com/pseudepigrapha/TheBookOfAdam.htm (accessed June 27, 2005); *Vita Adae Et Evae (The Life of Adam and Eve)*, 4:2, trans. R. H. Charles, *The Apocrypha and Pseudepigrapha of the Old Testament* (Oxford: Clarendon Press, 1913); *Saltair na Rann*, 1233-1240, trans. David Greene.

[14] Johann Andreas Eisenmenger, *The Traditions of the Jews, Contained in the Talmud and other Mystical Writings* (London: J. Robinson, 1748) 193; Robert Graves and Raphael Patai, *Hebrew Myths: The Book of Genesis* (Garden City, New York: Doubleday & Company, 1964), 78.

[15] *The Book of Adam*, [44]18.3, trans. J. P. Mahe, http://www.pseudepigrapha.com/pseudepigrapha/TheBookOfAdam.htm (accessed June 27, 2005).

[16] *The First Book of Adam and Eve (The Conflict of Adam and Eve with Satan)*, 13:16, trans. S. C. Malan (London: Williams and Norgate, 1882).

[17] *The Book of Adam*, [44]19.1-3, [44]20.4-5, trans. J. P. Mahe, http://www.pseudepigrapha.com/pseudepigrapha/TheBookOfAdam.htm (accessed June 27, 2005).

[18] *Armenian Apocrypha Relating to Adam and Eve*, 9 (notes), trans. Michael E. Stone (Leiden: E. J. Brill, 1996), 31.

[19] Louis Ginzberg, *The Legends of the Jews Volume V: Notes for Volume One and Two*, II. Adam, 131, trans. Henrietta Szold (Baltimore, Maryland: The Johns Hopkins University Press, 1909), 124; Robert Graves and Raphael Patai, *Hebrew Myths: The Book of Genesis* (Garden City, New York: Doubleday & Company, 1964), 86-87.

[20] G. H. Pember, M. A., *Earth's Earliest Ages and their Connection With Modern Spiritualism, Theosophy, and Buddhism* (Grand Rapids, Michigan: Kregel Publications, 1975), 127.

[21] Bentley Layton, *The Gnostic Scriptures*, "Other" Gnostic Teachings According to St. Irenaeus (New York: Doubleday, 1995), 181; Rabbi Leo Jung, Ph. D., *Fallen Angels in Jewish, Christian and Mohammedan Literature* (New York: KTAV Publishing House, 1974), 75-76; Robert Graves and Raphael Patai, *Hebrew Myths: The Book of Genesis* (Garden City, New York: Doubleday & Company, 1964), 85.

[22] Schatzhohle, III (Rabbi Leo Jung, Ph. D., *Fallen Angels in Jewish, Christian and Mohammedan Literature* (New York: KTAV Publishing House, 1974), 79).

[23] Johann Andreas Eisenmenger, *The Traditions of the Jews, Contained in the Talmud and Other Mystical Writings* (London: J. Robinson, 1748), 21.

[24] *The Zohar*, Volume 13, Pekudei, Section 21. Breastplate and Efod, 203, https://www2.kabbalah.com/k/index.php?p=zohar/zohar&vol=26&sec=912 (accessed Feb. 24, 2010).

[25] Alan Unterman, *Dictionary of Jewish Lore and Legend* (London: Thames and Hudson Ltd., 1991), 150.

[26] Wikipedia, the Free Dictionary, *Eve*, 4, http://en.wikipedia.org/wiki/Eve_%28Bible%29 (accessed Oct. 23, 2007).

[27] Greg Killian, *The Days of Noah*, 4, http://www.adamqadmon.com/nephilim/gkillian000 (accessed Dec. 6, 2000); Alan Unterman, *Dictionary of Jewish Lore and Legend* (New York: Thames and Hudson 1991), 176.

[28] Louis Ginzberg, *The Legends of the Jews Volume V: Notes for Volume One and Two*, II. Adam, 119, III. The Ten Generations, 3, trans. Henrietta Szold (Baltimore, Maryland: The Johns Hopkins University Press, 1909), 121, 133; James L. Kugel, *Traditions of the Bible* (Cambridge, Massachusetts: Harvard University Press, 1998), 130-131; Alan Unterman, *Dictionary of Jewish Lore and Legend* (London: Thames and Hudson Ltd., 1991), 150.

[29] *The Apocalypse of Moses / Apocalypsis Mosis*, 19:3, trans. R. H. Charles, http://www.pseudepigrapha.com/pseudepigrapha/aprmose.htm (accessed June 27, 2005).

[30] Andrew Collins, *From the Ashes of Angels: The Forbidden Legacy of a Fallen Race* (Rochester, Vermont: Bear and Company, 1996), 25.

[31] *The Book of Enoch*, 10:8, trans. R.H. Charles (Montana: Kessinger Publishing, 1912).

[32] Rabbi Leo Jung, Ph. D., *Fallen Angels in Jewish, Christian and Mohammedan Literature* (New York: KTAV Publishing House, 1974), 76.

[33] Merriam-Webster Dictionary, *Lasciviousness*, http://www.merriam-webster.com/dictionary/lasciviousness (accessed July 28, 2010); Rabbi Leo Jung, Ph. D., *Fallen Angels in Jewish, Christian and Mohammedan Literature* (New York: KTAV Publishing House, 1974), 78.

[34] Johann Andreas Eisenmenger, *The Traditions of the Jews, Contained in the Talmud and other Mystical Writings* (London: J. Robinson, 1748), 194; *The Armenian Apocryphal Adam Literature*, The History of the Creation and Transgression of Adam 20-26, History and Sermon: Concerning the Creation of Adam and the Incarnation of Christ Our God 19-31, trans. William Lowndes Lipscomb (Ann Arbor, Michigan: University Microfilms International, 1983), 122, 263; *The Book of Adam*, [44]19.1, trans. J. P. Mahe, http://www.pseudepigrapha.com/pseudepigrapha/TheBookOfAdam.htm (accessed June 27, 2005); *The Chronicles of Jerahmeel (The Hebrew Bible Historiale)*, 22:4-5, trans. M. Gaster, Ph. D. (London: The Royal Asiatic Society, 1899), 47.

[35] *Pirke De Rabbi Eliezer*, Chapter 13: The Serpent in Paradise [15A. ii.], trans. Gerald Friedlander (New York: Sepher-Hermon Press, 1981), 93.

[36] *The Book of Adam*, [45]32.2, trans. J. P. Mahe, http://www.pseudepigrapha.com/pseudepigrapha/TheBookOfAdam.htm (accessed June 27, 2005).

[37] *The Book of Adam*, [38]11.1-[38]11.2, trans. J. P. Mahe,
http://www.pseudepigrapha.com/pseudepigrapha/TheBookOfAdam.htm (accessed June 27, 2005).

[38] *The Book of Adam*, [44]21.2, trans. J. P. Mahe,
http://www.pseudepigrapha.com/pseudepigrapha/TheBookOfAdam.htm (accessed June 27, 2005).

[39] G. H. Pember, M. A., *Earth's Earliest Ages and their Connection With Modern Spiritualism, Theosophy, and Buddhism* (Grand Rapids, Michigan: Kregel Publications, 1975), 112; Malcolm Godwin, *Angels: An Endangered Species* (New York: Simon & Schuester, 1990), 26, 28, 104.

[40] *Saltair na Rann*, 1301-1316, trans. David Greene.

[41] *There Were Giants on the earth... The Nephilim*, 2, http://biblelight.net/nephilim.htm (accessed Feb. 3, 2010).

[42] *There Were Giants on the earth... The Nephilim*, 2, http://biblelight.net/nephilim.htm (accessed Feb. 3, 2010).

[43] Philo, *On the* Creation 151-152 (also 165-166) (James L. Kugel, *The Bible As It Was* (Cambridge, Massachusetts: Harvard University Press, 1997), 75).

[44] *The Gospel of Philip*, trans. Wesley W. Isenberg, http://www.gnosis.org/naghamm/gop.html (accessed Feb. 4, 2010).

[45] *The Midrash Rabbah*, Bereshith (Genesis) 34:12, trans. Rabbi Dr. H. Freedman and Maurice Simon (London: The Soncino Press, 1961).

[46] *The History of al-Tabari - Volume I: General Introduction and From the Creation to the Flood*, Adam and Eve's Place on Earth, 121, trans. Franz Rosenthal (Albany: New York Press, 1989), 292.

[47] *The First Book of Adam and Eve (The Conflict of Adam and Eve with Satan)*, 13:6-7, trans. S. C. Malan (London: Williams and Norgate, 1882).

[48] *The First Book of Adam and Eve (The Conflict of Adam and Eve with Satan)*, 32:7, 37:1, trans. S. C. Malan (London: Williams and Norgate, 1882).

[49] *The Apocalypse of Moses / Apocalypsis Mosis*, 24:4, trans. R. H. Charles, http://www.pseudepigrapha.com/pseudepigrapha/aprmose.htm (accessed June 27, 2005); *The Book of Adam*, [44]24:4, trans. J. P. Mahe, http://www.pseudepigrapha.com/pseudepigrapha/TheBookOfAdam.htm (accessed June 27, 2005); *The Armenian Apocryphal Adam Literature*, The History of the Repentance of Adam and Eve, the First Created Ones, and How They Did It 87-90, trans. William Lowndes Lipscomb (Ann Arbor, Michigan: University Microfilms International, 1983), 231.

[50] *The Book of the Bee*, 20, trans. Earnest A. Wallis Budge, M. A., http://www.sacred-texts.com/chr/bb/bb20.htm (accessed Oct. 10, 2004); *The Book of Adam*, [44]24.4, trans. J. P. Mahe, http://www.pseudepigrapha.com/pseudepigrapha/TheBookOfAdam.htm (accessed June 27, 2005).

[51] *The Armenian Apocryphal Adam Literature*, The History of the Repentance of Adam and Eve, The First Created Ones, and How They Did It 20, trans. William Lowndes Lipscomb (Ann Arbor, Michigan: University Microfilms International, 1983), 223-224.

[52] *The Babylonian Talmud*, Jews' College / Soncino English Translation, Sanhedrin 59a, http://www.halakhah.com/sanhedrin/sanhedrin_59.html (accessed Feb 3, 2010).

[53] *The Testimony of Truth*, trans. Soren Giversen and Birger A. Pearson, http://www.gnosis.org/naghamm/testruth.html (accessed Feb 3, 2010).

[54] *The Armenian Apocryphal Adam Literature*, History of the Creation and Transgression of Adam 41, trans. William Lowndes Lipscomb (Ann Arbor, Michigan: University Microfilms International, 1983), 125.

[55] *Saltair na Rann*, 1449-1456, trans. David Greene.

[56] *The Companion Bible*, Genesis 3:18 (notes) (Grand Rapids, Michigan: Kregel Publications, 1990), 8; Targum Neofiti 1: Genesis / translated, with apparatus and notes, 3:18, trans. Martin McNamara (Collegeville, Minnesota: Liturgical Press, 1992), 62; *The Armenian Apocryphal Adam Literature*, The Words of Adam to Seth 13, The History of the Repentance of Adam and Eve, the First Created Ones, and How They Did It 20, trans. William Lowndes Lipscomb (Ann Arbor, Michigan: University Microfilms International, 1983), 209, 224.

[57] Ellen Frankel, *The Classic Tales: 4000 Years of Jewish Lore* (Northvale, New Jersey: Jason Aronson Inc., 1989), 32.

[58] James L. Kugel, *Traditions of the Bible* (Cambridge, Massachusetts: Harvard University Press, 1998), 142; Johann Andreas Eisenmenger, *The Traditions of the Jews, Contained in the Talmud and other Mystical Writings* (London: J. Robinson, 1748), 23-24; Rabbi Leo Jung, Ph. D., *Fallen Angels in Jewish, Christian and Mohammedan Literature* (New York: KTAV Publishing House, 1974), 75.

[59] Rabbi Leo Jung, Ph. D., *Fallen Angels in Jewish, Christian and Mohammedan Literature* (New York: KTAV Publishing House, 1974), 75.

[60] James L. Kugel, *Traditions of the Bible* (Cambridge, Massachusetts: Harvard University Press, 1998), 142; Johann Andreas Eisenmenger, *The Traditions of the Jews, Contained in the Talmud and other Mystical Writings* (London: J. Robinson, 1748), 24; Rabbi Leo Jung, Ph. D., *Fallen Angels in Jewish, Christian and Mohammedan Literature* (New York: KTAV Publishing House, 1974), 75; Hyman E. Goldin, *The Book of Legends: Tales From the Talmud and Midrash* (New York: The Jordan Publishing Co., 1929), 25.

[61] *The Babylonian Talmud*, Jews' College / Soncino English Translation, Sotah 9a-9b, http://halakhah.com/sotah/sotah_9.html (accessed Jan. 31, 2011).

[62] *The Companion Bible*, Appendix 19 (Grand Rapids, Michigan: Kregel Publications, 1990), 24-25.

[63] *Psa.* 72:9 (KJV), *Isa.* 49:23 (KJV), Sherry Shriner, *Serpent Seedline*, 7-8, http://www.serpentseedline.com/

(accessed Sept. 5, 2007).

[64] Johann Andreas Eisenmenger, *The Traditions of the Jews, Contained in the Talmud and Other Mystical Writings* (London: J. Robinson, 1748), 198.

[65] *The Companion Bible*, Appendix 19 (Grand Rapids, Michigan: Kregel Publications, 1990), 24-25.

[66] *Psa.* 44:25 (KJV); Sherry Shriner, *Serpent Seedline*, 8, http://www.serpentseedline.com/ (accessed Sept. 5, 2007); *The Companion Bible*, Genesis 3:14 (notes) (Grand Rapids, Michigan: Kregel Publications, 1990), 7; *Prov.* 20:17 (KJV); *Psa.* 72:8 (KJV).

[67] *The Apocalypse of Moses / Apocalypsis Mosis*, 26:1-4, trans. R. H. Charles, http://www.pseudepigrapha.com/pseudepigrapha/aprmose.htm (accessed June 27, 2005).

[68] *Barhebraeus' Scholia on the Old Testament Part I: Genesis - II Samuel*, Genesis 3:14, trans. Martin Sprengling and William Creighton Graham (Chicago, Illinois: University of Chicago Press 1931), 27.

[69] S. Baring-Gould, *Legends of the Patriarchs and Prophets and Other Old Testament Characters* (New York: American Book Exchange, 1881), 43.

[70] Rabbi Leo Jung, Ph. D., *Fallen Angels in Jewish, Christian and Mohammedan Literature* (New York: KTAV Publishing House, 1974), 71; S. Baring-Gould, *Legends of the Patriarchs and Prophets and Other Old Testament Characters* (New York: American Book Exchange, 1881), 18.

[71] Shira Halevi, *The Life Story of Adam and Havah*, Genesis 3:15 (Northvale, New Jersey: Jason Aronson, Inc., 1997), 204.

[72] Rabbi Leo Jung, Ph. D., *Fallen Angels in Jewish, Christian and Mohammedan Literature* (New York: KTAV Publishing House, 1974), 71.

[73] S. Baring-Gould, *Legends of the Patriarchs and Prophets and Other Old Testament Characters* (New York: American Book Exchange, 1881), 16.

[74] Josephus, J*ewish Antiquities*, Book 1, 45-50, trans. H. ST. J. Thackeray (London: William Heinemann Ltd. 1961), 23.

[75] *Targum Pseudo-Jonathan (Targum of Palestine / Targum of Jonathan Ben Uzziel)*, On the Book of Genesis, Section III, Berashith, http://targum.info/pj/pjgen1-6.htm (accessed Oct. 2, 2009).

[76] Shira Halevi, *The Life Story of Adam and Havah*, Genesis 3:16 (Northvale, New Jersey: Jason Aronson, Inc., 1997), 204.

[77] *The Armenian Apocryphal Adam Literature*, History and Sermon: Concerning the Creation of Adam and the Incarnation of Christ Our God 42, trans. William Lowndes Lipscomb (Ann Arbor, Michigan: University Microfilms International, 1983), 261.

[78] *The Apocalypse of Moses / Apocalypsis Mosis*, 25:1-4, trans. R. H. Charles, http://www.pseudepigrapha.com/pseudepigrapha/aprmose.htm (accessed June 27, 2005).

[79] *The Apocalypse of Moses / Apocalypsis Mosis*, 25:2, trans. R. H. Charles, http://www.pseudepigrapha.com/pseudepigrapha/aprmose.htm (accessed June 27, 2005); *The Armenian Apocryphal Adam Literature*, 42, trans. William Lowndes Lipscomb (Ann Arbor, Michigan: University Microfilms International, 1983), 125.

[80] Robert Graves and Raphael Patai, *Hebrew Myths: The Book of Genesis* (Garden City, New York: Doubleday & Company, 1964), 87; *The History of al-Tabari - Volume I: General Introduction and From the Creation to the Flood*, God's Testing of Adam, 109, trans. Franz Rosenthal (Albany: New York Press, 1989), 280-281.

[81] *The History of al-Tabari - Volume I: General Introduction and From the Creation to the Flood*, God's Testing of Adam, 107, trans. Franz Rosenthal (Albany: New York Press, 1989), 278.

[82] *The Book of Adam*, [44] 25.1-4, trans. J. P. Mahe, http://www.pseudepigrapha.com/pseudepigrapha/TheBookOfAdam.htm (accessed June 27, 2005).

[83] S. Baring-Gould, *Legends of the Patriarchs and Prophets and Other Old Testament Characters* (New York: American Book Exchange, 1881), 43.

[84] James L. Kugel, *Traditions of the Bible* (Cambridge, Massachusetts: Harvard University Press, 1998), 143.

[85] James L. Kugel, *Traditions of the Bible* (Cambridge, Massachusetts: Harvard University Press, 1998), 143.

[86] Andrew Collins, *From the Ashes of Angels* ((Rochester, Vermont: Bear & Company, 1996), 40-41; *Armenian Apocrypha Relating to Adam and Eve*, History of the Forefathers, Adam and His Sons and Grandsons 32, trans. Michael E. Stone (Leiden: E. J. Brill, 1996), 196; Louis Ginzberg, *The Legends of the Jews Volume V: Notes for Volume One and Two*, III. The Ten Generations, 3, trans. Henrietta Szold (Baltimore, Maryland: The Johns Hopkins University Press, 1909), 134; Philip Gardiner, *Secrets of the Serpent: In Search of the Secret Past* (Foresthill Ca.: Reality press, 2006), 15, 17.

[87] *The Midrash Rabbah*, Bereshith (Genesis) 23:2, trans. Rabbi Dr. H. Freedman and Maurice Simon (London: The Soncino Press, 1961).

[88] *Saltair na Rann*, 1401-1404, trans. David Greene.

[89] *The Garden of Eden Bible Study*, 22, http://www.frank.germano.com/gardenofeden.htm (accessed Nov. 15, 2006).

[90] *Vita Adae Et Evae (The Life of Adam and Eve)*, 18:1-2, trans. R. H. Charles, *The Apocrypha and Pseudepigrapha of the Old Testament* (Oxford: Clarendon Press, 1913).

[91] *Vita Adae Et Evae (The Life of Adam and Eve)*, 18:3, trans. R. H. Charles, *The Apocrypha and Pseudepigrapha of*

the Old Testament (Oxford: Clarendon Press, 1913).

Chapter 8

[1] Shira Halevi, *The Life Story of Adam and Havah*, Genesis 3:13 (Northvale, New Jersey: Jason Aronson, Inc., 1997), 203.

[2] *The Book of the Mysteries of the Heavens and the Earth and Other Works of Bakhayla Mikael (Zosimas)*, trans. E.A. Wallis Budge (London: Oxford University Press, 1935), 26; G. H. Pember, M. A., *Earth's Earliest Ages and their Connection With Modern Spiritualism, Theosophy, and Buddhism* (Grand Rapids, Michigan: Kregel Publications, 1975), 100-101, 120.

[3] *The Book of Adam*, [44]26.3-4, trans. J. P. Mahe, http://www.pseudepigrapha.com/pseudepigrapha/TheBookOfAdam.htm (accessed June 27, 2005).

[4] *The Book of the Rolls (Kitab Al-Magall)*, trans. Margaret Dunlop Gibson, Apocrypha Arabica (London: C.J Clay and Sons, 1901), 10.

[5] Ed Tarkowski, *War of the Ages: 6000 Year Overview: Satan's Effort to Hinder God's Plan*, 3-4, http://www.adamqadmon.com/watchers/warofages.html (accessed Dec. 11, 2000).

[6] *The Companion Bible*, Appendix 19 (Grand Rapids, Michigan: Kregel Publications, 1990), 25.

[7] Rabbi Leo Jung, Ph. D., *Fallen Angels in Jewish, Christian and Mohammedan Literature* (New York: KTAV Publishing House, 1974), 70-71; Shira Halevi, *The Life Story of Adam and Havah*, Genesis 3:13 (Northvale, New Jersey: Jason Aronson, Inc., 1997), 203.

[8] *Targum Pseudo-Jonathan (Targum of Palestine / Targum of Jonathan Ben Uzziel)*, On the Book of Genesis, Section 3, Berashith, http://targum.info/pj/pjgen1-6.htm (accessed Oct. 2, 2009).

[9] Strong's G444 - *anthropos*, http://www.blueletterbible.org/lang/lexicon/lexicon.cfm?Strongs=G444&t=KJV.html (accessed Dec. 17, 2009).

[10] Garbiel Alvarez, *Historia Ecclesiae Antediluviana*, Madrid, 1713.

[11] *Luke* 3:23 (notes) (KJV (Scofield Reference Version)).

[12] Timothy Unruh, *The Days of Noah and the "Sons of God"*, 11, https://www.adamqadmon.com/watchers/sonsofgod002 (accessed Dec. 11, 2000).

[13] *2 Enoch (The Book of the Secrets of Enoch)*, 31:5, trans. W. R. Morfill, M. A. (Oxford: Clarendon Press, 1896).

[14] *The Zohar*, Volume 1. Beresheet A, Section 28. Hevel-Moshe, 286, https://www2.kabbalah.com/k/index.php?p=zohar/zohar&vol=2&sec=49 (accessed Feb. 24, 2010).

[15] *Book of the Glory of Kings (Kerba Nagast)*, 7. Concerning Noah, trans. Sir. E. A. Wallis Budge (London: Humphrey Milford, 1932).

[16] S. Baring-Gould, *Legends of the Patriarchs and Prophets and Other Old Testament Characters* (New York: American Book Exchange, 1881), 59.

[17] *Pirke De Rabbi Eliezer*, Chapter 21: Cain and Abel [25A. i.] (notes), trans. Gerald Friedlander (New York: Sepher-Hermon Press, 1981), 152.

[18] *The Book of Adam*, 21.2, trans. J. P. Mahe, http://www.pseudepigrapha.com/pseudepigrapha/TheBookOfAdam.htm (accessed June 27, 2005).

[19] Strong's H3045 - *yada*, http://www.blueletterbible.org/lang/lexicon/lexicon.cfm?Strongs=H3045&t=KJV (accessed Aug. 11, 2010); Strong's H853 - *eth*, http://www.blueletterbible.org/lang/lexicon/lexicon.cfm?Strongs=H853&t=KJV (accessed Aug. 11, 2010); Strong's H226 - *owth*, http://www.blueletterbible.org/lang/lexicon/lexicon.cfm?Strongs=H226&t=KJV (accessed Aug. 11, 2010); Strong's H2029 - *harah*, http://www.blueletterbible.org/lang/lexicon/lexicon.cfm?Strongs=H2029&t=KJV (accessed Aug. 16, 2010).

[20] James L. Kugel, *The Bible As It Was*, (Cambridge, Massachusetts: Harvard University Press, 1997), 86.

[21] *Pirke De Rabbi Eliezer*, Chapter 21, Cain and Abel [25A. i.], trans. Gerald Friedlander (New York: Sepher-Hermon Press, 1981), 151.

[22] *The Apocalypse of Moses / Apocalypsis Mosis*, 3:2, trans. R. H. Charles, http://www.pseudepigrapha.com/pseudepigrapha/aprmose.htm (accessed June 27, 2005).

[23] Johann Andreas Eisenmenger, *The Traditions of the Jews, Contained in the Talmud and Other Mystical Writings* (London: J. Robinson, 1748), 198.

[24] *Gen.* 1:1 (notes) (KJV (Scofield Reference Version)).

[25] James L. Kugel, *The Bible As It Was*, (Cambridge, Massachusetts: Harvard University Press, 1997), 86.

[26] *Targum Pseudo-Jonathan (Targum of Palestine / Targum of Jonathan Ben Uzziel)*, On the Book of Genesis, Section 2, Berashith, http://targum.info/pj/pjgen1-6.htm (accessed Oct. 2, 2009).

[27] *The Midrash Rabbah*, Bereshith (Genesis) 24:6, trans. Rabbi Dr. H. Freedman and Maurice Simon (London: The Soncino Press, 1961).

[28] James L. Kugel, *Traditions of the Bible* (Cambridge, Massachusetts: Harvard University Press, 1998), 157; Bentley Layton, *The Gnostic Scriptures*, The Holy Book of the Great Invisible Spirit, Mythic Characters: III. Humankind (New York: Doubleday, 1995), 103; Rabbi Leo Jung, Ph. D., *Fallen Angels in Jewish, Christian and Mohammedan Literature* (New York: KTAV Publishing House, 1974), 78; *Saltair na Rann*, 1961-1964, trans. David Greene; Alan

Unterman, *Dictionary of Jewish Lore and Legend* (London: Thames and Hudson Ltd., 1991), 44, 173.

[29] *The Works of Philo Judaeus*, Questions and Answers on Genesis 1, 81, trans. C. D. Yonge (London: H. G. Bohn, 1854-1855).

[30] Bentley Layton, *The Gnostic Scriptures*, The Reality of the Rulers, Cain and Abel, 11-29 (and notes) (New York: Doubleday, 1995), 72).

[31] *The Zohar*, Volume 5, Vayishlach, Section 28. "… who found Yemim in the wilderness", 261, https://www2.kabbalah.com/k/index.php/p=zohar/zohar&vol=10&sec=380 (accessed Feb. 24, 2010).

[32] Johann Andreas Eisenmenger, *The Traditions of the Jews, Contained in the Talmud and other Mystical Writings* (London: J. Robinson, 1748), 197; Rabbi Leo Jung, Ph. D., *Fallen Angels in Jewish, Christian and Mohammedan Literature* (New York: KTAV Publishing House, 1974), 92.

[33] Rabbi Leo Jung, Ph. D., *Fallen Angels in Jewish, Christian and Mohammedan Literature* (New York: KTAV Publishing House, 1974), 79.

[34] Johann Andreas Eisenmenger, *The Traditions of the Jews, Contained in the Talmud and Other Mystical Writings* (London: J. Robinson, 1748), 197.

[35] *The Book of Enoch*, 69:12, trans. R.H. Charles (Montana: Kessinger Publishing, 1912); Andrew Collins, *From the Ashes of Angels* (Rochester, Vermont: Bear & Company, 1996), 41.

[36] Rabbi Leo Jung, Ph. D., *Fallen Angels in Jewish, Christian and Mohammedan Literature* (New York: KTAV Publishing House, 1974), 78.

[37] *Pirke De Rabbi Eliezer*, Chapter 22: The Fall of the Angels [26A. i.], trans. Gerald Friedlander (New York: Sepher-Hermon Press, 1981), 158.

[38] Johann Andreas Eisenmenger, *The Traditions of the Jews, Contained in the Talmud and Other Mystical Writings* (London: J. Robinson, 1748), 198.

[39] Rabbi Leo Jung, Ph. D., *Fallen Angels in Jewish, Christian and Mohammedan Literature* (New York: KTAV Publishing House, 1974), 78.

[40] *Vita Adae Et Evae (The Life of Adam and Eve)*, 19.3, trans. R. H. Charles, The Apocrypha and Pseudepigrapha of the Old Testament (Oxford: Clarendon Press, 1913).

[41] *The Book of Adam*, 21.3a, trans. J. P. Mahe, http://www.pseudepigrapha.com/pseudepigrapha/TheBookOfAdam.htm (accessed June 27, 2005).

[42] Louis Ginzberg, *The Legends of the Jews Volume V: Notes for Volume One and Two*, III. The Ten Generations, 6, trans. Henrietta Szold (Baltimore, Maryland: The Johns Hopkins University Press, 1909), 135; Robert Graves and Raphael Patai, *Hebrew Myths: The Book of Genesis* (Garden City, New York: Doubleday & Company, 1964), 85.

[43] *The Apocalypse of Moses / Apocalypsis Mosis*, 21:3 (notes), trans. R. H. Charles, http://www.pseudepigrapha.com/pseudepigrapha/aprmose.htm (accessed June 27, 2005).

[44] *Targum Pseudo-Jonathan (Targum of Palestine / Targum of Jonathan Ben Uzziel)*, On the Book of Genesis, Section 4, Berashith, http://targum.info/pj/pjgen1-6.htm (accessed Oct. 2, 2009).

[45] Johann Andreas Eisenmenger, *The Traditions of the Jews, Contained in the Talmud and Other Mystical Writings* (London: J. Robinson, 1748), 198.

[46] Robert Bowie Johnson, Jr., *The Parthenon Code: Mankind's History in Marble* (Annapolis, Maryland: Solving Light Books, 2004), 193; *The World Before the Flood, and the History of the Patriarchs*, Chapter 1, 5, http://www.adamqadmon.com/watchers/pre-flood000.html (accessed Feb 10, 2001); James L. Kugel, *The Bible As It Was*, (Cambridge, Massachusetts: Harvard University Press, 1997), 87.

[47] James L. Kugel, *The Bible As It Was* (Cambridge, Massachusetts: Harvard University Press, 1997), 85.

[48] James L. Kugel, *The Bible As It Was* (Cambridge, Massachusetts: Harvard University Press, 1997), 87.

[49] *The Gospel of Judas: Cain - Cainites - Kenite - Rechabites*, 15, http://www.piney.com/Cain (accessed April 19, 2007).

[50] *The World Before the Flood and The History of the Patriarchs*, 5-6, www.adamqadmon.com/watchers/pre-flood000 (accessed Feb. 10, 2001).

[51] *The Penitence of our Forefather Adam*, 21.3a, trans. Gary A. Anderson and Michael E. Stone, http://www2.iath.virginia.edu/anderson/viat/english/vita.arm.html (accessed Dec 26, 2009).

[52] *The Book of Adam*, 21.3a, trans. J. P. Mahe, http://www.pseudepigrapha.com/pseudepigrapha/TheBookOfAdam.htm (accessed June 27, 2005).

[53] James L. Kugel, *The Bible As It Was* (Cambridge, Massachusetts: Harvard University Press, 1997), 85.

[54] *The Book of Adam*, 21.3a, trans. J. P. Mahe, http://www.pseudepigrapha.com/pseudepigrapha/TheBookOfAdam.htm (accessed June 27, 2005).

[55] Louis Ginzberg, *The Legends of the Jews Volume V: Notes for Volume One and Two*, III. The Ten Generations, 20, trans. Henrietta Szold (Baltimore, Maryland: The Johns Hopkins University Press, 1909), 140; Robert Graves and Raphael Patai, *Hebrew Myths: The Book of Genesis* (Garden City, New York: Doubleday & Company, 1964), 92.

[56] *The Book of Adam*, 21:3b-21:3c, trans. J. P. Mahe, http://www.pseudepigrapha.com/pseudepigrapha/TheBookOfAdam.htm (accessed June 27, 2005).

[57] *Barhebraeus' Scholia on the Old Testament Part I: Genesis - II Samuel*, Genesis 3:17, trans. Martin Sprengling and William Creighton Graham (Chicago, Illinois: University of Chicago Press 1931), 27.

[58] Bentley Layton, *The Gnostic Scriptures*, The Archontics According to St. Epiphanius, Cain and Abel, 40.5.3-4 (New York: Doubleday, 1995), 197.

[59] *The History of al-Tabari - Volume I: General Introduction and From the Creation to the Flood*, Cain and Abel, 137, 139, 146, trans. Franz Rosenthal (Albany: New York Press, 1989), 308, 310, 317; *Saltair na Rann*, 1969-1972, 2493-2496, trans. David Greene; *Barhebraeus' Scholia on the Old Testament Part I: Genesis - II Samuel*, Genesis 4:4, trans. Martin Sprengling and William Creighton Graham (Chicago, Illinois: University of Chicago Press 1931), 31; Louis Ginzberg, *The Legends of the Jews Volume I: From the Creation to Jacob*, trans. Henrietta Szold (Baltimore, Maryland: The Johns Hopkins University Press, 1909), 108; *The Armenian Apocryphal Adam Literature*, This Is the History of Abel and Cain the Sons of Adam 3-4, trans. William Lowndes Lipscomb (Ann Arbor, Michigan: University Microfilms International, 1983), 157-158.

[60] Robert Graves and Raphael Patai, *Hebrew Myths: The Book of Genesis* (Garden City, New York: Doubleday & Company, 1964), 99; *Pirke De Rabbi Eliezer*, Chap. 21: Cain and Abel [25A. i.], trans. Gerald Friedlander (New York: Sepher-Hermon Press, 1981), 152; *The History of al-Tabari - Volume I: General Introduction and From the Creation to the Flood,* Cain and Abel 137, 139-140, 147, trans. Franz Rosenthal (Albany: New York Press, 1989), 308, 310, 317; *The Garden of Eden Bible Study*, 17, http://www.frank.germano.com/gardenofeden.htm (accessed Nov. 15, 2006).

[61] *Pirke De Rabbi Eliezer*, Chapter 22: The Fall of the Angels [26A. i.] (notes), trans. Gerald Friedlander (New York: Sepher-Hermon Press, 1981), 158.

[62] *Pirke De Rabbi Eliezer*, Chap. 21: Cain and Abel [25A. i.], trans. Gerald Friedlander (New York: Sepher-Hermon Press, 1981), 152.

[63] *The Midrash Rabbah*, Bereshith (Genesis) 22:3, trans. Rabbi Dr. H. Freedman and Maurice Simon (London: The Soncino Press, 1961); *The Garden of Eden Bible Study*, 5, 17, http://www.frank.germano.com/gardenofeden.htm (accessed Nov. 15, 2006).

[64] Philip Gardiner, *Secrets of the Serpent: in Search of the Secret Past* (Foresthill Ca: Reality press, 2006), 18.

[65] *Gen.* 4:3-5 (KJV); *Sons of Cain: They Survived Noah's Flood*, 2, http://www.nfis.com/~danelady/sonsofcain.html (accessed June 5, 2000).

[66] Bentley Layton, *The Gnostic Scriptures*, The Secret Book According to John, Mythic characters II - III (New York: Doubleday, 1995), 25).

[67] *The Apocalypse of Moses / Apocalypsis Mosis*, 3:1 (notes), trans. R. H. Charles, The Apocrypha and Pseudepigrapha of the Old Testament, Volume Two (Berkeley, Ca.: Apocryphile Press, 2004).

[68] *Star Wars, Lesson Eight*, 4-5, http://usa-the-republic.com/religion/star%20wars/Star%20Wars%20-%20Lesson%20Eight.htm (accessed April 23, 2005).

[69] Richard Gan, *The Mark of the Wicked Ones*, 17, http://www.porpheticrevelation.net/w-ones.htm (accessed Aug. 22, 2007).

[70] William F. Dankenbring, *The Mark of Cain*, 2, http://www.triumphpro.com/the_mark_of_cain.htm (accessed Aug. 8, 2007).

[71] *The Zohar*, Volume 13, Pekudei, Section 21. Breastplate and Efod, 203, https://www2.kabbalah.com/k/index.php?p=zohar/zohar&vol=26&sec=912 (accessed Feb. 24, 2010).

[72] *The Zohar*, Volume 1, Beresheet A, Section 28. Hevel-Moshe, 285, https://www2.kabbalah.com/k/index.php?p=zohar/zohar&vol=2&sec=49 (accessed Feb. 24, 2010).

[73] Johann Andreas Eisenmenger, *The Traditions of the Jews, Contained in the Talmud and Other Mystical Writings* (London: J. Robinson, 1748), 197.

[74] *The World Before the Flood, and the History of the Patriarchs*, 6, http://www.adamqadmon.com/watchers/pre-flood000.htm (accessed Feb. 10, 2001); James E. Thorold, *Bible Folk-lore; A Study in Comparative Mythology* (London: Kegan Paul, Trench and Co, 1884), 11; James L. Kugel, *The Bible As It Was*, (Cambridge, Massachusetts: Harvard University Press, 1997), 87; G. H. Pember, M. A., *Earth's Earliest Ages and their Connection With Modern Spiritualism, Theosophy, and Buddhism* (Grand Rapids, Michigan: Kregel Publications, 1975), 117.

[75] *Book of the Glory of Kings (Kerba Nagast)*, 3. Concerning the Kingdom of Adam, 4. Concerning Envy, trans. Sir. E. A. Wallis Budge (London: Humphrey Milford, 1932).

[76] *The Book of the Rolls (Kitab Al-Magall)*, trans. Margaret Dunlop Gibson, Apocrypha Arabica, (London: C.J. Clay and Sons, 1901), 11.

[77] *Book of the Glory of Kings (Kerba Nagast)*, 4. Concerning Envy, trans. Sir. E. A. Wallis Budge (London: Humphrey Milford, 1932).

[78] *The Book of the Cave of Treasures*, The First Thousand Years: Adam to Yared (Jared), Adam's Expulsion from Paradise, trans. Sir E. A. Wallis Budge (London: The Religious Tract Society, 1927), 68-70.

Chapter 9

[1] answers.com, *basilisk*, http://www.answers.com/topic/basilisk (accessed Feb. 4, 2010).

[2] Johann Andreas Eisenmenger, *The Traditions of the Jews, Contained in the Talmud and other Mystical Writings* (London: J. Robinson, 1748), 197-198.

[3] *The Bible, The Koran, and the Talmud (Biblical Legends of the Mussulmans)*, Adam (A Mohammedan Legend),

trans. Dr. G. Weil (New York, 1863), 10; Robert Graves and Raphael Patai, *Hebrew Myths: The Book of Genesis* (Garden City, New York: Doubleday & Company, 1964), 92; S. Baring-Gould, *Legends of the Patriarchs and Prophets and Other Old Testament Characters* (New York: American Book Exchange, 1881), 68; *The History of al-Tabari - Volume I: General Introduction and From the Creation to the Flood*, Cain and Abel, 138, 141, trans. Franz Rosenthal (Albany: New York Press, 1989), 308, 311.

[4] G. H. Pember, M. A., *Earth's Earliest Ages and their Connection With Modern Spiritualism, Theosophy, and Buddhism* (Grand Rapids, Michigan: Kregel Publications, 1975), 118.

[5] G. H. Pember, M. A., *Earth's Earliest Ages and their Connection With Modern Spiritualism, Theosophy, and Buddhism* (Grand Rapids, Michigan: Kregel Publications, 1975), 118.

[6] Josephus, *Jewish Antiquities*, Book 1, 53-4, trans. H. ST. J. Thackeray (London: William Heinemann Ltd. 1961), 25.

[7] *The Works of Philo Judaeus*, Questions and Answers in Genesis 1, 59, trans. C. D. Yonge (London: H.G Bohn, 1854-1855).

[8] Louis Ginzberg, *The Legends of the Jews Volume I: From the Creation to Jacob*, trans. Henrietta Szold (Baltimore, Maryland: The Johns Hopkins University Press, 1909), 107.

[9] Louis Ginzberg, *The Legends of the Jews Volume I: From the Creation to Jacob*, trans. Henrietta Szold (Baltimore, Maryland: The Johns Hopkins University Press, 1909), 107-108.

[10] S. Baring-Gould, *Legends of the Patriarchs and Prophets and Other Old Testament Characters* (New York: American Book Exchange, 1881), 69; *The Armenian Apocryphal Adam Literature*, The History of Cain and Abel 7, trans. William Lowndes Lipscomb (Ann Arbor, Michigan: University Microfilms International, 1983), 270-271.

[11] G. H. Pember, M. A., *Earth's Earliest Ages and their Connection With Modern Spiritualism, Theosophy, and Buddhism* (Grand Rapids, Michigan: Kregel Publications, 1975), 118.

[12] *The Armenian Apocryphal Adam Literature*, This is the History of Abel and Cain the Sons of Adam 9, trans. William Lowndes Lipscomb (Ann Arbor, Michigan: University Microfilms International, 1983), 159.

[13] Louis Ginzberg, *The Legends of the Jews Volume V: Notes for Volume One and Two*, III. The Ten Generations, 12, trans. Henrietta Szold (Baltimore, Maryland: The Johns Hopkins University Press, 1909), 136; *The History of al-Tabari - Volume I: General Introduction and From the Creation to the Flood*, Cain and Abel, 140, trans. Franz Rosenthal (Albany: New York Press, 1989), 311.

[14] *Pirke De Rabbi Eliezer*, Chapter 21: Cain and Abel [25A. i.], trans. Gerald Friedlander (New York: Sepher-Hermon Press, 1981), 153-154.

[15] *The Armenian Apocryphal Adam Literature*, This is the History of Abel and Cain the Sons of Adam 12, trans. William Lowndes Lipscomb (Ann Arbor, Michigan: University Microfilms International, 1983), 160.

[16] *The Armenian Apocryphal Adam Literature*, This is the History of Abel and Cain the Sons of Adam 10, trans. William Lowndes Lipscomb (Ann Arbor, Michigan: University Microfilms International, 1983), 160.

[17] James L. Kugel, *Traditions of the Bible* (Cambridge, Massachusetts: Harvard University Press, 1998), 159.

[18] Louis Ginzberg, *The Legends of the Jews Volume V: Notes for Volume One and Two*, III. The Ten Generations, 13, trans. Henrietta Szold (Baltimore, Maryland: The Johns Hopkins University Press, 1909), 137; *Saltair na Rann*, 1957-1960, trans. David Greene; Shira Halevi, *The Life Story of Adam and Havah*, Genesis 4:5b (Northvale, New Jersey: Jason Aronson, Inc., 1997), 248; Wikipedia, the Free Encyclopedia, *Curse and Mark of Cain*, 2, http://en.wikipedia.org/wiki/Curse_and_mark_of_Cain (Oct. 09, 2007).

[19] Louis Ginzberg, *The Legends of the Jews Volume V: Notes for Volume One and Two*, III. The Ten Generations, 13, trans. Henrietta Szold (Baltimore, Maryland: The Johns Hopkins University Press, 1909), 137; *The Third Book of Adam and Eve (The Conflict of Adam and Eve with Satan)*, Chapter 4, trans. S. C. Malan (London: Williams and Norgate, 1882); *Saltair na Rann*, 1661-1664, trans. David Greene; Bentley Layton, *The Gnostic Scriptures*, Confrontation of Norea and the Rulers, 92 (New York: Doubleday, 1995), 73; *Targum Neofiti 1: Genesis / Translated, With Apparatus and Notes*, Genesis 4:7 (notes), trans. Martin McNamara (Collegeville, Minnesota: Liturgical Press, 1992).

[20] *Juvenile Instructor*, Vol. 26, p. 635.

[21] *The Armenian Apocryphal Adam Literature*, This is the History of Abel and Cain the Sons of Adam 10, trans. William Lowndes Lipscomb (Ann Arbor, Michigan: University Microfilms International, 1983), 160.

[22] Ellen Frankel, *The Classic Tales: 4000 Years of Jewish Lore* (Northvale, New Jersey: Jason Aronson Inc., 1989), 37.

[23] *Genizah Manuscripts of Palestinian Targum to the Pentateuch Volume One*, Genesis 4:7, trans. Michael L. Klein (Cincinnati: Hebrew Union College Press, 1986), 6.

[24] *Targum Pseudo-Jonathan (Targum of Palestine / Targum of Jonathan Ben Uzziel)*, On the Book of Genesis, Section 4, Berashith, http://targum.info/pj/pjgen1-6.htm (accessed Oct. 2, 2009).

[25] G. H. Pember, M. A., *Earth's Earliest Ages and their Connection With Modern Spiritualism, Theosophy, and Buddhism* (Grand Rapids, Michigan: Kregel Publications, 1975), 119.

[26] Louis Ginzberg, *The Legends of the Jews Volume V: Notes for Volume One and Two*, III. The Ten Generations, 7, trans. Henrietta Szold (Baltimore, Maryland: The Johns Hopkins University Press, 1909), 135.

[27] *The Book of Adam*, [23]3.2, trans. J. P. Mahe, http://www.pseudepigrapha.com/pseudepigrapha/TheBookOfAdam.htm (accessed June 27, 2005).

[28] *Targum Pseudo-Jonathan (Targum of Palestine / Targum of Jonathan Ben Uzziel)*, On the Book of Genesis, Section 4, Berashith, http://targum.info/pj/pjgen1-6.htm (accessed Oct. 2, 2009).

[29] *Targum Neofiti 1: Genesis / Translated, With Apparatus and Notes*, Genesis 4:8, trans. Martin McNamara (Collegeville, Minnesota: Liturgical Press, 1992).

[30] *Targum Pseudo-Jonathan (Targum of Palestine / Targum of Jonathan Ben Uzziel)*, On the Book of Genesis, Section 4, Berashith, http://targum.info/pj/pjgen1-6.htm (accessed Oct. 2, 2009).

[31] Robert Graves and Raphael Patai, *Hebrew Myths: The Book of Genesis* (Garden City, New York: Doubleday & Company, 1964), 91.

[32] *The History of al-Tabari - Volume I: General Introduction and From the Creation to the Flood,* Cain and Abel, 138, trans. Franz Rosenthal (Albany: New York Press, 1989), 308.

[33] Mikal Bin Gorion, *Mimekor Yisrael - Volume I*, Cain and Abel (Bloomington, Indiana: University Press, 1976), 7.

[34] Louis Ginzberg, *The Legends of the Jews Volume V: Notes for Volume One and Two*, III. The Ten Generations, 19, trans. Henrietta Szold (Baltimore, Maryland: The Johns Hopkins University Press, 1909), 139.

[35] James L. Kugel, *Traditions of the Bible* (Cambridge, Massachusetts: Harvard University Press, 1998), 162.

[36] Robert Graves and Raphael Patai, *Hebrew Myths: The Book of Genesis* (Garden City, New York: Doubleday & Company, 1964), 92.

[37] Mrs. Sydney Bristowe, *Sargon the Magnificent* (London: The Covenant Publishing Co., 1927), 4.

[38] *Yalkut Hadash* (Rabbi Leo Jung, Ph. D., Fallen Angels in Jewish, Christian and Mohammedan Literature (New York: KTAV Publishing House, 1974), 78).

[39] *The Gospel of Philip*, trans. Wesley W. Isenberg, http://www.gnosis.org/naghamm/gop.html (accessed Feb. 4, 2010).

[40] Robert Graves and Raphael Patai, *Hebrew Myths: The Book of Genesis* (Garden City, New York: Doubleday & Company, 1964), 92; Louis Ginzberg, *The Legends of the Jews Volume V: Notes for Volume One and Two*, III. The Ten Generations, 20, trans. Henrietta Szold (Baltimore, Maryland: The Johns Hopkins University Press, 1909), 139.

[41] James L. Kugel, *Traditions of the Bible* (Cambridge, Massachusetts: Harvard University Press, 1998), 160; *The Armenian Apocryphal Adam Literature*, This is the History of Abel and Cain the sons of Adam 18-29, 32-33, trans. William Lowndes Lipscomb (Ann Arbor, Michigan: University Microfilms International, 1983), 162-165.

[42] Shira Halevi, *The Life Story of Adam and Havah*, Genesis 4:8a (Northvale, New Jersey: Jason Aronson, Inc., 1997), 250.

[43] *The Armenian Apocryphal Adam Literature*, This is the History of Abel and Cain the Sons of Adam 33, trans. William Lowndes Lipscomb (Ann Arbor, Michigan: University Microfilms International, 1983), 165.

[44] *The Armenian Apocryphal Adam Literature*, This is the History of Abel and Cain the Sons of Adam 34, trans. William Lowndes Lipscomb (Ann Arbor, Michigan: University Microfilms International, 1983), 165.

[45] *The Armenian Apocryphal Adam Literature*, The History of the Repentance of Adam and Eve, the First Created Ones, and How They Did It 46, trans. William Lowndes Lipscomb (Ann Arbor, Michigan: University Microfilms International, 1983), 228.

[46] G. H. Pember, M. A., *Earth's Earliest Ages and their Connection With Modern Spiritualism, Theosophy, and Buddhism* (Grand Rapids, Michigan: Kregel Publications, 1975), 119.

[47] Louis Ginzberg, *The Legends of the Jews Volume I: From the Creation to Jacob*, trans. Henrietta Szold (Baltimore, Maryland: The Johns Hopkins University Press, 1909), 111.

[48] *The Companion Bible*, Genesis 4:13 (notes) (Grand Rapids, Michigan: Kregel Publications, 1990), 9; *Targum Neofiti 1: Genesis / Translated, With Apparatus and Notes*, Genesis 4:13, trans. Martin McNamara (Collegeville, Minnesota: Liturgical Press, 1992).

[49] *Genizah Manuscripts of Palestinian Targum to the Pentateuch Volume One*, Genesis 4:13, trans. Michael L. Klein (Cincinnati: Hebrew Union College Press, 1986), 7.

[50] *Targum Pseudo-Jonathan (Targum of Palestine / Targum of Jonathan Ben Uzziel)*, On the Book of Genesis, Section 4, Berashith, http://targum.info/pj/pjgen1-6.htm (accessed Oct. 2, 2009).

[51] William Dankenbring, *The Mark of Cain*, 5, http://www.triumphpro.com/the_mark_of_cain.htm (accessed Aug. 22, 2007).

[52] Ellen Frankel, *The Classic Tales: 4000 Years of Jewish Lore* (Northvale, New Jersey: Jason Aronson Inc., 1989), 37.

[53] Robert Graves and Raphael Patai, *Hebrew Myths: The Book of Genesis* (Garden City, New York: Doubleday & Company, 1964), 91.

[54] Robert Graves and Raphael Patai, *Hebrew Myths: The Book of Genesis* (Garden City, New York: Doubleday & Company, 1964), 91.

[55] *Genizah Manuscripts of Palestinian Targum to the Pentateuch Volume One*, Genesis 4:8, trans. Michael L. Klein (Cincinnati: Hebrew Union College Press, 1986), 10.

[56] Ellen Frankel, *The Classic Tales: 4000 Years of Jewish Lore* (Northvale, New Jersey: Jason Aronson Inc., 1989), 38-39.

[57] Ellen Frankel, *The Classic Tales: 4000 years of Jewish Lore* (Northvale, New Jersey: Jason Aronson Inc., 1989), 38.

[58] James R. Davis, *Have We Gone the Way of Cain?*, 6-7, http://www.focusongod.com/cain (accessed March 3, 2001).

[59] E. S. G. Bristowe, *Cain - An Argument* (Leicester: Edgar Backus, 1950), 59.

[60] Dictionary - MSN Encarta, *cynical*, http://www.encarta.msn.com/dictionary_/cynical (accessed Feb. 4, 2010).

[61] answers.com, *Cynics*, 1-2, http://www.answers.com/topic/cynic-1 (accessed Oct 18, 2007).

[62] *Cynical*, 1, http://encarta.msn.com/dictionary_/cynical.html (accessed Feb. 4, 2010); *Cynics*, 1-2,

http://www.answers.com/topic/cynic-1 (accessed Oct 18, 2007).

[63] Mrs. Sydney Bristowe, *Sargon the Magnificent* (London: The Covenant Publishing Co., 1927), 111.

[64] Mrs. Sydney Bristowe, *Sargon the Magnificent* (London: The Covenant Publishing Co., 1927), 111.

[65] Mrs. Sydney Bristowe, *Sargon the Magnificent* (London: The Covenant Publishing Co., 1927), 111.

[66] Mrs. Sydney Bristowe, *Sargon the Magnificent* (London: The Covenant Publishing Co., 1927), 112.

[67] Mrs. Sydney Bristowe, *Sargon the Magnificent* (London: The Covenant Publishing Co., 1927), 79.

[68] *The Armenian Apocryphal Adam Literature*, The History of the Repentance of Adam and Eve, the First Created Ones, and How They Did It 49, trans. William Lowndes Lipscomb (Ann Arbor, Michigan: University Microfilms International, 1983), 228.

[69] Mikal Bin Gorion, *Mimekor Yisrael - Volume I*, 7. Cain and Abel (Bloomington, Indiana: University Press, 1976), 9.

[70] James L. Kugel, *Traditions of the Bible* (Cambridge, Massachusetts: Harvard University Press, 1998), 165.

[71] *The Book of the Generations of Adam*, 5:11, http://www.earth-history.com/Pseudepigrapha/generations-adam.htm (accessed May 5, 2007).

[72] S. Baring-Gould, *Legends of the Patriarchs and Prophets and Other Old Testament Characters* (New York: American Book Exchange, 1881), 76.

[73] *The Armenian Apocryphal Adam Literature*, This is the History of Abel and Cain the sons of Adam 36, History of Cain and Abel 37, trans. William Lowndes Lipscomb (Ann Arbor, Michigan: University Microfilms International, 1983), 165, 271.

[74] *The History of al-Tabari - Volume I: General Introduction and From the Creation to the Flood*, Cain and Abel, 144, trans. Franz Rosenthal (Albany: New York Press, 1989), 315.

[75] Mikal Bin Gorion, *Mimekor Yisrael - Volume I*, 7. Cain and Abel (Bloomington, Indiana: University Press, 1976), 9.

[76] Richard Gan, *The Mark of the Wicked Ones*, 7, http://www.propheticrevelation.net/w-ones.htm (accessed Aug. 22, 2007).

[77] *The Armenian Apocryphal Adam Literature*, The History of the Repentance of Adam and Eve, The First Created Ones, and How They Did It 51-54, trans. William Lowndes Lipscomb (Ann Arbor, Michigan: University Microfilms International, 1983), 228.

[78] *The History of al-Tabari - Volume I: General Introduction and From the Creation to the Flood*, Cain and Abel 142, trans. Franz Rosenthal (Albany: New York Press, 1989), 312; *Barhebraeus' Scholia on the Old Testament Part I: Genesis - II Samuel*, Genesis 4:15, trans. Martin Sprengling and William Creighton Graham (Chicago, Illinois: University of Chicago Press 1931), 33.

[79] Mikal Bin Gorion, *Mimekor Yisrael - Volume I*, 7. Cain and Abel (Bloomington, Indiana: University Press, 1976), 9; *Barhebraeus' Scholia on the Old Testament Part I: Genesis - II Samuel*, Genesis 4:11, trans. Martin Sprengling and William Creighton Graham (Chicago, Illinois: University of Chicago Press 1931), 31.

[80] *Armenian Apocrypha Relating to Adam and Eve*, History of the Forefathers, Adam and His Sons and Grandsons 17, trans. Michael E. Stone (Leiden: E. J. Brill, 1996), 188-189.

[81] Louis Ginzberg, *The Legends of the Jews Volume V: Notes for Volume One and Two*, III. The Ten Generations, 26, trans. Henrietta Szold (Baltimore, Maryland: The Johns Hopkins University Press, 1909), 141.

[82] Mikal Bin Gorion, *Mimekor Yisrael - Volume I*, 7. Cain and Abel (Bloomington, Indiana: University Press, 1976), 9; *The History of al-Tabari - Volume I: General Introduction and From the Creation to the Flood*, Cain and Abel, 142, trans. Franz Rosenthal (Albany: New York Press, 1989), 312.

[83] Louis Ginzberg, *The Legends of the Jews Volume I: From the Creation to Jacob*, trans. Henrietta Szold (Baltimore, Maryland: The Johns Hopkins University Press, 1909), 111; Ellen Frankel, *The Classic Tales: 4000 years of Jewish Lore* (Northvale, New Jersey: Jason Aronson Inc., 1989), 39.

[84] S. Baring-Gould, *Legends of the Patriarchs and Prophets and Other Old Testament Characters* (New York: American Book Exchange, 1881), 73.

[85] *The History of al-Tabari - Volume I: General Introduction and From the Creation to the Flood*, Cain and Abel, 144, trans. Franz Rosenthal (Albany: New York Press, 1989), 315.

[86] Louis Ginzberg, *The Legends of the Jews Volume I: From the Creation to Jacob*, trans. Henrietta Szold (Baltimore, Maryland: The Johns Hopkins University Press, 1909), 111; Mikal Bin Gorion, *Mimekor Yisrael - Volume I*, 7. Cain and Abel (Bloomington, Indiana: University Press, 1976), 9.

[87] *The First Book of Adam and Eve (The Conflict of Adam and Eve with Satan)*, 79:24-26, trans. S. C. Malan (London: Williams and Norgate, 1882), 59.

[88] Mikal Bin Gorion, *Mimekor Yisrael - Volume I*, 7. Cain and Abel (Bloomington, Indiana: University Press, 1976), 9.

[89] S. Baring-Gould, *Legends of the Patriarchs and Prophets and Other Old Testament Characters* (New York: American Book Exchange, 1881), 70.

[90] *The Armenian Apocryphal Adam Literature*, The History of the Repentance of Adam and Eve, The First Created Ones, and How They Did It 60, trans. William Lowndes Lipscomb (Ann Arbor, Michigan: University Microfilms International, 1983), 229.

[91] James L. Kugel, *Traditions of the Bible* (Cambridge, Massachusetts: Harvard University Press, 1998), 163-164; *Armenian Apocrypha Relating to Adam and Eve*, History of the Forefathers, Adam and his Sons and Grandsons 7, trans. Michael E. Stone (Leiden: E. J. Brill, 1996), 185.

[92] Louis Ginzberg, *The Legends of the Jews Volume I: From the Creation to Jacob*, trans. Henrietta Szold (Baltimore, Maryland: The Johns Hopkins University Press, 1909), 111.

[93] *Armenian Apocrypha Relating to Adam and Eve*, History of the Forefathers, Adam and his Sons and Grandsons 21, trans. Michael E. Stone (Leiden: E. J. Brill, 1996), 191; S. Baring-Gould, *Legends of the Patriarchs and Prophets and Other Old Testament Characters* (New York: American Book Exchange, 1881), 74.

[94] *The First Book of Adam and Eve (The Conflict of Adam and Eve with Satan)*, 79:24-28, trans. S. C. Malan (London: Williams and Norgate, 1882).

[95] *Barhebraeus' Scholia on the Old Testament Part I: Genesis - II Samuel*, Genesis 4:12, trans. Martin Sprengling and William Creighton Graham (Chicago, Illinois: University of Chicago Press 1931), 31.

[96] *The First Book of Adam and Eve (The Conflict of Adam and Eve with Satan)*, 79:24-26, trans. S. C. Malan (London: Williams and Norgate, 1882), 59.

[97] *The Armenian Apocryphal Adam Literature*, This is the History of Abel and Cain the Sons of Adam 41, trans. William Lowndes Lipscomb (Ann Arbor, Michigan: University Microfilms International, 1983), 166.

[98] *The Armenian Apocryphal Adam Literature*, The History of the Repentance of Adam and Eve, The First Created Ones, and How They Did It 55-56, trans. William Lowndes Lipscomb (Ann Arbor, Michigan: University Microfilms International, 1983), 228.

[99] *Book of the Glory of Kings (Kerba Nagast)*, 4. Concerning Envy, trans. Sir. E. A. Wallis Budge (London: Humphrey Milford, 1932).

[100] S. Baring-Gould, *Legends of the Patriarchs and Prophets and Other Old Testament Characters* (New York: American Book Exchange, 1881), 74.

[101] *Barhebraeus' Scholia on the Old Testament Part I: Genesis - II Samuel*, Genesis 4:16, trans. Martin Sprengling and William Creighton Graham (Chicago, Illinois: University of Chicago Press 1931), 33.

[102] Robert Graves and Raphael Patai, *Hebrew Myths: The Book of Genesis* (Garden City, New York: Doubleday & Company, 1964), 93.

[103] *The Armenian Apocryphal Adam Literature*, This is the History of Abel and Cain the Sons of Adam 42-43, trans. William Lowndes Lipscomb (Ann Arbor, Michigan: University Microfilms International, 1983), 167.

[104] *The Armenian Apocryphal Adam Literature*, This is the History of Abel and Cain the Sons of Adam 44, 6, trans. William Lowndes Lipscomb (Ann Arbor, Michigan: University Microfilms International, 1983), 167.

[105] *The Armenian Apocryphal Adam Literature*, This is the History of Abel and Cain the Sons of Adam 57, trans. William Lowndes Lipscomb (Ann Arbor, Michigan: University Microfilms International, 1983), 170.

[106] J. Preston Eby, *The World System*, 3, http://www.theshop.net/giess/world.html (accessed Aug. 17, 2000); *The Book of the Cave of Treasures*, The First Thousand Years: Adam to Yared (Jared), Adam's Expulsion from Paradise, trans. Sir E. A. Wallis Budge (London: The Religious Tract Society, 1927), 68-70; *The World Before the Flood, and the History of the Patriarchs: Chapter 1*, 7, http://www.adamqadmon.com/watchers/pre-flood000.html (accessed Feb. 10, 2001); Moses Aberbach and Bernard Grossfield, *Targum Onkelos to Genesis: A Critical Analysis Together with an English Translation of the Text*, Genesis 4:16 (KTAV Publishing House, Inc., 1995), 42.

[107] *The Armenian Apocryphal Adam Literature*, The History of the Repentance of Adam and Eve, the First Created Ones, and How They Did It 57, trans. William Lowndes Lipscomb (Ann Arbor, Michigan: University Microfilms International, 1983), 228; Sir James George Frazer, *Folk-lore in the Old Testament: Studies in Comparative Religion, Legend and Law* (London: Macmillan and Co., Limited, 1923), 38.

[108] Theodor Gaster, *Myth, Legend, and Custom in the Old Testament* (New York: Harper & Row, 1969), 55; Sir James George Frazer, *Folk-lore in the Old Testament: Studies in Comparative Religion, Legend and Law* (London: Macmillan and Co., Limited, 1923), 38; *The Companion Bible*, Genesis 4:5 (notes) (Grand Rapids, Michigan: Kregel Publications, 1990), 9.

[109] Dick Fischer, *In Search of the Historical Adam*, 6, http://www.asa3.org/ASA/PSCF/1993/PSCF12-93Fischer.html (accessed April 12, 2005).

[110] Mrs. Sydney Bristowe, *Sargon the Magnificent* (London: The Covenant Publishing Co., 1927), 15.

[111] *Pirke De Rabbi Eliezer*, Chapter 21: Cain and Abel [25A. i.], trans. Gerald Friedlander (New York: Sepher-Hermon Press, 1981), 156; Robert Graves and Raphael Patai, *Hebrew Myths: The Book of Genesis* (Garden City, New York: Doubleday & Company, 1964), 96-97.

[112] Robert Graves and Raphael Patai, *Hebrew Myths: The Book of Genesis* (Garden City, New York: Doubleday & Company, 1964), 96-97; James L. Kugel, *Traditions of the Bible* (Cambridge, Massachusetts: Harvard University Press, 1998), 168-169.

[113] James L. Kugel, *Traditions of the Bible* (Cambridge, Massachusetts: Harvard University Press, 1998), 168.

[114] S. Baring-Gould, *Legends of the Patriarchs and Prophets and Other Old Testament Characters* (New York: American Book Exchange, 1881), 72.

[115] Rev. Alexander Hislop, *The Two Babylons* (Neptune, Jew Jersey: Loizeaux Brothers, 1959), 197-199.

[116] S. Baring-Gould, *Legends of the Patriarchs and Prophets and Other Old Testament Characters* (New York: American Book Exchange, 1881), 74; Alan Unterman, Dictionary of Jewish Lore and Legend (New York: Thames and Hudson 1991) 43-44.

[117] *Armenian Apocrypha Relating to Adam and Eve*, History of the Forefathers, Adam and his Sons and Grandsons 22,

trans. Michael E. Stone (Leiden: E. J. Brill, 1996), 191-192; S. Baring-Gould, *Legends of the Patriarchs and Prophets and Other Old Testament Characters* (New York: American Book Exchange, 1881), 74.

[118] *Armenian Apocrypha Relating to Adam and Eve*, History of the Forefathers, Adam and his Sons and Grandsons 22, trans. Michael E. Stone (Leiden: E. J. Brill, 1996), 192.

[119] *The Armenian Apocryphal Adam Literature*, This is the History of Abel and Cain the Sons of Adam 47, trans. William Lowndes Lipscomb (Ann Arbor, Michigan: University Microfilms International, 1983), 167.

[120] Colin Kidd, *The Forging of Races: Race and Scripture in the Protestant Atlantic World, 1600-2000* (Cambridge, New York: Cambridge University Press 2006), 75.

[121] James E. Thorold Rogers, *Bible Folk-Lore; a Study in Comparative Mythology* (London: Kegan Paul, Trench and Co., 1884), 12.

[122] James L. Kugel, *The Bible As It Was* (Cambridge, Massachusetts: Harvard University Press, 1997), 85; *Fallen Angels and Genetic Science*, 3, http://www.angelfire.com/home/thefaery/hafgan.html (accessed Sept. 13, 2007).

[123] Richard Gan, *The Mark of the Wicked Ones*, 10-1, http://www.propheticrevelation.net/w-ones.htm (accessed Aug. 22, 2007).

[124] E. S. G. Bristowe, *Cain - An Argument* (Leicester: Edgar Backus, 1950), 75; Mrs. Sydney Bristowe, *Sargon the Magnificent* (London: The Covenant Publishing Co., 1927), 83; Richard Gan, *The Mark of the Wicked Ones*, 10-11, http://www.propheticrevelation.net/w-ones.htm (accessed Aug. 22, 2007).

[125] Mrs. Sydney Bristowe, *Sargon the Magnificent* (London: The Covenant Publishing Co., 1927), 15-16.

[126] *Barhebraeus' Scholia on the Old Testament Part I: Genesis - II Samuel*, Genesis 4:16, trans. Martin Sprengling and William Creighton Graham (Chicago, Illinois: University of Chicago Press 1931), 33.

[127] *The Midrash Rabbah*, Bereshith (Genesis) 22:12 (and notes), trans. Rabbi Dr. H. Freedman and Maurice Simon (London: The Soncino Press, 1961).

[128] James R. Davis, *Have We Gone the Way of Cain?*, 8, http://www.focusongod.com/cain (accessed March 3, 2001).

[129] Josephus, *Jewish Antiquities*, Book 1, 59-64, trans. H. ST. J. Thackeray (London: William Heinemann Ltd. 1961), 29.

[130] William F. Dankerbring, *The Mark of Cain*, 6, www.triumphro.com (accessed Aug. 22, 2007).

[131] Dictionary.com, *perdition*, http://www.dictionary.reference.com/browse/perdition (accessed Feb. 4, 2011).

[132] Your Dictionary.com, *perdition*, http://www.yourdictionary.com/perdition (accessed Feb. 4, 2010).

[133] Merriam-Webster Online Dictionary, *Loss*, 1, http://www.m-w.com/dictionary/loss (accessed June 7, 2007).

[134] *The Apocalypse of Abraham*, 24:5-6, translator unknown, http://www.pseudepigrapha.com/pseudepigrapha/Apocalypse_of_Abraham.html (accessed Oct 5, 2006).

[135] *The Book of the Generations of Adam*, 9:6, http://www.earth-history.com/Pseudepigrapha/generations-adam.htm (accessed May 5, 2007).

[136] Rabbi Leo Jung, Ph. D., *Fallen Angels in Jewish, Christian and Mohammedan Literature* (New York: KTAV Publishing House, 1974), 155.

[137] *The Writings of Abraham*, 40:2-4, http://www.earth-history.com/Pseudepigrapha/Mormonism/writings-abraham-1.htm (accessed May 10, 2007); *The Armenian Apocryphal Adam Literature*, The History of the Repentance of Adam and Eve, the First Created Ones, and How They Did It 14, trans. William Lowndes Lipscomb (Ann Arbor, Michigan: University Microfilms International, 1983), 222.

[138] Strongs's G684 - *apoleia* (Thayer's Lexicon), http://www.blueletterbible.org/lang/lexicon/lexicon.cfm?Strongs=G684&t=KJV# (accessed Dec. 30, 2010); Greg Killian, *The Days of Noah*, 20, http://www.adamqadmon.com/nephilim/gkillian000.html (accessed Dec. 6, 2000).

[139] *The Book of the Generations of Adam*, 5:8, http://www.earth-history.com/Pseudepigrapha/generations-adam.htm (accessed May 5, 2007).

[140] Vines Expository Dictionary of New Testament Words, *Perdition*, 1, http://www.blueletterbible.org/lang/lexicon/lexicon.cfm?Strongs=G684&t=KJV (accessed May 5, 2007).

Chapter 10

[1] *Jude* 1:13 (Mrs. Sydney Bristowe, *Sargon the Magnificent* (London: The Covenant Publishing Co., 1927), 153).

[2] Robert Bowie Johnson, Jr., *The Parthenon Code: Mankind's History in Marble* (Annapolis, Maryland: Solving Light Books, 2004), 9.

[3] Robert Bowie Johnson, Jr., *The Parthenon Code: Mankind's History in Marble* (Annapolis, Maryland: Solving Light Books, 2004), 26.

[4] Mrs. Sydney Bristowe, *Sargon the Magnificent* (London: The Covenant Publishing Co., 1927), 160; Robert Bowie Johnson, Jr., *The Parthenon Code: Mankind's History in Marble* (Annapolis, Maryland: Solving Light Books, 2004), 192.

[5] Robert Bowie Johnson, Jr., *The Parthenon Code: Mankind's History in Marble* (Annapolis, Maryland: Solving Light Books, 2004), 13.

[6] Britannica Online Encyclopedia, *Cainite*, 5, www.members.eb.com/Ebchecked/topics/88487/Cainites (accessed March 2, 2010).

[7] Britannica Online Encyclopedia, *Cainite*, 5, www.members.eb.com/Ebchecked/topics/88487/Cainites (accessed

March 2, 2010).

[8] *An Historical Treatise of the Travels of Noah Into Europe: Containing the first inhabitation and peopling thereof*, (also Summary, p. 2), trans. Richard Lynche (1601), http://www.annomundi.com/history/travels_of_noah.htm (accessed Dec. 7, 2007); Robert Bowie Johnson, Jr., *The Parthenon Code: Mankind's History in Marble* (Annapolis, Maryland: Solving Light Books, 2004), 80-81; Robert Bowie Johnson, Jr., *Noah in Ancient Greek Art* (Annapolis, Maryland: Solving Light Books, 2007), 44-46.

[9] Josephus, *Jewish Antiquities*, Book 1, 59-64, trans. H. ST. J. Thackeray (London: William Heinemann Ltd. 1961), 29.

[10] Robert Bowie Johnson, Jr., *The Parthenon Code: Mankind's History in Marble* (Annapolis, Maryland: Solving Light Books, 2004), 17.

[11] *The Midrash Rabbah*, Bereshith (Genesis) 22:13, trans. Rabbi Dr. H. Freedman and Maurice Simon (London: The Soncino Press, 1961).

[12] Mrs. Sydney Bristowe, *Sargon the Magnificent* (London: The Covenant Publishing Co., 1927), 79.

[13] William F. Dankenbring, *The Mark of Cain*, 5, http://www.triumphpro.com/the_mark_of_cain.htm (accessed Aug. 22, 2007).

[14] William F. Dankenbring, *The Mark of Cain*, 3, http://www.triumphpro.com/the_mark_of_cain.htm (accessed Aug. 22, 2007).

[15] Mrs. Sydney Bristowe, *Sargon the Magnificent* (London: The Covenant Publishing Co., 1927), 31.

[16] Mrs. Sydney Bristowe, *Sargon the Magnificent* (London: The Covenant Publishing Co., 1927), 21.

[17] E. S. G. Bristowe, *Cain - An Argument* (Leicester: Edgar Backus, 1950), 19.

[18] E. S. G. Bristowe, *Cain - An Argument* (Leicester: Edgar Backus, 1950), 18; Mrs. Sydney Bristowe, *Sargon the Magnificent* (London: The Covenant Publishing Co., 1927), 26.

[19] Mrs. Sydney Bristowe, *Sargon the Magnificent* (London: The Covenant Publishing Co., 1927), 150.

[20] Mrs. Sydney Bristowe, *Sargon the Magnificent* (London: The Covenant Publishing Co., 1927), 22.

[21] Mrs. Sydney Bristowe, *Sargon the Magnificent* (London: The Covenant Publishing Co., 1927), 84.

[22] Mrs. Sydney Bristowe, *Sargon the Magnificent* (London: The Covenant Publishing Co., 1927), 89.

[23] *Jude* 1:11 (notes) (KJV (*The Schofield Reference Bible*)).

[24] *The Book of the Generations of Adam*, 5:5, http://www.earth-history.com/Pseudepigrapha/generations-adam.htm (accessed May 5, 2007).

[25] Mrs. Sydney Bristowe, *Sargon the Magnificent* (London: The Covenant Publishing Co., 1927), 117.

[26] Socrates (Mrs. Sydney Bristowe, *Sargon the Magnificent* (London: The Covenant Publishing Co., 1927), 70).

[27] Mrs. Sydney Bristowe, *Sargon the Magnificent* (London: The Covenant Publishing Co., 1927), 63.

[28] E. S. G. Bristowe, *Cain - An Argument* (Leicester: Edgar Backus, 1950), 46.

[29] Mrs. Sydney Bristowe, *Sargon the Magnificent* (London: The Covenant Publishing Co., 1927), 62-63.

[30] Mrs. Sydney Bristowe, *Sargon the Magnificent* (London: The Covenant Publishing Co., 1927), 57.

[31] Mrs. Sydney Bristowe, *Sargon the Magnificent* (London: The Covenant Publishing Co., 1927), 57.

[32] Mrs. Sydney Bristowe, *Sargon the Magnificent* (London: The Covenant Publishing Co., 1927), 70.

[33] Mrs. Sydney Bristowe, *Sargon the Magnificent* (London: The Covenant Publishing Co., 1927), 67, 70, 72-73, 75-77; Robert Bowie Johnson, Jr., *The Parthenon Code: Mankind's History in Marble* (Annapolis, Maryland: Solving Light Books, 2004), 11, 185; E. S. G. Bristowe, *Cain - An Argument* (Leicester: Edgar Backus, 1950), 41.

[34] Mrs. Sydney Bristowe, *Sargon the Magnificent* (London: The Covenant Publishing Co., 1927), 54, 72-76, 81, 84, 106, 166; Wikipedia, the free encyclopedia, *Eve*, 1, http://en.wikipedia.org/wiki/Eve_%28Bible%29 (accessed Oct. 23, 2007).

[35] E. S. G. Bristowe, *Cain - An Argument* (Leicester: Edgar Backus, 1950), 47, 62, 63; Mrs. Sydney Bristowe, *Sargon the Magnificent* (London: The Covenant Publishing Co., 1927), 72.

[36] E. S. G. Bristowe, *Cain - An Argument* (Leicester: Edgar Backus, 1950), 8.

[37] Mrs. Sydney Bristowe, *Sargon the Magnificent* (London: The Covenant Publishing Co., 1927), 76-7, 81, 91; E. S. G. Bristowe, *Cain - An Argument* (Leicester: Edgar Backus, 1950), 17, 41.

[38] Mrs. Sydney Bristowe, *Sargon the Magnificent* (London: The Covenant Publishing Co., 1927), 115.

[39] Mrs. Sydney Bristowe, *Sargon the Magnificent* (London: The Covenant Publishing Co., 1927), 151.

[40] Mrs. Sydney Bristowe, *Sargon the Magnificent* (London: The Covenant Publishing Co., 1927), 49.

[41] E. S. G. Bristowe, *Cain - An Argument* (Leicester: Edgar Backus, 1950), 3, 69; Mrs. Sydney Bristowe, *Sargon the Magnificent* (London: The Covenant Publishing Co., 1927), 39, 58-60, 66-67, 70, 87, 94, 103-104, 112, 161-162.

[42] Mrs. Sydney Bristowe, *Sargon the Magnificent* (London: The Covenant Publishing Co., 1927), 151.

[43] E. S. G. Bristowe, *Cain - An Argument* (Leicester: Edgar Backus, 1950), 10.

[44] Robert Bowie Johnson, Jr., *The Parthenon Code: Mankind's History in Marble* (Annapolis, Maryland: Solving Light Books, 2004), 194.

[45] E. S. G. Bristowe, *Cain - An Argument* (Leicester: Edgar Backus, 1950), 5.

[46] Mrs. Sydney Bristowe, *Sargon the Magnificent* (London: The Covenant Publishing Co., 1927), 84.

[47] Mrs. Sydney Bristowe, *Sargon the Magnificent* (London: The Covenant Publishing Co., 1927), 151.

[48] E. S. G. Bristowe, *Cain - An Argument* (Leicester: Edgar Backus, 1950), 40.

[49] E. S. G. Bristowe, *Cain - An Argument* (Leicester: Edgar Backus, 1950), 62.

[50] Mrs. Sydney Bristowe, *Sargon the Magnificent* (London: The Covenant Publishing Co., 1927), 151.

[51] Mrs. Sydney Bristowe, *Sargon the Magnificent* (London: The Covenant Publishing Co., 1927), 73.

[52] *Creation Mythology: Atum the Creator*, http://www.egyptartsite.com/crea.html (accessed Aug. 12, 2010).

[53] Robert Bowie Johnson, Jr., *The Parthenon Code: Mankind's History in Marble* (Annapolis, Maryland: Solving Light Books, 2004), 9.

[54] Robert Bowie Johnson, Jr., *The Parthenon Code: Mankind's History in Marble* (Annapolis, Maryland: Solving Light Books, 2004), 173.

[55] E. S. G. Bristowe, *Cain - An Argument* (Leicester: Edgar Backus, 1950), 44.

[56] Donald Mackenzie, *Myths of Babylonia and Assyria*, Chapter 10 (1915), 35.

[57] Mrs. Sydney Bristowe, *Sargon the Magnificent* (London: The Covenant Publishing Co., 1927), 95.

[58] Mrs. Sydney Bristowe, *Sargon the Magnificent* (London: The Covenant Publishing Co., 1927), 150.

[59] Mrs. Sydney Bristowe, *Sargon the Magnificent* (London: The Covenant Publishing Co., 1927), 71.

[60] Mrs. Sydney Bristowe, *Sargon the Magnificent* (London: The Covenant Publishing Co., 1927), 100 (and notes).

[61] Mrs. Sydney Bristowe, *Sargon the Magnificent* (London: The Covenant Publishing Co., 1927), 55.

[62] Mrs. Sydney Bristowe, *Sargon the Magnificent* (London: The Covenant Publishing Co., 1927), 150.

[63] Mrs. Sydney Bristowe, *Sargon the Magnificent* (London: The Covenant Publishing Co., 1927), 93.

[64] Mrs. Sydney Bristowe, *Sargon the Magnificent* (London: The Covenant Publishing Co., 1927), 93.

[65] E. S. G. Bristowe, *Cain - An Argument* (Leicester: Edgar Backus, 1950), 8.

[66] E. S. G. Bristowe, *Cain - An Argument* (Leicester: Edgar Backus, 1950), 45.

[67] Mrs. Sydney Bristowe, *Sargon the Magnificent* (London: The Covenant Publishing Co., 1927), 80-81.

[68] E. S. G. Bristowe, *Cain - An Argument* (Leicester: Edgar Backus, 1950), 66.

[69] Mrs. Sydney Bristowe, *Sargon the Magnificent* (London: The Covenant Publishing Co., 1927), 151; E. S. G. Bristowe, *Cain - An Argument* (Leicester: Edgar Backus, 1950), 45.

[70] Philip Gardiner, Secrets of the Serpent: in Search of the Secret Past (Foresthill Ca: Reality press, 2006), 42.

[71] E. S. G. Bristowe, *Cain - An Argument* (Leicester: Edgar Backus, 1950), 45.

[72] A. H. Sayce, *Hibbert Lectures, 1887: Lectures on the Origin and Growth of Religion* (Williams and Northgate, 1898), 154.

[73] E. S. G. Bristowe, *Cain - An Argument* (Leicester: Edgar Backus, 1950), 127.

[74] Mrs. Sydney Bristowe, *Sargon the Magnificent* (London: The Covenant Publishing Co., 1927), 64.

[75] Robert Bowie Johnson, Jr., *The Parthenon Code: Mankind's History in Marble* (Annapolis, Maryland: Solving Light Books, 2004), 17.

[76] Philip Gardiner, *Secrets of the Serpent: in Search of the Secret Past* (Foresthill Ca.: Reality press, 2006), 18.

[77] Mrs. Sydney Bristowe, *Sargon the Magnificent* (London: The Covenant Publishing Co., 1927), 70-71.

[78] Mrs. Sydney Bristowe, *Sargon the Magnificent* (London: The Covenant Publishing Co., 1927), 81.

[79] Mrs. Sydney Bristowe, *Sargon the Magnificent* (London: The Covenant Publishing Co., 1927), 151.

[80] Robert Bowie Johnson, Jr., *The Parthenon Code: Mankind's History in Marble* (Annapolis, Maryland: Solving Light Books, 2004), 7.

[81] Robert Bowie Johnson, Jr., *The Parthenon Code: Mankind's History in Marble* (Annapolis, Maryland: Solving Light Books, 2004), 189.

[82] Robert Bowie Johnson, Jr., *The Parthenon Code: Mankind's History in Marble* (Annapolis, Maryland: Solving Light Books, 2004), 244.

[83] Robert Graves and Raphael Patai, *Hebrew Myths: The Book of Genesis* (Garden City, New York: Doubleday & Company, 1964), 75.

[84] Robert Bowie Johnson, Jr., *The Parthenon Code: Mankind's History in Marble* (Annapolis, Maryland: Solving Light Books, 2004), 12.

[85] Mrs. Sydney Bristowe, *Sargon the Magnificent* (London: The Covenant Publishing Co., 1927), 74.

[86] Robert Bowie Johnson, Jr., *The Parthenon Code: Mankind's History in Marble* (Annapolis, Maryland: Solving Light Books, 2004), 6, 22.

[87] Robert Bowie Johnson, Jr., *The Parthenon Code: Mankind's History in Marble* (Annapolis, Maryland: Solving Light Books, 2004), 12, 99, 169-170.

[88] Robert Bowie Johnson, Jr., *The Parthenon Code: Mankind's History in Marble* (Annapolis, Maryland: Solving Light Books, 2004), 171, 244.

[89] Louis Ginzberg, *The Legends of the Jews Volume I: From the Creation to Jacob*, trans. Henrietta Szold (Baltimore, Maryland: The Johns Hopkins University Press, 1909), 105.

[90] S. Baring-Gould, *Legends of the Patriarchs and Prophets and Other Old Testament Characters* (New York: American Book Exchange, 1881), 75.

[91] *The History of al-Tabari - Volume I: General Introduction and From the Creation to the Flood,* Adam's Descendants to Jared, 167, trans. Franz Rosenthal (Albany: New York Press, 1989), 337.

[92] *The Book of the Generations of Adam*, 5:5, http://www.earth-history.com/Pseudepigrapha/generations-adam.htm (accessed May 5, 2007).

[93] Theodor Gaster, *Myth, Legend, and Custom in the Old Testament* (New York: Harper & Row, 1969), 51.

[94] Theodor Gaster, *Myth, Legend, and Custom in the Old Testament* (New York: Harper & Row, 1969), 51-52.

[95] Theodor Gaster, *Myth, Legend, and Custom in the Old Testament* (New York: Harper & Row, 1969), 52; Wikipedia, the Free Encyclopedia, *Lamech*, 2, http://en.wikipedia.org/wiki/Lamech (accessed Aug. 28, 2007).

[96] Robert Bowie Johnson, Jr., *The Parthenon Code: Mankind's History in Marble* (Annapolis, Maryland: Solving Light Books, 2004), 16-18, 192; James E. Thorold Rogers, *Bible Folk-Lore: A Study in Comparative Mythology* (London: Kegan Paul, Trench & Co., 1884), 11.

[97] Robert Bowie Johnson, Jr., *The Parthenon Code: Mankind's History in Marble* (Annapolis, Maryland: Solving Light Books, 2004), 192.

[98] Herman L. Hoeh, *Compendium of World History*, Volume 2, Chapter 18, 9-10, www.earth-history.com/Various/Compendium/hhc2ch18 (accessed July 12, 2007).

[99] Mrs. Sydney Bristowe, *Sargon the Magnificent* (London: The Covenant Publishing Co., 1927), 126.

[100] Robert Graves and Raphael Patai, *Hebrew Myths: The Book of Genesis* (Garden City, New York: Doubleday & Company, 1964), 94; *The Chronicles of Jerahmeel (The Hebrew Bible Historiale)*, 24:1, trans. M. Gaster, Ph. D. (London: The Royal Asiatic Society, 1899), 50.

[101] E. S. G. Bristowe, *Cain - An Argument* (Leicester: Edgar Backus, 1950), 66; Mrs. Sydney Bristowe, *Sargon the Magnificent* (London: The Covenant Publishing Co., 1927), 152.

[102] Josephus, *Jewish Antiquities*, Book 1, 59-64, trans. H. ST. J. Thackeray (London: William Heinemann Ltd. 1961), 29; Louis Ginzberg, *The Legends of the Jews Volume V: Notes for Volume One and Two*, III. The Ten Generations, 41, trans. Henrietta Szold (Baltimore, Maryland: The Johns Hopkins University Press, 1909), 144.

[103] Robert Bowie Johnson, Jr., *Athena and Kain: The True Meaning of Greek Myth* (Annapolis, Maryland: Solving Light Books, 2003), 54.

[104] Louis Ginzberg, *The Legends of the Jews Volume I: From the Creation to Jacob*, trans. Henrietta Szold (Baltimore, Maryland: The Johns Hopkins University Press, 1909), 115.

[105] *Pseudo-Philo (The Biblical Antiquities of Philo)*, 2:3-4, trans. M. R. James (1917), http://www.sacred-texts.com/bib/bap/bap19.htm (accessed July 13, 2006); Mrs. Sydney Bristowe, *Sargon the Magnificent* (London: The Covenant Publishing Co., 1927), 151.

[106] Mrs. Sydney Bristowe, *Sargon the Magnificent* (London: The Covenant Publishing Co., 1927), 14.

[107] Josephus, *Jewish Antiquities*, Book 1, 59-64, trans. H. ST. J. Thackeray (London: William Heinemann Ltd. 1961), 29; *The Chronicles of Jerahmeel (The Hebrew Bible Historiale)*, 24:1, trans. M. Gaster, Ph. D. (London: The Royal Asiatic Society, 1899), 50.

[108] *The Chronicles of Jerahmeel (The Hebrew Bible Historiale)*, 26:11, trans. M. Gaster, Ph. D. (London: The Royal Asiatic Society, 1899), 55.

[109] Mrs. Sydney Bristowe, *Sargon the Magnificent* (London: The Covenant Publishing Co., 1927), 152.

[110] Louis Ginzberg, *The Legends of the Jews Volume I: From the Creation to Jacob*, trans. Henrietta Szold (Baltimore, Maryland: The Johns Hopkins University Press, 1909), 117.

[111] S. Baring-Gould, *Legends of the Patriarchs and Prophets and Other Old Testament Characters* (New York: American Book Exchange, 1881), 75.

[112] Rev. G. Oliver, *The Antiquities of Freemasonry; Comprising Illustrations of the Five Grand Periods of Masonry, From The Creation of the World to the Dedication of King Solomon's Temple* (London: Richard Spencer, 1843), 46; *The Chronicles of Jerahmeel (The Hebrew Bible Historiale)*, 24:1, trans. M. Gaster, Ph. D. (London: The Royal Asiatic Society, 1899), 50.

[113] Mrs. Sydney Bristowe, *Sargon the Magnificent* (London: The Covenant Publishing Co., 1927), 70-71 (and notes).

[114] E. S. G. Bristowe, *Cain - An Argument* (Leicester: Edgar Backus, 1950), 65.

[115] *Gen.* 4:17 (KJV); E. S. G. Bristowe, *Cain - An Argument* (Leicester: Edgar Backus, 1950), 5, 9; Mrs. Sydney Bristowe, *Sargon the Magnificent* (London: The Covenant Publishing Co., 1927), 27, 53-54, 72, 80, 150; Mysterious World: *Ah, Osiria! Part III: Nimrod Hunting*, 13, http://www.mysteriousworld.com/Journal/2003/Autumn/Osiria/ (accessed July 12, 2007).

[116] Mrs. Sydney Bristowe, *Sargon the Magnificent* (London: The Covenant Publishing Co., 1927), 80.

[117] Mrs. Sydney Bristowe, *Sargon the Magnificent* (London: The Covenant Publishing Co., 1927), 80.

[118] I. P. Cory, *Ancient Fragments* (1832), Berossus, Of the Cosmology and Deluge, http://www.sacred-texts.com/cla/af/index.htm (accessed Aug. 14, 2007).

[119] Mrs. Sydney Bristowe, *Sargon the Magnificent* (London: The Covenant Publishing Co., 1927), 142 (notes).

[120] E. S. G. Bristowe, *Cain - An Argument* (Leicester: Edgar Backus, 1950), 7.

[121] Mrs. Sydney Bristowe, *Sargon the Magnificent* (London: The Covenant Publishing Co., 1927), 15-16.

[122] Strong's Exhaustive Concordance, *Qayin (7014)*, 1, http://www.strongsnumbers.com/hebrew/7014 (accessed March 17, 2010),

[123] Mrs. Sydney Bristowe, *Sargon the Magnificent* (London: The Covenant Publishing Co., 1927), 144, 148-149; E. S. G. Bristowe, *Cain - An Argument* (Leicester: Edgar Backus, 1950), 58.

[124] Mrs. Sydney Bristowe, *Sargon the Magnificent* (London: The Covenant Publishing Co., 1927), 148-149.

[125] Mrs. Sydney Bristowe, *Sargon the Magnificent* (London: The Covenant Publishing Co., 1927), 151.

[126] Mrs. Sydney Bristowe, *Sargon the Magnificent* (London: The Covenant Publishing Co., 1927), 129; James L.

Kugel, *Traditions of the Bible* (Cambridge, Massachusetts: Harvard University Press, 1998), 169.

[127] Mrs. Sydney Bristowe, *Sargon the Magnificent* (London: The Covenant Publishing Co., 1927), 129.

[128] Mrs. Sydney Bristowe, *Sargon the Magnificent* (London: The Covenant Publishing Co., 1927), 88 (notes).

Made in the USA
Monee, IL
22 October 2021